The Sphere Project

Humanitarian Charter and Minimum Standards in Disaster Response

Humanitarian Charter and Minimum Standards in Disaster Response

Contents

Introduction

Meeting essential needs and restoring life with dignity are core principles that should inform all humanitarian action.

The purpose of the Humanitarian Charter and the Minimum Standards is to increase the effectiveness of humanitarian assistance, and to make humanitarian agencies more accountable. It is based on two core beliefs: first, that all possible steps should be taken to alleviate human suffering that arises out of conflict and calamity, and second, that those affected by a disaster have a right to life with dignity and therefore a right to assistance.

This book is the result of more than two years of inter-agency collaboration to frame a Humanitarian Charter, and to identify Minimum Standards to advance the rights set out in the Charter. These standards cover disaster assistance in water supply and sanitation, nutrition, food aid, shelter and site planning, and health services.

Humanitarian Charter

The cornerstone of the book is the Humanitarian Charter (Part 1). Based on the principles and provisions of international humanitarian law, international human rights law, refugee law, and the *Code of Conduct for the International Red Cross and Red Crescent Movement and (NGOs) in Disaster Relief*, the Charter describes the core principles that govern humanitarian action and asserts the right of populations to protection and assistance.

The Charter defines the legal responsibilities of states and parties to guarantee the right to assistance and protection. When states are unable to respond, they are obliged to allow the intervention of humanitarian organisations.

The Minimum Standards

The Minimum Standards (Part 2) were developed using broad networks of experts in each of the five sectors. Most of the standards, and the indicators that accompany them, are not new, but consolidate and adapt existing knowledge and practice. Taken as whole, they represent a remarkable consensus across a broad spectrum of agencies, and mark a new determination to ensure that humanitarian principles are realised in practice.

Scope and limitations of the Humanitarian Charter and Minimum Standards

Agencies' ability to achieve the Minimum Standards will depend on a range of factors, some of which are within their control, while others such as political and security factors, lie outside their control. Of particular importance will be the extent to which agencies have access to the affected population, whether they have the consent and cooperation of the authorities in charge, and whether they can operate in conditions of reasonable security. Availability of sufficient financial, human and material resources is also essential. This document cannot alone constitute a complete evaluation guide or set of criteria for humanitarian action.

While the Charter is a general statement of humanitarian principles, the Minimum Standards do not attempt to deal with the whole spectrum of humanitarian concerns or actions. First, they do not cover all the possible forms of appropriate humanitarian assistance. Second, and more importantly, they do not deal with the larger issues of humanitarian protection.

Humanitarian agencies are frequently faced with situations where human acts or obstruction threaten the fundamental well-being or security of whole communities or sectors of a population – such as to constitute violations of international law. This may take the form of direct threats to people's well-being, or to their means of survival, or to their safety. In the context of armed conflict, the paramount humanitarian concern will be to protect people against such threats.

Comprehensive strategies and mechanisms for ensuring access and protection are not detailed in this document. However, it is important to stress that the form of relief assistance and the way in which it is provided can have a significant impact (positive or negative) on the affected population's security. The Humanitarian Charter recognises that the attempt to provide assistance in situations of conflict 'may potentially render civilians more vulnerable to attack, or bring unintended advantage to one or more of the warring parties', and it commits agencies to minimising such adverse effects of their interventions as far as possible.

The Humanitarian Charter and Minimum Standards will not solve all the problems of humanitarian response, nor can they prevent all human suffering. What they offer is a tool for humanitarian agencies to enhance the effectiveness and quality of their assistance and thus to make a significant difference to the lives of people affected by disaster.

Part 1

The
Humanitarian
Charter

The Humanitarian Charter

Humanitarian agencies committed to this Charter and to the Minimum Standards will aim to achieve defined levels of service for people affected by calamity or armed conflict, and to promote the observance of fundamental humanitarian principles.

The Humanitarian Charter expresses agencies' commitment to these principles and to achieving the Minimum Standards. This commitment is based on agencies' appreciation of their own ethical obligations, and reflects the rights and duties enshrined in international law in respect of which states and other parties have established obligations.

The Charter is concerned with the most basic requirements for sustaining the lives and dignity of those affected by calamity or conflict. The Minimum Standards which follow aim to quantify these requirements with regard to people's need for water, sanitation, nutrition, food, shelter and health care. Taken together, the Humanitarian Charter and the Minimum Standards contribute to an operational framework for accountability in humanitarian assistance efforts.

1 Principles

We reaffirm our belief in the humanitarian imperative and its primacy. By this we mean the belief that all possible steps should be taken to prevent or alleviate human suffering arising out of conflict or calamity, and that civilians so affected have a right to protection and assistance.

It is on the basis of this belief, reflected in international humanitarian law and based on the principle of humanity, that we offer our services as humanitarian agencies. We will act in accordance with the principles of humanity and impartiality, and with the other principles set out in the *Code of Conduct for the International Red Cross and Red Crescent Movement and Non-Governmental Organizations in Disaster Relief* (1994).

The Humanitarian Charter affirms the fundamental importance of the following principles:

1.1 The right to life with dignity

This right is reflected in the legal measures concerning the right to life, to an adequate standard of living and to freedom from cruel, inhuman or degrading treatment or punishment. We understand an individual's right to life to entail the right to have steps taken to preserve life where it is threatened, and a corresponding duty on others to take such steps. Implicit in this is the duty not to withhold or frustrate the provision of life-saving assistance. In addition, international humanitarian law makes specific provision for assistance to civilian populations during conflict, obliging states and other parties to agree to the provision of humanitarian and impartial assistance when the civilian population lacks essential supplies.[1]

1.2 The distinction between combatants and non-combatants

This is the distinction which underpins the 1949 Geneva Conventions and their Additional Protocols of 1977. This fundamental principle has been increasingly eroded, as reflected in the enormously increased proportion of civilian casualties during the second half of the twentieth century. That internal conflict is often referred to as 'civil war' must not blind us to the need to distinguish between those actively engaged in hostilities, and civilians and others (including the sick, wounded and prisoners) who play no direct part. Non-combatants are protected under international humanitarian law and are entitled to immunity from attack.[2]

1.3 The principle of non-refoulement

This is the principle that no refugee shall be sent (back) to a country in which his or her life or freedom would be threatened on account of race, religion, nationality, membership of a particular social group or political opinion; or where there are substantial grounds for believing that s/he would be in danger of being subjected to torture.[3]

2 Roles and Responsibilities

2.1 We recognise that it is firstly through their own efforts that the basic needs of people affected by calamity or armed conflict are met, and we acknowledge the primary role and responsibility of the state to provide assistance when people's capacity to cope has been exceeded.

2.2 International law recognises that those affected are entitled to protection and assistance. It defines legal obligations on states or warring parties to provide such assistance or to allow it to be provided, as well as to prevent and refrain from behaviour that violates fundamental human rights. These rights and obligations are contained in the body of international human rights law, international humanitarian law and refugee law. (See sources listed below.)

2.3 As humanitarian agencies, we define our role in relation to these primary roles and responsibilities. Our role in providing humanitarian assistance reflects the reality that those with primary responsibility are not always able or willing to perform this role themselves. This is sometimes a matter of capacity. Sometimes it constitutes a wilful disregard of fundamental legal and ethical obligations, the result of which is much avoidable human suffering.

2.4 The frequent failure of warring parties to respect the humanitarian purpose of interventions has shown that the attempt to provide assistance in situations of conflict may potentially render civilians more vulnerable to attack, or may on occasion bring unintended advantage to one or more of the warring parties. We are committed to minimising any such adverse effects of our interventions in so far as this is consistent with the obligations outlined above. It is the obligation of warring parties to respect the humanitarian nature of such interventions.

2.5 In relation to the principles set out above and more generally, we recognise and support the protection and assistance mandates of the International Committee of the Red Cross and of the United Nations High Commissioner for Refugees under international law.

3 Minimum Standards

The Minimum Standards which follow are based on agencies' experience of providing humanitarian assistance. Though the achievement of the standards depends on a range of factors, many of which may be beyond our control, we commit ourselves to attempt consistently to achieve them and we expect to be held to account accordingly. We invite other humanitarian actors, including states themselves, to adopt these standards as accepted norms.

By adhering to the standards set out in chapters 1 – 5 we commit ourselves to make every effort to ensure that people affected by disasters have access to at least the minimum requirements (water, sanitation, food, nutrition, shelter and health care) to satisfy their basic right to life with dignity. To this end we will continue to advocate that governments and other parties meet their obligations under international human rights law, international humanitarian law and refugee law.

We expect to be held accountable to this commitment and undertake to develop systems for accountability within our respective agencies, consortia and federations. We acknowledge that our fundamental accountability must be to those we seek to assist.

Notes

1. Articles 3 and 5 of the *Universal Declaration of Human Rights* 1948; Articles 6 and 7 of the *International Covenant on Civil and Political Rights* 1966; common Article 3 of the four *Geneva Conventions* of 1949; Articles 23, 55 and 59 of the *Fourth Geneva Convention*; Articles 69 to 71 of *Additional Protocol I* of 1977; Article 18 of *Additional Protocol II* of 1977 as well as other relevant rules of international humanitarian law; *Convention against Torture and Other Cruel, Inhuman or Degrading Treatment or Punishment* 1984; Articles 10, 11 and 12 of the *International Covenant on Economic, Social, and Cultural Rights* 1966; Articles 6, 37, and 24 of the *Convention on the Rights of the Child* 1989; and elsewhere in international law.

2. The distinction between combatants and non-combatants is the basic principle underlying international humanitarian law. See in particular common Article 3 of the four *Geneva Conventions* of 1949 and Article 48 of *Additional Protocol I* of 1977. See also Article 38 of the *Convention on the Rights of the Child.*

3. Article 33 of the *Convention on the Status of Refugees* 1951; Article 3 of the *Convention against Torture and Other Cruel, Inhuman* or *Degrading Treatment or Punishment* 1984; Article 22 of the *Convention on the Rights of the Child* 1989.

Sources

The following instruments inform this Charter:

Universal Declaration of Human Rights 1948.

International Covenant on Civil and Political Rights 1966.

International Covenant on Economic, Social and Cultural Rights 1966.

The four *Geneva Conventions* of 1949 and their two *Additional Protocols* of 1977.

Convention on the Status of Refugees 1951 *and the Protocol relating to the Status of Refugees* 1967.

Convention against Torture and Other Cruel, Inhuman or Degrading Treatment or Punishment 1984.

Convention on the Prevention and Punishment of the Crime of Genocide 1948.

Convention on the Rights of the Child 1989.

Convention on the Elimination of All Forms of Discrimination Against Women 1979.

Guiding Principles on Internal Displacement 1998.

Part 2
The Minimum
Standards

Minimum Standards in Water Supply and Sanitation

Minimum Standards in Water Supply and Sanitation

Part 2:1

Contents

For the general glossary and acronyms, see Annexes 1 and 2 at the end of the book.

Minimum Standards in Water Supply and Sanitation

Introduction

The minimum standards for Water Supply and Sanitation are a practical expression of the principles and rights embodied in the Humanitarian Charter. The Charter is concerned with the most basic requirements for sustaining the lives and dignity of those affected by calamity or conflict, as reflected in the body of international human rights, humanitarian, and refugee law. It is on this basis that agencies offer their services. They undertake to act in accordance with the principles of humanity and impartiality, and with the other principles set out in the *Code of Conduct for the International Red Cross and Red Crescent Movement and NGOs in Disaster Relief.* The Humanitarian Charter reaffirms the fundamental importance of three key principles:

- the right to life with dignity
- the distinction between combatants and non-combatants
- the principle of non-refoulement

The minimum standards fall into two broad categories: those that relate directly to people's rights; and those that relate to agency processes which help ensure people acquire these rights. Some of the minimum standards combine both of these categories.

1 The importance of water supply and sanitation in emergencies

People affected by disasters are more likely to become ill and to die from diseases related to inadequate sanitation and water supplies than from any other single cause. The most important of these are diarrhoeal diseases and others transmitted by the faeco-oral route. Their transmission is encouraged by inadequate sanitation, poor hygiene and contaminated water supplies. Other water and sanitation-related diseases include those carried by vectors associated with solid waste and water.

The main purposes of emergency water supply and sanitation programmes are to provide a minimum quantity of clean drinking water, and to reduce the transmission of faeco-oral diseases and exposure to disease-bearing vectors. A further important objective is to help establish the conditions that allow people to live and to perform daily tasks, such as going to the toilet, and washing with dignity, comfort and security.

In most emergency situations the responsibility for procuring water falls to women and children. However, when using communal water and sanitation facilities, for example in refugee or displaced situations, women and adolescent girls are also more vulnerable to sexual violence or exploitation. It is important, therefore, to encourage women's participation in water supply and sanitation programmes wherever possible. Their involvement will help to ensure that the entire affected population has safe and easy access to water supply and sanitation services, and that services are equitable and appropriate.

2 Finding your way around this chapter

The chapter is divided into eight sections (analysis, water supply, excreta disposal etc), each of which includes the following:

● **The minimum standards:** these specify the minimum levels to be attained in each area.

● **Key indicators:** these are 'signals' that show whether the standard has been attained. They provide a way of measuring and communicating both the impact, or result, of programmes as well as the process, or methods, used. The indicators may be qualitative or quantitative.

● **Guidance notes:** these include specific points to consider when applying the standard in different situations, guidance on tackling practical difficulties and advice on priority issues. They may also include critical issues relating to the standard or indicators, and describe dilemmas, controversies or gaps in current knowledge. Filling these gaps will help improve the minimum standards for water supply and sanitation in the future.

Further relevant information, including a bibliography, is supplied in the Appendices. The particular good practice features for the water and sanitation sector are described in Appendix 3.

The organisation of the chapter reflects the division of activities and responsibilities that commonly occurs in emergency situations. Action in each of these areas contributes to the overall aims of the water and sanitation programme as defined above, and is closely linked both epidemiologically and operationally to the objectives and activities of the other sectors. The analysis standards proposed for assessment, monitoring and evaluation relate to all areas within the water supply and sanitation sector.

Progress in achieving standards in one area determines the importance of progress in other areas. For instance, in situations where excreta disposal and hygiene facilities are inadequate, it is more urgent to reach the minimum water quantity standard than in situations where the environment is relatively free of pathogens due to adequate sanitation and hygiene conditions. Priorities should be decided on the basis of sound information shared between sectors as the situation evolves.

Reference to other sectors' technical standards is made where relevant. The purpose of this is to highlight how work in one sector is closely linked to work in other sectors, and that progress in one is dependent on progress in other areas.

Part 2:1

The Minimum Standards

1 Analysis

Programmes that meet the needs of disaster-affected populations must be based on a clear understanding of the current situation, including political and security factors, and anticipated developments. The people affected by the disaster, agencies, donors and local authorities need to know that interventions are appropriate and effective. Analysis of the effects of the disaster, and of the impact of the water supply and sanitation programme itself, are therefore critical. If the problem is not correctly identified and understood then it will be difficult, if not impossible, to make the right response.

Standardised methods of analysis that are used across the sectors have great potential to rapidly identify acute humanitarian needs and to ensure that resources are directed accordingly. This section sets out agreed standards and indicators for collecting and analysing information to identify needs, to design programmes, to monitor and evaluate their effectiveness, and to ensure the participation of the affected population.

The standards for analysis apply before any programme takes place and throughout the programme cycle. Analysis starts with an immediate initial assessment that identifies the impact of the disaster and whether and how to respond. It continues with monitoring, which identifies how well the programme is meeting needs and determines whether changes are required; and with evaluation, which determines the overall effectiveness of the programme and identifies lessons for the future.

The sharing of information and knowledge among all those involved is fundamental to achieving a full understanding of the problem and coordinated assistance. Documenting and disseminating information from the analysis process contributes to a broad understanding of the adverse public health and other consequences of disasters, and can assist in the development of improved disaster prevention and mitigation strategies.

Analysis standard 1: initial assessment

Programme decisions are based on a demonstrated understanding of the emergency situation and on a clear analysis of the health risks and needs relating to water supply and sanitation.

Part 2:1

Key indicators

● An immediate initial assessment that follows internationally accepted procedures is carried out by appropriately experienced personnel.

● The assessment is conducted in cooperation with a multi-sectoral team (water and sanitation, nutrition, food, shelter and health), local authorities, women and men from the affected population and humanitarian agencies intending to respond to the situation.

● The information is gathered and presented in a way that allows for transparent and consistent decision making.

● Data are disaggregated by sex, and by age where feasible.

● The information gathered identifies needs and health risks related to water supply and sanitation for different gender, social and age groups, and provides baseline data for monitoring and evaluation.

● All working and damaged water and sanitation systems are inspected.

● The assessment considers the national standards for water supply and sanitation in the country where the disaster has occurred, and in the country where humanitarian assistance is provided, if different.

● In situations of prevailing insecurity, the assessment includes an analysis of factors affecting the personal safety and security of the affected population.

● Recommendations are made about the need for external assistance. If assistance is required, recommendations are made on priorities, a strategy for intervention and resources needed. There is consideration of:

  – The social and political structure of the population, including cultural and gender factors relating to access and use of water and sanitation facilities.

  – The estimated number of people affected and demographic characteristics.

  – Local capacity and resources.

  – Special attention for groups at risk.

  – Access to the affected population and constraints on their freedom of movement.

  – Political, security and operating environment.

  – The possible long-term implications and environmental impact of the interventions proposed.

● The specific security threats faced by vulnerable groups, especially women and girls, are taken into account in the design of water and sanitation facilities.

● An assessment report is produced that covers key areas and appropriate recommendations.

● Assessment findings are made available to other sectors, national and local authorities, participating agencies, and male and female representatives from the affected population.

Guidance notes

1. *Internationally accepted procedures for initial assessment:* see Davis, J and Lambert, R (1995), and Pesigan, A M and Telford, J (1996).

2. *Timeliness:* timeliness is of the essence for the initial assessment, which should be carried out as soon as possible after the disaster. If required there should be an immediate response to critical needs at the same time. As a general rule, a report should be generated within a week of arrival at the site of the disaster, though this depends on the particular event and the wider situation.

3. *People conducting the assessment:* people who are able to collect information from all groups in the affected population in a culturally acceptable manner should be included, especially with regard to gender analysis and language skills. Ideally, there should be a balance in the numbers of men and women taking part.

4. *Assessment procedure:* the procedure for conducting the assessment should be agreed upon by all participants before field work begins and specific tasks contributing to the assessment should be assigned accordingly.

5. *Gathering information:* there are several different techniques for information gathering and these should be chosen carefully to match the situation and the type of information required. As a general rule, information should be gathered more frequently when the situation is changing more rapidly, and when there are critical developments such as new population movements or an epidemic outbreak of diarrhoea. Initial assessments may be quick and unrefined but analysis improves as more time and data are available. Checklists are a useful way of ensuring that all the key questions have been examined. See Appendix 1 for an example checklist.

6. *Sources of information:* information for the assessment report can be compiled from existing literature, relevant historical material, pre-emergency data and from discussions with appropriate, knowledgeable people including donors, agency staff, government personnel, local specialists, female and male community leaders,

elders, participating health staff, teachers, traders and so on. National or regional level preparedness plans may also be an important source of information. Group discussions with members of the affected population can yield useful information on beliefs and practices.

The methods used for collecting information and the limits of its reliability must be clearly communicated. Information should never be presented in such a way as to provide a misleading picture of the actual situation.

7. *Underlying issues:* an awareness of the rights of those affected by disasters, under international law, should underpin the assessment. Initial assessment and subsequent analysis should demonstrate an awareness of underlying structural, political, security, economic, demographic and environmental issues operating in the area. It is imperative that prior experience and the views of the people affected by the disaster are taken into consideration when analysing the dynamics and impact of the new emergency. This requires inclusion of local expertise and knowledge in data collection and analysis of resources, capacities, vulnerabilities and needs. The current and pre-emergency living conditions of displaced and non-displaced people in the area must also be considered.

8. *Groups at risk:* the needs of groups that are at risk of additional harm such as women, adolescents, unaccompanied minors, children, elderly people, and people with disabilities must be considered. Gender roles within the social system need to be identified.

9. *Recovery:* thinking and analysis concerning the post-disaster recovery period should be part of the initial assessment, so that interventions to meet immediate emergency requirements can serve to foster recovery among the affected population.

10. *Relationship with host population:* providing water and sanitation facilities for displaced populations in settlements can cause resentment among communities in the area, especially where existing resources such as water sources are inadequate or have to be shared with the new arrivals. In order to minimise the potential

for tension, the hosts should be consulted, and (where appropriate) work done to enhance the existing infrastructure. Likewise, where displaced populations are dispersed amongst a host population, planning should take account of the fact that they will place additional stress on the infrastructure and available resources.

Analysis standard 2: monitoring and evaluation

The performance of the water supply and sanitation programme, its effectiveness in responding to health problems related to water and sanitation, and changes in the context are monitored and evaluated.

Key indicators

● The information collected for monitoring and evaluation is timely and useful; it is recorded and analysed in an accurate, logical, consistent and transparent manner.

● Systems are in place that ensure systematic collection of information on:

    – Water consumption.

    – Water quality.

    –– Water supply system and operation.

    – Access to water points.

    – Access to toilets.

    – Activities in vector control, solid waste management and drainage.

● The use of water and sanitary facilities and goods is monitored.

● Access to water and sanitation, and water supply and sanitation-related health problems for the population surrounding the emergency settlement are monitored.

● Safety of water and sanitation facilities for vulnerable groups, particularly women and adolescent girls, is monitored.

● Women, men and children from the affected population are regularly consulted, and are involved in monitoring activities.

● There is regular analytical reporting on the impact of the water supply and sanitation programme on the affected population. There is also reporting of any contextual changes and other factors that may necessitate adjustment to the programme.

● Systems are in place that enable an information flow between the programme, other sectors, the affected population, the relevant local authorities, donors and others as needed. There is a regular exchange of information between the water supply and sanitation sector and the health information system. (See Health Services, chapter 5.)

● Monitoring activities provide information on the effectiveness of the programme in meeting the needs of target groups within the affected population.

● The programme is evaluated with reference to stated objectives and agreed minimum standards to measure its overall effectiveness and impact on the affected population.

Guidance notes

1. *Use of monitoring information:* emergencies are volatile and dynamic by definition. Regular and current information is therefore vital in ensuring that programmes remain relevant. Information derived from continual monitoring of programmes should be fed into reviews and evaluations. In some circumstances a shift in strategy may be required to respond to major changes in the context or needs. See Appendix 4 for suggested reading on assessment, monitoring and evaluation.

2. *Cooperation with other sectors:* information generated by the assessment process is used as an initial baseline for the health information system (see Health Services, chapter 5) and for monitoring and evaluation activities for the water supply and sanitation programme. Monitoring and evaluation activities require close cooperation with other sectors.

3. *Using and disseminating information:* information collected should be directly relevant to the programme, in other words it should be useful and should be used. It should also be made available as needed to other sectors and agencies, and to the affected populations. The means of communication used (dissemination methods, language and so on) must be appropriate for the intended audience.

4. *People involved in monitoring:* when monitoring requires consultation, people who are able to collect information from all groups in the affected population in a culturally acceptable manner should be included, especially with regard to gender and language skills. Women's involvement should be encouraged.

5. *Use of facilities:* people's use of the facilities and goods provided may be affected by factors such as security, convenience, quality, and whether they are appropriate to needs and customs. For example, monitoring of water points and toilets is critical to the safety of women and children because sexual violence often occurs at these locations. Wherever possible factors that limit the use of facilities should be dealt with through changes to the programme. It is essential to ensure that consultation before and during the programme includes adequate discussion with women, for whom the constraints on use are likely to be greatest.

6. *Evaluation:* evaluation is important because it measures effectiveness, identifies lessons for future preparedness, mitigation and assistance, and promotes accountability. Evaluation refers here to two, linked processes:

   a) Internal programme evaluation is normally carried out by staff as part of the regular analysis and review of monitoring information. The agency must also evaluate the effectiveness of all its programmes in a given disaster situation or compare its programmes across different situations.

   b) External evaluation may by contrast be part of a wider evaluation exercise by agencies and donors, and may take place, for example, after the acute phase of the emergency. When evaluations are carried out it is important that the techniques and resources used are consistent with the scale and nature of the programme, and that the report describes the methodology employed and the processes followed in reaching conclusions. Outcomes of evaluations should be disseminated to all the humanitarian actors, including the affected population.

Analysis standard 3: participation

The disaster-affected population has the opportunity to participate in the design and implementation of the assistance programme.

Key indicators

● Women and men from the disaster-affected population are consulted, and are involved in decision-making that relates to needs assessment, programme design and implementation.

● Women and men from the disaster-affected population receive information about the assistance programme, and have the opportunity to comment back to the assistance agency about the programme.

Guidance notes

1. *Equity:* the participation of disaster-affected people in decision-making, programme design and implementation helps to ensure that programmes are equitable and effective. Special effort should be made to ensure the participation of women and balanced male and female representation within the assistance programme. Participation in the water supply and sanitation programme may also serve to reinforce people's sense of dignity and worth in times of crisis. It generates a sense of community and ownership which can help ensure the safety and security of those who are receiving assistance, as well as those who are responsible for its implementation.

2. *People can be involved in water supply and sanitation programmes in different ways:* for example through involvement in the assessment team; involvement in decision-making (eg establishing conditions that allow people to go to the toilet and wash with dignity, comfort and security); disseminating information including cultural and gender factors relating to access and use of facilities; assisting in identifying security issues.

3. *Coordination committees:* coordination committees help ensure people's involvement in the assistance programme. Gender, age, ethnicity and socio-economic status should be taken into consideration in order to ensure that committees adequately represent the affected population. Acknowledged political leaders, female and male community leaders and religious leaders should also be represented. The roles and functions of a coordination committee should be agreed upon when it is set up.

4. *Seeking views and opinions:* participation can also be achieved through regular polling and discussions. This can take place during distribution, through home visits or when addressing individual concerns. Group discussions with members of the affected community can yield useful information on cultural beliefs and practices.

Part 2:1

2 Water Supply

Water is universally essential for drinking, cooking and personal and domestic hygiene. In extreme situations, there may not be enough water available to meet physiological needs, and in these cases a survival level of potable drinking water is of critical importance. In most cases however, the main health problems associated with inadequate water supply are caused by poor hygiene due to lack of water, and by the consumption of water that is contaminated at some stage.

Water supply standard 1: access and water quantity

All people have safe access to a sufficient quantity of water for drinking, cooking and personal and domestic hygiene. Public water points are sufficiently close to shelters to allow use of the minimum water requirement.

Key indicators

- At least 15 litres of water per person per day is collected.

- Flow at each water collection point is at least 0.125 litres per second.

- There is at least 1 water point per 250 people.

- The maximum distance from any shelter to the nearest water point is 500 metres.

Water supply standard 2: water quality

Water at the point of collection is palatable, and of sufficient quality to be drunk and used for personal and domestic hygiene without causing significant risk to health due to water-borne diseases, or to chemical or radiological contamination from short term use.

Key indicators

● There are no more than 10 faecal coliforms per 100 ml at the point of delivery for undisinfected supplies.

● Sanitary survey indicates low risk of faecal contamination.

● For piped water supplies to populations over 10,000 people, or for all water supplies at times of risk or presence of diarrhoea epidemic, water is treated with a residual disinfectant to an acceptable standard (eg residual free chlorine at the tap is 0.2-0.5 mg per litre and turbidity is below 5 NTU).

● Total dissolved solids are no more than 1,000 mg per litre (approximately 2,000 µs/cm electrical conductivity for simple field measurement), and water is palatable to users.

● No significant negative health effect due to chemical or radiological contamination from short term use, or from the planned duration of use of the water source, is detected (including carry-over of treatment chemicals), and assessment shows no significant probability of such an effect.

Water supply standard 3: water use facilities and goods

People have adequate facilities and supplies to collect, store and use sufficient quantities of water for drinking, cooking and personal hygiene, and to ensure that drinking water remains sufficiently safe until it is consumed.

Key indicators

● Each household has two water collecting vessels of 10-20 litres, plus water storage vessels of 20 litres. Water collection and storage vessels have narrow necks and/or covers.

● There is 250g of soap available per person per month.

● Where communal bathing facilities are necessary, there are sufficient bathing cubicles for bathing at an acceptable frequency and at an acceptable time, with separated cubicles for men and for women.

● Where communal laundry facilities are necessary, there is 1 washing basin per 100 people; private laundering areas are available for women to wash and dry undergarments and sanitary cloths.

Guidance notes

1. *Needs:* the exact quantities of water needed for domestic use may vary according to the climate, the sanitation facilities available, people's normal habits, their religious and cultural practices, the food they cook, the clothes they wear etc. In some situations water may be needed in large quantities for specific purposes, for instance for pour-flush toilets, to keep an existing sewer system or urban water distribution system functioning, or to water animals which may be vital to the livelihoods and well-being of the people affected by the disaster. Quantities needed for these uses are not included in the standards and should be added to the minimum figure if necessary. Quantities of water needed for health centres, therapeutic feeding centres, orphanages etc are not included in the standard figures, and should be added if necessary. See Appendix 2 for guidance on the additional quantities needed.

2. *Microbiological water quality:* in most emergency situations, water-related disease transmission is due as much to insufficient water for personal and domestic hygiene as to contaminated water supplies. When applying standards for microbiological water quality in an emergency situation, consideration should be given to the risk of excess infection from water-borne disease posed by the

water supplied, and what other water sources people may be likely to use. For longer-term supplies, refer to WHO *Guidelines for Drinking Water Quality* (1984).

3. *Water disinfection:* water should be treated with a residual disinfectant such as chlorine if there is a significant risk of water source or post-collection contamination. This risk will be determined by conditions in the settlement, such as population density, excreta disposal arrangements, hygiene practices, the prevalence of water-borne disease etc. As a general rule, any piped water supply for a large and concentrated population should be treated with a residual disinfectant such as chlorine, and in the case of a threat or existence of a diarrhoea epidemic, all drinking water supplies should be treated before distribution or in the home.

4. *Chemical and radiological contamination:* where hydrogeological records or knowledge of industrial activity suggest that water supplies may carry chemical or radiological health risks, those risks should be assessed rapidly. A decision that balances short - term public health risks and benefits should then be made. A decision about using possibly contaminated water for longer term supplies should be made on the basis of a more thorough assessment and analysis. For longer-term supplies, refer to WHO *Guidelines for Drinking Water Quality* (1984).

5. *Palatability:* while taste is not a direct problem for health, if the safe water supply does not taste good to the consumers they may drink from unsafe sources and put their health at risk. This may also be a risk when chlorinated water is supplied. Palatability depends on what the consumer is used to and should therefore be verified in the field to make a final decision on whether or not the water is acceptable, or whether promotional activities are needed to ensure that only safe supplies are used.

6. *Water quality for health centres:* apart from small quantities of very pure water needed for some medical equipment, water supplied to health centres does not need to be of better quality than that supplied to the general population, unless the concentration of certain chemicals is particularly high. However, given the likely

Part 2:1

numbers of pathogenic organisms present in health centres and the vulnerability of patients, water should be disinfected with chlorine or another residual disinfectant, and water storage equipment designed and managed to control contamination. Very young children may be susceptible to certain chemical contaminants and this should be checked with medical staff.

7. *Quality / quantity:* during the emergency attention must be given to the quantity of water that is available as well as its quality. Until minimum standards for both quantity and quality are met, the priority should be to provide equitable access to an adequate quantity of water of intermediate quality, rather than to provide an inadequate quantity of water which meets the minimum standard for quality. If there are serious doubts about the microbiological quality of the water, it should be treated with a residual disinfectant as a first measure to improve quality.

8. *Access and equity:* even if a sufficient quantity of water is available to meet minimum needs, additional measures may be needed to ensure that access is equitable. Unless water points are sufficiently close to their dwellings, people will not be able to collect enough water for their needs. In urban situations, it may be necessary to have water supplied into individual buildings to ensure that toilets continue to function. Water may need to be rationed to ensure that everyone's basic needs are met. If water is rationed or pumped at given times, this should be at times that are convenient to women and others who have responsibility for collecting water. Women and men from the affected population should be informed about their entitlements, and should also be involved in monitoring the equitable distribution of water.

9. *Water collection and storage:* people need vessels to collect water, to store it and to use it for washing, cooking and bathing. These vessels should be hygienic and appropriate to local needs and habits, in terms of size, shape and design.

10. *Communal washing and bathing facilities:* people may need a space where they can bathe in privacy. If this is not possible at the family shelter, some central facilities may be needed. Washing

clothes is an essential activity for hygiene, particularly for children, and cooking and eating utensils need washing. It is not possible to define universal standards relating to these activities, but if some facilities are needed for them to be carried out then they should be available. The design, numbers and location of these facilities should be decided in consultation with the intended users, especially women. Among the essential factors to consider are the safety, appropriateness and convenience of facilities for the users, especially women and girls, whose views on siting and design should be sought. As with latrines, facilities that are remote from the centre of a settlement are likely to pose additional risk of attack to female users.

3 Excreta Disposal

Proper disposal of human excreta creates the first barrier to excreta-related disease, helping to reduce disease transmission through direct and indirect routes. Excreta disposal is therefore a first priority, and in most emergency situations should be addressed with as much speed and effort as water supply. Appropriate facilities for defecation are one of a number of emergency interventions essential for people's dignity, safety, health and well-being.

Excreta disposal standard 1: access to, and numbers of toilets

People have sufficient numbers of toilets, sufficiently close to their dwellings to allow them rapid, safe and acceptable access at all times of the day and night.

Key indicators

- Maximum of 20 people per toilet.

- Use of toilets is arranged by household(s) and/or segregated by sex.

- Toilets are no more than 50 metres from dwellings, or no more than one minute's walk.

- Separate toilets for women and men are available in public places (markets, distribution centres, health centres etc).

Excreta disposal standard 2: design and construction

People have access to toilets which are designed, constructed and maintained in such a way as to be comfortable, hygienic and safe to use.

Key indicators

● Technically sound design and construction specifications, approved by the intended users, are used for all forms of household and public toilets.

● Cleaning and maintenance routines for public toilets are in place and function correctly.

● Toilets are designed, built and located to have the following features:

   – They are easy to keep clean enough to invite use and not to present a health hazard.

   – They are accessible and easy to use by all sections of the population including children, old people, pregnant women and physically and mentally disabled people.

   – They are lit at night if necessary for security or convenience.

   – Hand washing facilities are close by.

   – They minimise fly and mosquito breeding.

   – They allow for the disposal of women's sanitary protection, or provide women with the necessary privacy for washing and drying sanitary protection cloths.

   – They provide a degree of privacy in line with the norms of the users.

● Latrines and soakaways in most soils are at least 30 metres from any groundwater source and the bottom of any latrine is at least 1.5 metres above the water table. Drainage or spillage from defecation systems does not run towards any surface water source or shallow groundwater source.

● People are provided with tools and materials for constructing, maintaining and cleaning their own toilets if appropriate.

Guidance notes

1. *Acceptable facilities:* successful excreta disposal programmes are based on an understanding of peoples' varied needs, and on the participation of the users in the use of facilities they may not be accustomed to and which they may not find easy or attractive to use. Design, construction and location of toilets must take account of the preferences of the intended users, and women and other members of the population should be consulted.

2. *Children's faeces:* particular attention should be given to children's faeces, which are commonly more dangerous than those of adults. Parents or caregivers need to be involved, and facilities should be designed and installed with children in mind. It may be necessary to provide parents or caregivers with information about safe disposal of infant faeces and nappy (diaper) laundering practices.

3. *Anal cleansing:* water should be provided for people who use it. For other people it may be necessary to provide some sort of paper or other material for anal cleansing. Users should be consulted on the most appropriate materials.

4. *Hand washing:* users should have the means to wash their hands after defecation, with soap or an alternative, and should be encouraged to do so if necessary. This provides an important barrier to the spread of disease.

5. *Menstruation:* women and girls of reproductive age should have access to suitable materials for the absorption and disposal of menstrual blood. If these materials are to be provided by the agency, women should be consulted on what is appropriate. Where cloths are washed, dried and re-used, women should have access to a private place to do this in a hygienic way.

6. *Hygienic toilets:* if toilets are not kept clean they may be a focus for disease transmission and people will prefer not to use them. Cleaning and maintenance of all types of toilet should be addressed.

Toilets are more likely to be kept clean if users have a sense of ownership. This is encouraged by having them close to where people sleep, avoiding large blocks and involving users, where possible, in decisions about their design and construction.

7. *Shared facilities:* it is not always possible to provide one toilet per 20 people or per family immediately. In the short term, shared facilities are usually needed. Access to these shared facilities can be ensured by working with the intended users to decide who will have access to the toilet and how the sharing and responsibility for cleaning will be organised. It may be that men and women use different toilets, or that several families all use the same toilet. As the numbers of toilets are increased the sharing arrangements will change. In some situations it may be necessary to provide, clean and maintain public toilets for some or all of the population. It is important both that sufficient numbers of toilets are available and that every person can identify and gain access to a toilet when necessary.

8. *Distance of defecation systems from water sources:* the distances given above may be increased for fissured rocks and limestone, or decreased for fine soils. Groundwater pollution may not be a concern if the groundwater is not consumed.

9. *Security:* especially in crowded settlements, it is vital to consider the security of those using sanitation facilities, in particular women and girls. Latrines that are far from inhabited areas, or which are poorly lit, expose women and girls to additional risk of attack.

Part 2:1

4 Vector Control

Vector-borne diseases are a major cause of sickness and death in many emergency situations. Although malaria is probably the vector-borne disease of greatest public health concern, a number of others can pose a major threat to health. Flies may play an important role in the transmission of diarrhoeal disease. The control of vector-borne disease involves efforts in several areas, including health services, shelter, site selection and planning, and environmental health services, including water supply, excreta disposal, solid waste management and drainage. Although the nature of vector-borne disease is complex and addressing vector-related problems often demands specialist attention, there is much that can be done with simple and effective measures once the disease, the vector and their interaction with the beneficiary population have been identified.

Although not of primary public health concern, so-called nuisance pests, such as bed bugs, can cause significant discomfort and loss of sleep and are often worthy of attention for their indirect impact on health.

Vector control standard 1: individual and family protection

People have the means to protect themselves from disease vectors and nuisance pests when they are estimated to be a significant risk to health or well-being.

Key indicators

● All populations associated with a vector-borne disease risk have access to shelters equipped with insect control.

● Control of human lice is carried out to an agreed standard where louse-borne typhus or relapsing fever are a threat.

Vector control standard 2: physical, environmental and chemical protection measures

The number of disease-bearing vectors and nuisance animals that pose a risk to people's health and well-being are kept to an acceptable level.

Key indicators

● Vulnerable populations are settled outside the malarial zone.

● The population of malaria-bearing mosquitoes is kept low enough to avoid the risk of excessive malaria infection.

● Vector breeding or resting sites are modified where necessary and practicable.

● Rats, flies and other nuisance pests are kept within acceptable levels.

● Intensive fly control is carried out in high density settlements when there is a risk or presence of diarrhoea epidemic.

Vector control standard 3: good practice in the use of chemical vector control methods

Vector control measures that make use of pesticides are carried out in accordance with agreed international norms to ensure that staff, the people affected by the disaster and the local environment are adequately protected, and to avoid creating resistance to pesticides.

Key indicators

● Personnel are protected by the provision of training, protective clothing, supervision and a restriction on the number of hours handling pesticides.

● The purchase, transport, storage and disposal of pesticides and application equipment follows international norms, and can be accounted for at all times.

● People are informed about the potential risks of pesticides and about the schedule for application. They are protected during and after the application of pesticides according to internationally agreed procedures.

● The choice of pesticide and application method conform to national and international protocols.

● The quality of pesticide and of treated bednets conforms to international norms.

Guidance notes

1. *Links with other sectors:* site selection is important in limiting the exposure of the population to vector-borne disease risk. The risk of vector-borne disease is one of the key questions considered when choosing possible sites. Health service activities may help reduce pathogen prevalence by effective treatment, immunisation or prophylaxis, and vector-borne disease control should be undertaken with activities in both the health sector and the water supply and sanitation sector. Both health service and nutrition activities can help reduce vector-borne disease incidence by their impact on general health and nutritional status.

2. *Defining vector-borne disease risk:* decisions about vector control interventions should be based on an assessment of excess disease risk, as well as on clinical evidence of a vector-borne disease problem. Factors influencing this risk include:

   – Immune status - previous exposure, nutritional stress and other stresses.

   – Pathogen type and prevalence - in both vectors and humans.

   – Vector species and ecology.

   – Vector numbers (season, breeding sites etc).

   – Existing individual protection and avoidance measures.

3. *Individual protection measures:* it is recommended that if there is a risk of excess malaria, individual protection measures such as treated bednets are provided systematically and at an early stage. Impregnated bednets have the added advantage of giving some protection against lice, bedbugs and sandflies. Other individual protection measures which may be appropriate and which are commonly used already by people familiar with mosquitoes include the use of long sleeved clothing, household fumigants, mosquito screens and repellents. It is vital to ensure that users can accept and use these individual protection measures if they are to be effective.

4. *Environmental and chemical vector control:* there are a number of basic environmental engineering measures which can be taken to reduce the opportunities for vector breeding within the settlement. These include disposal of human and animal excreta and refuse for controlling flies, and drainage of standing water for controlling mosquitoes. Most priority environmental health measures such as excreta disposal and refuse disposal will have some impact on the populations of some vectors, but not all. However, it may not be possible to have sufficient impact on all the breeding, feeding and resting sites within and nearby the settlement, even in the longer term, and localised chemical control measures or individual protection measures may be needed. In some circumstances, space spraying may be justified and effective in reducing numbers of adult insects, for example for reducing fly numbers in anticipation of, or during, a diarrhoea epidemic.

5. *Household and personal insecticide treatment:* household treatment with residual insecticide can be effective in controlling the spread of malaria. Louse-borne typhus and relapsing fever may be avoided by personal treatment for the control of body lice by means of a mass campaign, and as newly displaced people arrive in a settlement.

6. *Indicators for vector control programmes:* the simplest indicators for measuring the impact of most vector control activities are disease incidence and parasite counts (for malaria). However, these are insensitive indicators which should be used with caution and interpreted in the light of other factors.

Part 2:1

7. ***Designing a response:*** vector control programmes may have no impact on disease if they target the wrong vector, use ineffective methods, or target the right vector in the wrong place or at the wrong time. Health data can help identify and monitor a vector problem, but designing an effective response requires more detailed study and, often, expert advice. This advice should be discussed with national and international health organisations, to ensure that national and international protocols are followed to identify the appropriate response and to ensure the correct choice and application of any chemicals used. Local advice should be sought on local disease problems, breeding sites, seasonal variations in vector numbers etc.

5 Solid Waste Management

If organic solid waste is not disposed of, the major risks posed are fly and rat breeding (see vector control) and surface water pollution. Uncollected and accumulating solid waste and the debris left after a natural disaster or conflict may also create a depressing and ugly environment, discouraging efforts to improve other aspects of environmental health. Solid waste may block drainage channels and lead to environmental health problems associated with stagnant and polluted surface water.

Solid waste management standard 1: solid waste collection and disposal

People have an environment that is acceptably free of solid waste contamination, including medical wastes.

Key indicators

● Domestic refuse is removed from the settlement or buried on site before it becomes a nuisance or a health risk.

● There are no contaminated or dangerous medical wastes (needles, glass, dressings, drugs etc) at any time in the living area or public spaces.

● There is a correctly designed, constructed and operated incinerator with deep ash pit within the boundaries of each health facility.

● There are refuse pits, bins or specified areas at markets and slaughtering areas, with a daily collection system.

● Final disposal of solid waste is carried out in such a place and in such a way as to avoid creating health and environmental problems.

Solid waste management standard 2: solid waste containers/pits

People have the means to dispose of their domestic waste conveniently and effectively.

Key indicators

● No dwelling is more than 15 metres from a refuse container or household refuse pit, or 100 metres from a communal refuse pit.

● One 100 litre refuse container is available per 10 families, where domestic refuse is not buried on site.

Guidance notes

1. *Refuse type and quantity:* refuse in emergency settlements varies widely in composition and quantity, according to the amount and type of economic activity and the staple foods consumed. The extent to which solid waste has an impact on people's health should be assessed in a logical manner to identify whether action is needed and what that action should be. If solid waste is recycled within the community this should be encouraged, as long as it presents no significant health risk. Distribution of commodities that produce a large amount of solid waste because of the way they are packaged or processed on site should be avoided.

2. *Participation:* most solid waste management programmes depend on the participation of the population concerned for placing their refuse in containers provided, or burying it where appropriate. Parents and children should be made aware of the dangers of playing with or recycling medical wastes.

3. *Medical waste:* special provision is needed for medical waste. It should be disposed of within the perimeter of a medical facility, cholera isolation centre, feeding centre etc, and not mixed in with the general settlement refuse. Responsibility for disposing of medical waste should be clearly defined.

4. *Market waste:* most market waste can be treated in the same way as domestic refuse. Slaughter house waste may need special treatment and special facilities to deal with the liquid wastes produced, and to ensure slaughtering is carried out in hygienic conditions.

5. *The dead:* mortality rates are often high during the early stages of emergencies, or directly after a natural disaster, demanding mass management of dead bodies, usually by burial in large graves. Graveyards and mass graves must be located at least 30 metres from groundwater sources used for drinking water, with the bottom of any grave at least 1.5 metres above the groundwater table.

A common myth associated with natural disasters is that human remains are responsible for epidemics. In many cases, the management of human remains rests on the false belief that they represent an epidemic hazard if not immediately buried or burned. In fact, the health hazard associated with dead bodies is negligible. However, in special cases such as during cholera or typhus epidemics, human remains may pose special health risks.

In general, families should be allowed to bury or cremate their own dead in their traditional way. Cemeteries or cremation facilities should be planned for and provided early on in the life of a new settlement, in consultation with members of the affected population. Provision should be made for monitoring funerals for mortality data. It may be necessary to provide cloth or other materials for families to wrap their dead before burial or cremation. Depending on circumstances, the recovery and identification of the bodies of family members may be the primary concern of survivors. When those being buried are the victims of violence, forensic issues should be considered.

Part 2:1

6. *Disposal of solid waste:* whatever means of final disposal is chosen, for instance burial or incineration, this should be done in such a way as to avoid creating health and environmental problems.

6 Drainage

Surface water in and near emergency settlements may come from household and water point wastewater, leaking latrines and sewers, rain water and rising floodwater. The main health problems associated with this water are contamination of water supplies and the living environment, damage to latrines and shelters, vector breeding and drowning. Surface water in and near the settlement may provide health and other benefits, enabling people to wash themselves, their cooking utensils and their clothes. An appraisal of the benefits and risks presented should be made when deciding whether or not to drain such water bodies. This section addresses small scale drainage problems and activities. Large scale drainage is generally determined by site selection and development. (See Shelter and Site Planning, chapter 4.)

Drainage standard 1: drainage works

People have an environment that is acceptably free from risk of water erosion and from standing water, including storm water, flood water, domestic wastewater and wastewater from medical facilities.

Key indicators

● There is no standing wastewater around water points or elsewhere in the settlement.

● Storm water flows away.

● Shelters, paths and water and sanitation facilities are not flooded or eroded by water.

Drainage standard 2: installations and tools

People have the means (installations, tools etc) to dispose of domestic wastewater and water point wastewater conveniently and effectively, and to protect their shelters and other family or communal facilities from flooding and erosion.

Key indicators

● Sufficient numbers of appropriately designed tools are provided to people for small drainage works and maintenance where necessary.

● Water point drainage is well planned, built and maintained. This includes drainage from washing and bathing areas as well as water collection points.

Guidance notes

1. *Site selection and planning:* the most effective way to avoid drainage problems is in the choice and lay out of the emergency settlement. (See Shelter and Site Planning, site selection standards, in chapter 4.) It may not be practicable to address the drainage problems of some sites, or of nearby water bodies.

2. *Promotion:* where small-scale drainage works are necessary to protect latrines and shelters, and to avoid stagnating household and water point wastewater, it may be appropriate to involve the population concerned. Technical support and tools may then be needed. It may also be necessary to provide information and alternatives if nearby water bodies pose health risks such as schistosomiasis or hazards from consumption of the water.

3. *Drainage and excreta disposal:* special care is needed to ensure that latrines and sewers are protected from flooding in order to avoid structural damage and leakage.

7 Hygiene Promotion

Hygiene behaviour is a crucial factor in the transmission of water and sanitation-related disease, and hygiene promotion is widely considered to be an essential element of an effective emergency water supply and sanitation response. It is difficult measure the impact of hygiene promotion programmes in emergencies. However, such programmes may be effective if they are assessed, planned and implemented in a systematic way, and if they focus on a very small number of important practices which can be rapidly influenced. It must be stressed that hygiene promotion should never substitute for good sanitation and water supplies, which are the key to good hygiene.

Definition of hygiene promotion

Hygiene promotion is defined here as the mix between the population's knowledge, practice and resources, and agency knowledge and resources which together enable risky hygiene behaviours to be avoided. Effective hygiene promotion relies on an exchange of information between the agency and the affected community in order to identify key hygiene problems, and to design, implement and monitor a programme to promote hygiene practices that will deal with these problems. This definition recognises that hygiene behaviour and the material means for healthy living should be promoted together.

Hygiene promotion standard 1: hygiene behaviour and use of facilities

All sections of the affected population are aware of priority hygiene practices that create the greatest risk to health and are able to change them. They have adequate information and resources for the use of water and sanitation facilities to protect their health and dignity.

Key indicators

1 Water supply

● People use the highest quality of readily available water.

● Public hygiene facilities (showers, laundry basins etc) are used appropriately and equitably.

● Average water use for drinking, cooking and personal hygiene in any household is at least 15 litres per person per day.

● Covers (where provided) are placed on water containers.

● Mean faecal contamination in potable water containers is indicated by less than 50 faecal coliforms per 100 ml.

2 Excreta disposal

● People use the toilets available and children's faeces are disposed of immediately and hygienically.

● People use toilets in the most hygienic way, both for their own health and for the health of others.

● Household toilets are cleaned and maintained in such a way that they are used by all intended users and are hygienic and safe to use.

● Parents and other caregivers demonstrate awareness of the need to dispose of children's faeces safely.

● Families and individuals participate in a family latrine programme by registering with the agency, digging pits or collecting materials.

● People wash their hands after defecation and handling children's stools and before cooking and eating.

3 Vector control

● Bedding and clothing is aired and washed regularly.

● In malaria-endemic areas:

 – People with treated mosquito nets keep, use and retreat them correctly.

- People avoid exposure to mosquitoes during biting times using the means available to them.

- Containers which may be mosquito breeding sites are removed, emptied of water regularly or covered.

4 Solid waste management

● Waste is put in containers daily for collection, or buried in a specified refuse pit.

● Parents, other caregivers and children are aware of the danger of touching needles and dressings from medical facilities, in cases where the minimum standard for the disposal of medical waste is not met.

5 Drainage

● Areas around shelters and water points are free of standing wastewater, and local stormwater drains are kept clear.

● There is a demand for tools for drainage works.

● People avoid entering water bodies where there is a schistosomiasis risk.

6 Funerals

● People have the resources and information necessary to carry out funerals in a manner which respects their culture and does not create a risk to health.

Hygiene promotion standard 2: programme implementation

All facilities and resources provided reflect the vulnerabilities, needs and preferences of all sections of the affected population. Users are involved in the management and maintenance of hygiene facilities where appropriate.

Key indicators

- Key hygiene risks of public health importance are identified in assessments and in the objectives for hygiene promotion activities.

- The design and implementation process for water supply and sanitation programmes includes and operates a mechanism for representative input from all users.

- All groups within the population have access to the resources or facilities needed to achieve the hygiene practices that are promoted.

- Hygiene promotion activities address key behaviours of importance for public health and they target priority groups.

- Hygiene and behaviour messages, where used, are understood and accepted by the intended audience.

- Users take responsibility for the management and maintenance of water supply and sanitation facilities as appropriate.

Guidance notes

1. *Agencies and the affected population share responsibility for hygiene practice:* as with all of the other standards, action by agencies on hygiene promotion will not necessarily be required, but these are points which need monitoring so that action can be taken if necessary. The ultimate responsibility for hygiene practice lies with all members of the affected population. The responsibility of humanitarian agencies is to enable hygienic practice by ensuring that both knowledge and facilities are accessible, and to be able to demonstrate that this is achieved. As a part of this process, they should engage women from the affected population in developing hygiene messages and in distributing related materials and supplies to the community.

2. *Targeting priority hygiene risks and behaviours:* the objectives of hygiene promotion activities and communication strategies should be clearly defined in order to avoid diluting key messages, confusing people or sending messages to the wrong people. The understanding gained through assessing hygiene risks should be used to plan and

prioritise material assistance, so that information flows usefully between the agency and the population concerned.

An assessment is needed to identify the key hygiene behaviours to be addressed and the likely success of promotional activity. This assessment should look at resources available to the population as well as behaviours, so that messages do not promote the impossible.

3. *Reaching all sections of the population:* hygiene messages must be delivered by people who have access to all members of the population. For example, in some cultures it is not acceptable for women to speak to unknown men. Materials should be designed so that messages reach illiterate members of the population.

Part 2:1

8 Human Resource Capacity and Training

All aspects of humanitarian assistance rely on the skills, knowledge and commitment of staff and volunteers working in difficult and sometimes insecure conditions. The demands placed on them can be considerable, and if they are to conduct their work to a level where minimum standards are assured, it is essential that they are suitably experienced and trained and that they are adequately managed and supported by their agency.

Capacity standard 1: competence

Water supply and sanitation programmes are implemented by staff who have appropriate qualifications and experience for the duties involved, and who are adequately managed and supported.

Key indicators

- All staff working on a water supply and sanitation programme are informed of the purpose and method of the activities they are asked to carry out.

- Assessments, programme design and key technical decision-making are carried out by staff with relevant technical qualifications and previous emergency experience.

- Staff and volunteers are aware of gender issues relating to the affected population. They know how to report incidents of sexual violence.

- Staff with technical and management responsibilities have access to support for informing and verifying key decisions.

- Staff or volunteers involved in information gathering are thoroughly briefed and regularly supervised.

- Staff or volunteers involved in hygiene education have the ability or aptitude for this activity and receive appropriate training and supervision.

- Staff and volunteers involved in construction and other manual activities are trained, supervised and equipped adequately to ensure their work is carried out efficiently and safely.

Guidance notes

1. *See:* ODI/People In Aid (1998), *Code of Best Practice in the Management and Support of Aid Personnel.*

2. *Staffing:* staff and volunteers should demonstrate capabilities equal to their respective assignments. They should also be aware of key aspects of human rights conventions, international humanitarian law and the *Guiding Principles on Internal Displacement* (see the Humanitarian Charter).

   Providing training and support as a part of emergency preparedness is important to ensure that skilled personnel are available to deliver quality services. Given that emergency preparedness cannot be assured in many countries, humanitarian agencies should ensure that qualified and competent staff are identified and properly prepared before eventual assignment to an emergency situation.

   When deploying staff and volunteers, agencies should seek to ensure that there is a balance in the number of women and men on emergency teams.

Appendix 1

Initial Needs Assessment Questions, Water Supply and Sanitation

This list of questions is primarily for use to assess needs, identify indigenous resources and describe local conditions. It does not include questions to determine external resources needed in addition to those immediately and locally available.

1 General

- How many people are affected and where are they?

- What are people's likely movements? What are the security factors for the people affected and for potential relief interventions?

- What are the current or threatened water and sanitation-related diseases? What is the distribution and expected evolution of problems?

- Who are the key people to consult or contact?

- Who are the vulnerable people in the population? What special security risks exist for women and girls?

2 Water supply

- What is the current water source?

- How much water is available per person per day?

- What is the daily/weekly frequency of the water supply?

- Is the water available at the source enough for short term and longer term needs?

- Are water collection points close enough to where people live? Are they safe?

● Is the current water supply reliable? How long will it last?

● Do people have enough water containers of the right size and type?

● Is the water source contaminated or at risk of contamination (microbiological and chemical/radiological)?

● Is treatment necessary? Is treatment possible? What treatment is necessary?

● Is disinfection necessary, even if supply is not contaminated?

● Are there alternative sources nearby?

● Are there any obstacles to using available supplies?

● Is it possible to move the population if water sources are inadequate?

● Is it possible to tanker water if water sources are inadequate?

● What are the key hygiene issues related to water supply?

● Do people have the means to use water hygienically in this situation?

3 Excreta disposal

● What is the current defecation practice? If it is open defecation, is there a designated area? Is the area safe?

● Are there any existing facilities? If so are they used, are they sufficient and are they operating successfully? Can they be extended or adapted?

● Is the current defecation practice a threat to water supplies or living areas?

● Is the current defecation practice a health threat to users?

● Are people familiar with the construction and use of toilets?

● Are people prepared to use latrines, defecation fields, trenches etc?

● What are the current beliefs and practices, including gender-specific practices, concerning excreta disposal?

● Is there sufficient space for defecation fields, pit latrines etc?

● What is the slope of the terrain?

● What is the level of the groundwater table?

● Are soil conditions suitable for on-site excreta disposal?

● What local materials are available for constructing toilets?

● Do current excreta disposal arrangements encourage vectors?

● Do people have access to water and soap for washing hands after defecation?

● Are there materials or water available for anal cleansing?

● How do women manage issues related to menstruation? Are there appropriate materials or facilities available for this?

4 Vector-borne disease

● What are the vector-borne disease risks and how serious are those risks? (See Vector Control section for determining risk.)

● If vector-borne disease risks are high, do people at risk have access to individual protection?

● Is it possible to make changes to the local environment (by drainage, scrub clearance, excreta disposal, refuse disposal etc) to discourage vector breeding?

● Is it necessary to control vectors by chemical means? What programmes, regulations and resources for vector control and use of chemicals are there?

● What information and safety precautions need to be provided to households?

5 Solid waste disposal

● Is solid waste a problem?

● How do people dispose of their waste?

- What type and quantity of solid waste is produced?

- Can solid waste be disposed of on site, or does it need to be collected and disposed of off site?

- Are there medical facilities and activities producing waste? How is this being disposed of? Who is responsible?

6 Drainage

- Is there a drainage problem? (Flooding shelters and latrines, vector breeding sites, polluted water contaminating living areas or water supplies.)

- Do people have the means to protect their shelters and latrines from local flooding?

Appendix 2

Water Quantities in Addition to the Minimum Standard for Basic Domestic Consumption

Public toilets	1-2 litres/user/day for hand washing 2-8 litres/cubicle/day for cleaning toilet
All flushing toilets	20-40 litres/user/day for conventional flushing toilets 3-5 litres/user/day for pour-flush toilets
Anal washing	1-2 litres/person/day
Health centres and hospitals	5 litres/outpatient 40-60 litres/inpatient/day Additional quantities may be needed for some laundry equipment, flushing toilets etc
Cholera centres	60 litres/patient/day 15 litres/carer/day
Therapeutic feeding centres	15-30 litres/person/day 15 litres/carer/day
Livestock	20-30 litres/large or medium animal/day 5 litres/small animal/day

Appendix 3

Good Practice in Water Supply and Sanitation Programmes

Emergency water supply and sanitation programmes should have the following good practice features in order to support the implementation of the standards. They:

- Respond to unmet needs identified by an assessment which meets minimum standards (see Analysis section).

- Consult with and encourage the participation of women in formulating objectives and identifying key public health issues that relate to the special needs of women.

- Are based on clear objectives which address priority public health issues.

- Ensure sustained, equitable application of minimum standards or better within three to six months.

- Are coordinated to ensure that priorities are met and gaps and overlaps are avoided.

- Are phased, addressing immediate needs then achieving minimum standards as quickly as possible, giving priority to the most important needs at the time.

- Are routinely and systematically monitored to ensure the progress of planned activities and to allow timely programme changes where needed (see Analysis standards).

- Involve a representative, gender-balanced cross-section of the affected population in decision-making and in project implementation (design, construction, operation and maintenance), in line with their capacity to participate in these activities.

- Complement and build on local capacities, respect local programmes and involve local authorities as appropriate.

- Consider the local context – economic, social, political and environmental – in planning and implementation.

- Recognise the needs of local people as well as those directly affected by the disaster, including avoiding pollution of local water supplies.

- Use equipment and provide facilities which are sensitive to the traditional practices of the affected population and which ensure a minimum level of dignity and comfort.

- Are sensitive to the varied needs of different social groups, at the household level and at the population level, and the impact of the programme on them.

- Are rapid in impact, but long-term in perspective, and create favourable conditions for positive developments.

- Ensure the safety of staff, volunteers and other members of the affected population involved in programme implementation and participatory activities.

- Are implemented by staff with appropriate qualifications and experience for the duties involved, who are adequately managed and supported.

- Use equipment and techniques that may be managed and maintained with local skills and resources.

Appendix 4

Select Bibliography

Almedom, A, Blumenthal, U and Manderson, L (1997), *Hygiene Evaluation Procedures: Approaches and Methods for Assessing Water- and Sanitation-Related Hygiene Practices*. International Nutrition Foundation for Developing Countries. Available from London School of Hygiene and Tropical Medicine, Keppel Street, London WC1, UK.

Cairncross, S and Feachem, R (1993), *Environmental Health Engineering in the Tropics: An Introductory Text*. John Wiley and Sons. Chichester.

Davis, J and Lambert, R (1995), *Engineering in Emergencies: A Practical Guide for Relief Workers*. RedR/IT Publications. London. This book contains reference information on all the areas covered by the standards for this sector.

House, S and Reed, R (1997), *Emergency Water Sources: Guidelines for Selection and Treatment*. WEDC. Loughborough University. Loughborough.

MSF (1992), *Public Health Technician in Emergency Situation*. First Edition. Médecins Sans Frontières. Paris.

Overseas Development Institute/People In Aid (1998), *Code of Best Practice in the Management and Support of Aid Personnel*. ODI/People In Aid. London.

Pesigan, A M and Telford, J (1996), Needs and Resources Assessment. In: *Preliminary Proceedings of the First International Emergency Settlement Conference: New Approaches to New Realities, Topic 3*. University of Wisconsin Disaster Management Center.

Pickford, J (1995), *Low Cost Sanitation: A Survey of Practical Experience*. IT Publications. London.

Thomson, M (1995), *Disease Prevention though Vector Control: Guidelines for Relief Organisations*. Oxfam. Oxford.

UNHCR (1991), *Guidelines on the Protection of Refugee Women.* UNHCR. Geneva.

UNHCR (1982), *Handbook for Emergencies.* UNHCR. Geneva.

UNHCR (1994), *Technical Approach: Environmental Sanitation.* PTSS/UNHCR. Geneva.

UNHCR (1992), *Water Manual for Refugee Situations.* PTSS/UNHCR. Geneva.

WCRWC/UNICEF (1998), *The Gender Dimensions of Internal Displacement.* Women's Commission for Refugee Women and Children. New York.

WHO (1984), *Guidelines for Drinking Water Quality*, Vol. I. WHO. Geneva.

Minimum Standards in Nutrition

Minimum Standards
in Nutrition

Contents

For the general glossary and acronyms, see Annexes 1 and 2 at the end of the book.

Part 2:2

Minimum Standards
in Nutrition

Introduction

The minimum standards for Nutrition are a practical expression of the principles and rights embodied in the Humanitarian Charter. The Charter is concerned with the most basic requirements for sustaining the lives and dignity of those affected by calamity or conflict, as reflected in the body of international human rights, humanitarian, and refugee law. It is on this basis that agencies offer their services. They undertake to act in accordance with the principles of humanity and impartiality, and with the other principles set out in the *Code of Conduct for the International Red Cross and Red Crescent Movement and NGOs in Disaster Relief*. The Humanitarian Charter reaffirms the fundamental importance of three key principles:

● the right to life with dignity

● the distinction between combatants and non-combatants

● the principle of non-refoulement

The minimum standards fall into two broad categories: those that relate directly to people's rights; and those that relate to agency processes which help ensure people acquire these rights. Some of the minimum standards combine both of these categories.

1 The importance of nutrition in emergencies

Access to food and maintenance of adequate nutritional status is a critical determinant of people's survival in the initial stages of an emergency. Malnutrition can be the most serious public health problem and may be a leading cause of death, whether directly or indirectly. Those most commonly affected are children between the ages of six months and five years, though younger infants, older children, adolescents, pregnant women, breastfeeding women and other adults may also be affected.

The purpose of nutrition programmes is to correct and to prevent malnutrition. Programmes aiming to correct malnutrition may consider appropriate feeding, medical treatment and/or supportive care. Preventative programmes aim to ensure that the population has equal access to food of adequate quantity and quality and has the means and know-how to prepare and consume it safely, and that individuals receive nutritional support as required.

As women usually assume overall responsibility for food in the household, they have an important role to play in helping to ensure that nutrition programmes are equitable, appropriate and accessible. For example, they can provide valuable information about feeding hierarchies, and how food is acquired by the affected population; they can also contribute to an understanding of gender roles and the cultural practices that affect how different members of the population access nutrition programmes. It is therefore important to encourage women's participation in the design and implementation of nutrition programmes wherever possible.

2 Finding your way around this chapter

This chapter is divided into four sections, each of which includes the following:

● **The minimum standards:** these specify the minimum levels to be attained in each area.

● **Key indicators:** these are 'signals' that show whether the standard has been attained. They provide a way of measuring and communicating both the impact, or result, of programmes as well as the process, or methods, used. The indicators may be qualitative or quantitative.

● **Guidance notes:** these include specific points to consider when applying the standard and indicators in different situations, guidance on tackling practical difficulties, advice on priority issues. They may also include critical issues relating to the standard or indicators, and describe dilemmas, controversies or gaps in current knowledge.

Filling these gaps will help improve the minimum standards for nutrition in the future.

The first three sections of the chapter, Analysis, General Nutritional Support to the Population and Nutritional Support to Those Suffering From Malnutrition reflect the logical process which nutritionists usually follow in responding to a new emergency. Firstly, they need to understand the nature of the problem. Secondly, they deal with the largest group (ie the general population) to avoid further deterioration and thirdly, they take steps to reduce the risks of death and illness for those who are already malnourished. The fourth section, Human Resource Capacity and Training, applies to all work and deals with issues related to the human capacity required to implement effective nutrition programmes.

There are four appendices giving: the definitions of terms and acronyms; minimum nutritional requirements for emergency affected populations; minimum nutrient densities for minerals not included in Appendix 2; and a select bibliography.

Reference to other sectors' technical standards is made where relevant. The purpose of this is to highlight how work in one sector is closely linked to work in other sectors, and that progress in one is dependent on progress in other areas.

In particular, there are close connections between the nutrition sector standards and those in food aid. The two sectors overlap in terms of the information required for assessment of the situation and identification of needs. There is also commonality with respect to defining nutritional (and hence food) requirements.

The two have been kept as separate chapters for three reasons. First, nutrition in emergencies is concerned with more than simply making decisions about food aid needs. Second, food aid programming carries with it specific requirements regarding financial and logistical management procedures; merging the two sectors would have made the chapter too long and too broad. Third, nutrition is associated with broader issues of food security rather than simply food aid. Food aid might be one component of a food security response but further standards are needed to cover this area.

The Minimum Standards

1 Analysis

Nutrition is not a subject that can be considered in isolation from others. Health, agriculture, water, economics, religious and traditional beliefs, social practice and welfare systems are some of the most important factors affecting nutritional status. Analysis of the underlying causes of malnutrition may be a complex process but it is vital if we are to ensure that effective programmes are put in place.

Programmes that meet the needs of disaster-affected populations must be based on a clear understanding of the current situation, including political and security factors, and anticipated developments. The people affected by the disaster, agencies, donors and local authorities need to know that interventions are appropriate and effective. Analysis of the effects of the disaster, its impact on those factors which affect nutritional status and, eventually, the impact of the programme itself are therefore critical. If the problem is not correctly identified and understood then it will be difficult, if not impossible, to make the right response.

Standardised methods of analysis that are used across the sectors have great potential to rapidly identify acute humanitarian needs and to ensure that resources are appropriately directed. This section sets out agreed standards and indicators for collecting and analysing information to identify needs, to design programmes, to monitor and evaluate their effectiveness, and to ensure the participation of the affected population.

The standards for analysis apply before any programme takes place and throughout the programme cycle. Analysis starts with an immediate initial assessment that identifies the impact of the disaster and whether and how to respond. It continues with monitoring, which identifies how well the programme is responding to needs and determines whether changes are required; and with evaluation, which determines the overall effectiveness of the programme and identifies lessons for the future.

The sharing of information and knowledge among all those involved is fundamental to achieving a full understanding of the problem and coordinated assistance. Documenting and disseminating information from the analysis process contributes to a broad understanding of the adverse public health and other consequences of disasters, and can assist in the development of improved disaster prevention and mitigation strategies.

The UNICEF conceptual framework for nutrition in emergencies has been used as a basis for the standards in this section. See the diagram below.

Before reading this section please see the definitions for *access, food security, malnutrition* and *social and care environment* in Appendix 1.

Part 2:2

Conceptual Model of the Causes of Malnutrition in Emergencies

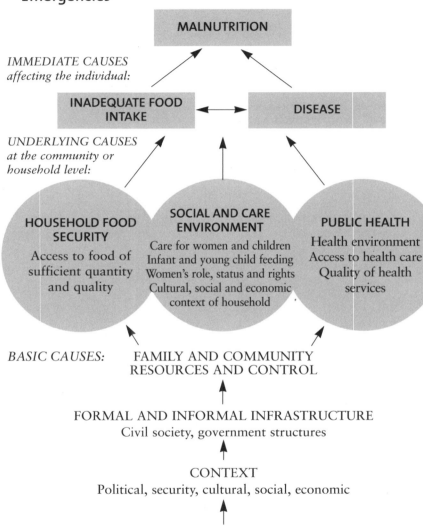

Adapted from UNICEF (1997b) and Oxfam (1997 draft)

Analysis standard 1: initial assessment

Before any programme decisions are made, there is a demonstrated understanding of the basic nutritional situation and conditions which may create risk of malnutrition.

Key indicators

● An immediate initial assessment that follows internationally accepted procedures is carried out by appropriately experienced personnel.

● The assessment is conducted in cooperation with a multi-sectoral team (water and sanitation, nutrition, food, shelter, health), local authorities, women and men from the affected population and humanitarian agencies intending to respond to the situation.

● The information gathered considers the national standards for nutrition in the country where the disaster has occurred, or in the country where humanitarian assistance is provided, if different.

● The needs of groups that are at risk of additional harm are considered.

● The information is gathered and presented in a way that allows for transparent and consistent decision making.

● Data are disaggregated by sex and age.

● An assessment report is produced, covering the following areas:

– *Basic causes of malnutrition:*

Human, structural, natural and economic resources.

The political and security context.

Formal and informal infrastructure.

Population movements and constraints on freedom of movement.

Part 2:2

– *Underlying causes of malnutrition:*

Food security.

Public health.

Social and care environment.

– *Outcomes of nutritional stress:*

Malnutrition.

Mortality.

Morbidity.

● In situations of prevailing insecurity, the assessment includes an analysis of factors affecting the personal safety and security of affected populations.

● Recommendations are made about the need for external assistance.

● Assessment findings are made available to other sectors, national and local authorities, participating agencies and male and female representatives from the affected population.

Guidance notes

1. *Internationally accepted procedures for initial assessment:* see MSF (1995), Save the Children Fund (1995), Young (1992) and WFP/UNHCR (December 1997).

2. *Timeliness:* timeliness is of the essence for the initial assessment, which should be carried out as soon as possible after the disaster. As a general rule, a report should be generated within a week of arrival at the site of the disaster, though this depends on the particular event and the wider situation.

3. *People conducting the assessment:* people who are able to collect information from all groups in the affected population in a culturally acceptable manner should be included, especially with regard to gender analysis and language skills. Ideally, there should be a balance in the numbers of men and women taking part.

4. *Assessment procedure:* the procedure for conducting the assessment should be agreed upon by all participants before field work begins and specific tasks contributing to the assessment should be assigned accordingly.

5. *Sources of information:* information for the assessment report can be compiled from existing literature, relevant historical material, pre-emergency data and from discussions with appropriate, knowledgeable people including donors, agency staff, government personnel, local specialists, female and male community leaders, elders, health staff, teachers, traders and so on. Appropriate sources of pre-emergency data may be found from documents such as: health and nutrition surveillance data; demographic and health survey reports from the country of origin (produced by Macro International); refugee nutrition information system reports (ACC/SCN); data bases (eg MEDLINE) for published literature and documents within relevant line ministries or Universities; and material from UN, donor and non-governmental agencies already working with the population. National or regional level preparedness plans may also be an important source of information. Group discussions with members of the affected population can yield useful information on beliefs and practices.

The methods used for collecting information and the limits of its reliability must be clearly communicated. Information should never be presented in such a way as to provide a misleading picture of the actual situation.

6. *Assessment report:* the assessment report should make clear how information was gathered and what gaps remain to be filled in the next stage of programme design. In the discussion on the underlying causes of malnutrition, it is valuable to highlight whether any pre-existing nutritional problems, including micronutrient deficiencies, are likely to have been worsened by the emergency, and whether there are particular groups which may be experiencing greater nutritional stress (eg pregnant and lactating women, adolescents, unaccompanied minors, children, elderly people, and people with disabilities).

Part 2:2

7. ***Underlying issues:*** an awareness of the rights of those affected by disasters, under international law, should underpin the assessment. Initial assessment and subsequent analysis should demonstrate an awareness of underlying structural, political, security, economic, demographic and environmental issues operating in the area. It is imperative that prior experience and the views of people affected by the disaster are taken into consideration when analysing the dynamics and impact of the new emergency. This requires inclusion of local expertise and knowledge in data collection and analysis of resources, capacities, vulnerabilities and needs. The current and pre-emergency living conditions of displaced and non-displaced people in the area must be considered. Gender roles within the social system also need to be taken into account, including cultural practices that contribute to women's nutritional vulnerability. For example, in certain cultures, women eat after everyone else.

8. ***Recovery:*** thinking and analysis concerning the post-disaster recovery period should be part of the initial assessment, so that interventions to meet immediate emergency requirements can serve to foster recovery among the affected population.

Analysis standard 2: response

If a nutrition intervention is required, there is a clear description of the problem(s) and a documented strategy for the response.

Key indicators

● Information on the following underlying causes of malnutrition is available and is analysed with regard to the nature and severity of the problem(s) and those worst affected:

– Food security (regional, sub-group, household, individual): eg markets, production, livestock, assets, remittances, employment, food gathering, sufficiency of food (see Appendix 2 for population based nutritional requirements), food preparation, fuel, breastfeeding, endemic micronutrient deficiencies etc.

– Public health: eg disease patterns; health care services; environmental risk factors: water, sanitation, vector-borne diseases, average parasite load; hygiene measures; traditional medicinal practices etc. (See Water Supply and Sanitation, chapter 1 and Health Services, chapter 5.)

– Social and care environment: especially with respect to: marginalised or separated groups; pregnant and adolescent women; breastfeeding mothers; infant and young child feeding practices; shelter/crowding conditions; social support systems etc.

● Implementation strategies incorporate consideration of:

– The estimated number of people affected and demographic characteristics.

– The social and political structure of the population.

– Special attention to groups at risk.

– Access to the affected population and constraints on their freedom of movement.

– Political security and operating environment.

– Existing policies concerning nutrition.

– Local capacity and resources.

– Local infrastructure and existing facilities and services.

– The possible long-term implications and environmental impact of the situation and interventions proposed.

Part 2:2

Guidance notes

1. *See also:* guidance notes for Nutrition analysis standard 1, above.

2. *Sources of information for these indicators might include:* the initial assessment report; minutes of coordination meetings; project proposals; analysis of relevant existing data, eg health and nutrition surveillance; burial counts and so on. This information may be followed up with quantitative and/or qualitative data gathering exercises to enable a more thorough analysis of the problem. Basic principles of transparency, validity and reliability must be respected and there are many different types of assessment protocol available which enable adherence to these principles. When anthropometric surveys are conducted, results must always be interpreted in the light of other factors relating to food security, public health and the social and care environment.

3. *Using different types of information:* the indicators for programme design are presented separately but in practice many types of information may have to be considered concurrently. For example, information that informs commodity selection in a food aid programme would need to be considered alongside those factors that inform the method of distribution. The system of assessment and analysis is flexible rather than rigid, and there are many linkages and overlaps that must be understood and accommodated.

4. *Sound methods and analysis:* information and sound methods must be accompanied by documented analysis. Assessment conclusions need to be internally coherent, clearly based on the information collected and linked to existing theory. (See nutrition analysis standard 1 and the conceptual framework, above.)

5. *Estimating requirements:* in order to assess the extent to which people are managing to meet their nutritional needs, it is necessary to have some reference for comparison. This is drawn from current WHO, UNHCR and WFP average requirements for population groups (see Appendix 2). However, there are two important points to consider before these requirements are used:

Firstly, the mean per capita requirements for population groups incorporate the requirements of all age groups and both sexes. They are therefore not specific to any single age/sex group and should not be used to assess requirements for an individual.

Secondly, these requirements are based on a series of assumptions which, unless true for the particular population, will lead to errors. Calculations for the requirements were based on a particular demographic profile:

Group	% of population
0-4 years:	12.37
5-9 years:	11.69
10-14 years:	10.53
15-19 years:	9.54
20-59 years:	48.63
60+ years:	7.24
pregnant:	2.4
lactating:	2.6
male/female:	50.84 / 49.16

See WFP/UNHCR (December 1997), and WHO (1997).

As the demographic structure of different populations varies, this will affect the nutritional requirements of the population concerned. For example if 26% of a refugee population were under 5 year olds, and the population was 50% males and 50% females, the requirement is reduced to 1,940 kcals.

Estimates of requirements must therefore be used with reference to information that is specific to the context. This enables the validity of the underlying assumptions to be tested. The following information is needed:

- Size of the population.

- The demographic structure of the population, in particular the percentage of under 5 year olds and the percentage of females.

- Mean adult weights and actual, usual or desirable body weight. Requirements will increase if the mean body weight for adult men exceeds 60kg and the mean body weight for adult females exceeds 52kg.

- Activity levels to maintain productive life. Requirements will increase if activity levels exceed light (ie 1.55 x Basal Metabolic Rate for men and 1.56 x Basal Metabolic Rate for women).

- Average temperature, and shelter and clothing capacities. Requirements will increase if the mean ambient temperature is less than 20°C.

- Non-nutritional needs which affect food needs: ie the potential role of food as a social and economic resource. Requirements will increase if there are any non-nutritional food needs such as religious festivals.

- The nutritional status of the population. Requirements will increase if the population is malnourished and has extra requirements for catch-up growth.

If it is not possible to incorporate this kind of information into the initial assessment, the figures in Appendix 1 may be used as a minimum in the first instance.

6. *Micronutrients – issues:* there are currently no estimates for population-level (rather than individual) requirements for most of the minerals, despite evidence highlighting their importance. As an interim guide, and pending further expert consultation by WHO, minimum nutrient densities (per 100 kcal) are proposed in Appendix 3.

For populations dependent on food aid, the choice of commodities (including decisions on fortification levels), should be based on the requirements of the population and the availability of foods which the population can access independently. Some of the food rations used currently for populations that are fully dependent on food aid may not be sufficient to meet requirements (particularly riboflavin (vitamin B^2), niacin (vitamin B^3), vitamin C, iron and folic acid). All micronutrients are vital for healthy life. Therefore where the assessment suggests that certain micronutrient requirements will not be met by the population themselves, the intervention must plan to meet the shortfall.

Even if the foods provided to a population meet the specified requirements, this cannot be taken as a proxy of adequate intake and utilisation by the body of micronutrients. Discrepancies that can occur at ration distribution or as a result of meal sharing within households affect the quantity of food eaten by individuals. Micronutrient losses can occur in other ways as well. For example losses can occur during transportation and storage of food; during processing (eg the reduction of B vitamins during milling); as a result of prolonged cooking, particularly for the water-soluble vitamins; and as a result of nutrients combining with binding agents in the diet which prohibit their absorption in the gut (eg phytates impair the absorption of iron originating from vegetable sources). Losses may also occur as a consequence of disease, in particular parasite loads, where the body's ability to access and utilise the nutrients is restricted. It is therefore essential that monitoring of nutritional status is a component of all programmes.

See also Human Resource Capacity standard 1.

Part 2:2

Analysis standard 3: monitoring and evaluation

The performance and effectiveness of the nutrition programme and changes in the context are monitored and evaluated.

Key indicators

● The information that is collected for monitoring and evaluation is timely and useful; it is recorded and analysed in an accurate, logical, consistent and transparent manner.

● Systems are in place that enable the impact (positive or negative) of the intervention on people's nutritional status to be monitored. This might include an active surveillance system if micronutrient deficiencies have been observed. (See Health Services, analysis standards for the health information system in chapter 5.)

● There is regular analytical reporting on the impact of the emergency and of the programme on the nutrition situation. There is also reporting of any contextual changes and other factors that may necessitate adjustment to the programme.

● Systems are in place that enable an information flow between the programme, other sectors, the affected population, the relevant local authorities, donors and others as needed.

● Monitoring activities provide information on the effectiveness of the programme in meeting the needs of different groups within the affected population.

● Women, men and children from the affected population are regularly consulted, and are involved in monitoring activities.

● The programme is evaluated with reference to stated objectives and agreed minimum standards to measure its overall effectiveness and impact on the affected population.

Guidance notes

1. *Use of monitoring information:* emergencies are volatile and dynamic by definition. Regular and current information is therefore vital in ensuring that programmes remain relevant. Information derived from continual monitoring of programmes should be fed into reviews and evaluations. In some circumstances, a shift in strategy may be required to respond to major changes in the context or needs.

2. *Cooperation with other sectors:* information generated by the assessment process is used as an initial baseline for the health information system (see Health Services, chapter 5) and for monitoring and evaluation activities for the nutrition programme. Monitoring and evaluation activities require close cooperation with other sectors.

3. *Using and disseminating information:* information collected should be directly relevant to the programme, in other words it should be useful and should be used. It should also be made available as needed to other sectors and agencies, and to the affected populations. The means of communication used (dissemination methods, language and so on) must be appropriate for the intended audience.

4. *Constraints:* monitoring activity can be constrained by the difficulty of gathering reliable, valid information in a volatile and changing situation. For example, when a population is in a continual state of flux, moving to and fro across a border, over a prolonged period of time, there can be no assurance that measurements made in one instance relate to the same population in a different place or time. In such situations, therefore, data needs to be interpreted very carefully.

5. *People involved in monitoring:* when monitoring requires consultation, people who are able to collect information from all groups in the affected population in a culturally acceptable manner should be included, especially with regard to gender and language skills. Women's involvement should be encouraged.

Part 2:2

6. *Evaluation:* evaluation is important because it measures effectiveness, identifies lessons for future preparedness, mitigation and assistance, and promotes accountability. Evaluation refers here to two, linked processes:

a) Internal programme evaluation is normally carried out by staff as part of the regular analysis and review of monitoring information. The agency must also evaluate the effectiveness of all its programmes in a given disaster situation or compare its programmes across different situations.

b) External evaluation may by contrast be part of a wider evaluation exercise by agencies and donors, and may take place, for example, after the acute phase of the emergency. When evaluations are carried out it is important that the techniques and resources used are consistent with the scale and nature of the programme, and that the report describes the methodology employed and the processes followed in reaching conclusions. Outcomes of evaluations should be disseminated to all the humanitarian actors, including the affected population.

Analysis standard 4: participation

The disaster-affected population has the opportunity to participate in the design and implementation of the assistance programme.

Key indicators

● Women and men from the disaster-affected population are consulted, and are involved in decision-making that relates to needs assessment, programme design and implementation.

● Women and men from the disaster-affected population receive information about the assistance programme, and have the opportunity to comment back to the assistance agency about the programme.

Guidance notes

1. *Equity:* the participation of disaster-affected people in decision-making, programme design and implementation helps to ensure that programmes are equitable and effective. Special effort should be made to ensure the participation of women and balanced male and female representation within the assistance programme. Participation in the nutrition programme may also serve to reinforce people's sense of dignity and worth in times of crisis. It generates a sense of community and ownership which can help ensure the safety and security of those who are receiving the aid, as well as those who are responsible for its distribution.

2. *People can be involved in nutrition programmes in different ways:* for example through involvement in the assessment team; provision of paid and volunteer labour in feeding programmes; through participation in decisions over selection of food commodities; by disseminating information about the use of any unfamiliar food aid commodities; by supplying information about people with special nutrition needs and supplying household lists.

3. *Coordination committees:* coordination committees help ensure people's involvement in the assistance programme. Gender, age, ethnicity and socio-economic status should be taken into consideration in order to ensure that committees adequately represent the affected population. Acknowledged political leaders, female and male community leaders and religious leaders should also be represented. The roles and functions of a coordination committee should be agreed upon when it is set up.

4. *Seeking views and opinions:* participation can also be achieved through regular polling and discussions. This can take place during distribution, through home visits or when addressing individual concerns. Group discussions with members of the affected community can yield useful information on cultural beliefs and practices.

Part 2:2

2 General Nutritional Support to the Population

This section considers the nutritional resources and services required to ensure that the needs of the general population are met. Unless and until these needs are met, any targeted nutrition interventions are likely to have limited impact since those who recover would return to a context of inadequate nutritional support. They would therefore be likely to deteriorate once again.

Before reading the standards, please see the definitions for the *International Unit* (IU) and *malnutrition* in Appendix 1.

General nutritional support standard 1: nutrient supply

The nutritional needs of the population are met.

Key indicators

- Levels of moderate malnutrition are stable at, or declining to, acceptable levels.

- There are no cases of scurvy, pellagra or beri-beri.

- Rates of xerophthalmia or iodine deficiency disorders are not of public health significance (see guidance notes below).

- There is access to a range of foods – staple (cereal or tuber), pulses (or animal products), fat sources etc.

● There is access to vitamin C rich or fortified foods or appropriate supplements.[1]

● There is access to iodised salt for the majority (>90%) of households where iodine deficiency disorders are endemic.

● There is access to vitamin A rich or fortified foods or appropriate supplements.

● There is access to additional sources of niacin (eg pulses, nuts, offal) if the staple is maize or sorghum.

● There is access to additional sources of thiamine (eg pulses, nuts, eggs) if the staple is polished rice.

● Infants under six months have access to breastmilk (or appropriate substitute).

● Children aged from about six months[2] have access to nutritious energy-dense foods.

● There is no indication that the extra nutritional needs of pregnant and breastfeeding women and adolescents are not being met.

Guidance notes

1. *Malnutrition rates:* Improving trends in malnutrition might be indicated by health centre records, growth monitoring (health centre or community based), random sample nutrition surveys, results from screening, reports from the community or reports by community workers.

   Nutrition survey results provide an estimate of the prevalence of malnutrition. The most widely accepted practice is to assess the level of malnutrition in children under five years old as a proxy for the rest of the population. However, even when there is no

---

Notes

1. Access to vitamin C is important not only to avoid scurvy but to enhance iron absorption.
2. World Health Assembly Resolution 47.5.9 May 1994 (A47/VR/11).

indication of malnutrition in under-five year olds, older children, adolescents or adult women and men may be affected. Care should thus be taken in making assumptions about the general population based on the conditions of young children. When there is reason to believe that other specific groups may be unduly affected, then they should also be assessed.

Deciding whether levels of malnutrition are acceptable (see general nutritional support standard 1) requires analysis of the current situation in the light of local norms. These might include levels of malnutrition in the population before the emergency; or levels of malnutrition in the host population if the affected population is displaced into a context where environmental and other external factors which increase mortality risk differ from those of their home area. Thus acceptable levels of malnutrition are those that are not associated with excess risk of mortality.

The risks associated with inadequate nutrient intakes for pregnant and breastfeeding women and adolescents include: pregnancy complications, maternal mortality, low birth weight and impaired lactation performance. It is assumed that food allocations within households account for these extra nutritional needs (pregnant women on average require an extra 285 kcal per day; lactating mothers require an extra 500 kcal). In some situations though, this may not be valid and women may need to be monitored, particularly with respect to iron, folic acid and vitamin A status. The prevalence of low birth weight babies (below 2.5kg) may also be a useful monitoring tool in some contexts. WHO recommend that if the prevalence exceeds 15%, then this indicates the need for a different level of public health response.

2. *Micronutrient deficiencies:* The indicators for general nutritional support standard 1 serve to highlight the importance of dietary quality. If these indicators are met, then deterioration of the micronutrient status of the population should be prevented.

   There is a range of possible options for prevention of micronutrient deficiencies. These include: increasing the quantity of food in the general ration to allow more food exchanges; improving the nutritional quality of the ration; local purchase of commodities to provide nutrients otherwise missing in the ration; measures to promote local production of foods contributing nutrients estimated to be low; provision of micronutrient rich food stuffs as a supplement to rations; appropriate fortification of staple foods or blended foods; and/or medicinal supplementation.

Three micronutrient deficiencies (scurvy, pellagra and beri-beri) have been highlighted as these are the most commonly observed deficiencies to have resulted from inadequate humanitarian assistance. They are specified here because they are avoidable. Individual cases of scurvy, pellagra and beri-beri presenting at health centres, for example, are likely to be a result of restricted access to certain types of food and are therefore probably indicative of a population-wide problem. As such, they should be tackled by population-wide interventions. (In any context where there is clear evidence that these micronutrient deficiencies are an endemic problem, levels should be reduced to at least those that would have been expected had the emergency not occurred.)

Iron deficiency anaemia, particularly in pregnant women and growing adolescents is one example of other micronutrient deficiencies which may be important contributors to mortality. The emergency may or may not have elevated the prevalence of the deficiency. In situations where a chronic endemic situation is exacerbated by the emergency, special attention must be paid to possible prevention and correction measures (see above and targeted nutritional support standard 3). Indicators of programme performance will be context specific.

Tackling micronutrient deficiencies within the first phase of an emergency is complicated by difficulties in identifying them (see targeted nutritional support standard 3). The exceptions are xerophthalmia and goitre for which clear 'field-friendly' identification criteria are available. These deficiencies can be tackled by population level interventions (ie high-dose supplementation for children (see below) and salt iodisation respectively).

Part 2:2

Indicators of clinical vitamin A deficiency (xerophthalmia) in children 6-71 months of age

(prevalence of one or more indicators signifies a public health problem)

Indicator	Minimum prevalence
Night blindness (present at 24-71 months)	>1%
Conjunctival xerosis with Bitot spots	>0.5%
Corneal xerosis / ulceration / keratomalacia	>0.01%
Corneal scars	>0.05%

See Sommer, A (1995)

When measles or other immunisation is carried out, which is often routine in emergencies resulting in displacement, it is usual practice to provide a vitamin A supplement to all children under five years of age, according to the following schedule:

- Infants 6-12 months: 100,000 IU orally (repeat every 4-6 months).

- Children >12 months: 200,000 IU orally (repeat every 4-6 months).

For clinical treatment of vitamin A deficiency, or in the case management of measles, WHO recommends:

- Infants <6 months: 50,000 IU orally on day one; 50,000 IU orally on day two.

- Infants 6-12 months: 100,000 IU orally on day one; 100,000 IU orally on day two.

– Children >12 months: 200,000 IU orally on day one; 200,000 IU orally on day two.

This helps reduce mortality associated with measles. Furthermore, it is recommended where feasible that mothers receive a high dose of vitamin A (200,000 IU orally) as soon as possible after delivery and within 8 weeks. (See: WHO (1997) and Health Services standards for measles control, in chapter 5.)

Indicators of iodine deficiency – goitre

(prevalence of (ideally) two indicators signifies a public health problem)

Indicator	Target population	Severity of public health problem (prevalence)		
		Mild	Moderate	Severe
Goitre grade >0	school age children*	5.0-19.9%	20.0-29.9%	≥30.0%
Thyroid volume >97th centile by ultra sound	school age children	5.0-19.9%	20.0-29.9%	≥30.0%
Median urinary iodine level (µg/l)	school age children	50-99	20-49	<20
Thyroid Stimulating Hormone >5U/l whole blood	neonates	3.0-19.9%	20.0-39.9%	≥40.0%
Median Thyroglobulin (ng/ml serum)	children and adults	10.0-19.9	20.0-39.9	≥40.0

*preferably children aged 6-12 years

See WHO/UNICEF/ICCIDD (1994), *Indicators for assessing iodine deficiency disorders and their control through salt iodisation.* Document WHO/NUT/94.6, WHO, Geneva.

Part 2:2

These indicators of iodine deficiency may be problematic: the biochemical indicators may not be possible in many emergency contexts, and the clinical assessments risk high levels of inaccuracy. Nevertheless, while assessment of urinary iodine is necessary to get a full picture of iodine status, a rough indication of the severity of the situation can be obtained by clinical examination of a valid sample of children aged 6 to 12 years.

3. ***Dietary quality:*** The indicators measure the quality of the diet but do not quantify nutrient availability. This is impracticable as it would impose unrealistic requirements for information collection.

   Indicators can be measured using information from various sources gathered by different techniques. These might include: monitoring the food basket at the household level; assessing food prices and food availability on the markets; monitoring the routes along which food is moved; assessing the nutrient content of distributed food using food composition tables (or Nutcalc, see Appendix 4); examination of food aid distribution plans and records; conducting food security assessments; household surveys and/or reviewing existing literature, eg agency reports.

4. ***Infant and young child feeding:*** breastfeeding is the healthiest way to feed a baby in most circumstances, particularly in an emergency in which normal hygiene procedures may have been disrupted and rates of infection may have increased.

   In situations where some mothers are not breastfeeding their infants there are three options:

   a) Relactation, where mothers are informed, supported and encouraged by experienced individuals.

   b) Formula feeding, if the milk can be prepared safely and where supplies can be guaranteed.

   c) Traditional alternative feeding, supporting other methods mothers may be familiar with to ensure they are safe and appropriate.

It is normally very rare for mothers not to be able to produce breast milk (only 1 or 2 per 10,000 mothers). However mothers may die or be separated from their infant. If it is not possible for the infant to have access to breastmilk (either from the mother, a wet nurse or a milk bank), then the provision of infant formula will be necessary. Whenever food commodities such as infant formula or commercial weaning foods are distributed, an intensive educational component must be an integral part of the work. This might involve intensive support for the infants' carers on methods for safe feeding (see general nutritional support standard 4); training of health professionals in lactation management; and promotion of, and support for, pregnant women and mothers of new-borns to breastfeed.

When infant formula is provided, there must be a guarantee that its provision can continue for as long as the infant needs it. The procurement of infant formula in emergencies must also adhere to the stipulations of the *International Code of Marketing of Breastmilk Substitutes* (WHO, 1981) which protects breastfeeding from commercial interests.

Young children require energy-dense foods since they are unable to eat large meals but have relatively high requirements given their body size. It is recommended that 30% of the energy content of their diet comes from fat sources. In cases where infants aged 6-24 months do not have access to breastmilk, nutritious energy-dense foods must be sufficient to fully replace the nutrients that would have been derived from breastmilk and complementary foods. For further information on complementary feeding, see WHO, 1998a.

5. *Support for breastfeeding women:* the implications of severe malnutrition, trauma and stress on the capacity of the mother to breastfeed are not known. Although the breastfeeding mechanism itself is robust, research has shown clearly that the psychological state of the mother can affect the release of milk. In situations where the breastfeeding mother is affected by severe malnutrition, trauma or stress, she should, in the first instance, receive adequate support in order to encourage lactation.

Part 2:2

6. ***Breastfeeding and HIV transmission:*** the HIV virus can be transmitted from mother to infant. A child stands the greatest risk – believed to be 20% – of vertical or mother-to-child transmission during the time of late pregnancy and childbirth. There is an additional risk that an infant will be infected through breastmilk. However, in situations where sanitation is inadequate and families are poorly resourced, death from diarrhoea is 14 times higher in artificially-fed infants that in those who are breastfed. In an emergency context, these risks must be carefully considered. It is important that breastfeeding is not undermined, particularly in situations where the HIV status of the mother is unknown.

General nutritional support standard 2: food quality and safety

Food that is distributed is of sufficient quality and is safely handled so as to be fit for human consumption.

Key indicators

● There are no outbreaks of food-borne diseases caused by distributed food.

● There are no unreasonable complaints about the quality of foods distributed – from recipients or programme staff.

● Suppliers of food commodities carry out regular quality control and produce commodities which meet the official government standards or Codex Alimentarius Standards (eg with regard to packaging, labelling, shelf life etc).

● All foods supplied are systematically checked by independent quality surveyors.

● All food received in the country of distribution, for the disaster-affected population, has a minimum six-month shelf life (except fresh produce and whole maize meal) and is distributed to the population before the expiry date.

● Adequate storage structures (in line with current recommendations) are in place and proper management of stores is conducted (see Food Aid resource management standard, in chapter 3).

● Staff have adequate knowledge about potential health hazards caused by improper handling, storage and distribution of food.

Guidance notes

1. *Sources of information:* information to find out whether the indicators have been achieved may be obtained from: quality control inspection reports, food labels, warehouse reports and protocols etc.

2. *Purchase of commodities:* the purchase of commodities is best done by specialists, for example at headquarters, regional offices or in specialised agencies (see Food Aid logistics standard, in chapter 3). If errors are made, they are extremely difficult to correct at field level.

3. *Milling of maize meal:* whole maize meal has a shelf life of 6-8 weeks. Milling should therefore take place immediately prior to consumption. Alternatively, low extraction milling can be used; this removes the germ, the oil and enzymes which cause rapid rancidity.

4. *Storage:* see also Walker, D J (ed) (1992).

5. *FAO/WHO (mixed years), Codex Alimentarius:* see the select bibliography for the full reference.

General nutritional support standard 3: food acceptability

Foods that are provided are appropriate and acceptable to the entire population.

Key indicators

● People are consulted on the acceptability and appropriateness of the foods being distributed and results are fed into programme decisions.

Part 2:2

● Foods distributed do not conflict with the religious or cultural traditions of the recipient or host populations (this includes any food taboos for pregnant or breastfeeding women).

● The staple food distributed is familiar to the population.

● Complementary foods for young children are palatable and digestible.

● There is no distribution of free or subsidised milk powder to the general population.

● People have access to culturally important condiments (such as sugar or chilli).

Guidance notes

1. *Monitoring of sales:* in any humanitarian intervention which involves the distribution of foods, it is important to monitor any sales and reasons why these are occurring. This would help interpret any change in trends as well as monitor effects on the local economy.

2. *Looting:* looting or theft of food, for example before distribution to families when bulk quantities might be stolen, could indicate that the commodity is seen as more valuable economically than nutritionally. If the staple food is looted, this may have important implications for the viability of the food aid programme. All looting incidents should be reported to the coordinating authorities immediately. (See Food Aid resource management standard, in chapter 3.)

   Food aid is a valuable commodity and, as with other goods, its distribution carries security risks. It may be hazardous for people to go to the distribution point, as they may be exposed to attack. People may also risk attack by armed persons for their rations on their way back from distribution points. Where appropriate, alternatives such as provision of cooked meals should be considered. (See also Food Aid distribution standard, in chapter 3.)

3. *Support for breastfeeding women:* in populations where the habitual practice in infant feeding was to use breastmilk substitute, and where processed commercial products were given as weaning foods to young children, it might be necessary to support mothers in adopting new techniques during the emergency. Particularly important are measures to promote and support breastfeeding (see general nutritional support standard 1). In this sense, the emergency can sometimes provide an opportunity to change practices which pose health risks. However, an emergency is rarely the right time to encourage behavioural change which is not an absolute necessity.

4. *Powdered milk:* powdered or modified milks that have not been mixed with other commodities should not be included in a general food distribution because their indiscriminate use could result in serious problems. Of particular concern are the potential health hazards that are likely to occur as a consequence of inappropriate dilution, germ contamination or lactose intolerance.

Part 2:2

General nutritional support standard 4: food handling and safety

Food is stored, prepared and consumed in a safe and appropriate manner, both at household and community level.

Key indicators

● There are no outbreaks of food-borne disease linked to a local food distribution site occurring as a consequence of hazardous food preparation.

● The coordinating body has received no reports from representatives of the affected population concerning difficulties in storing, preparing, cooking and consuming the food being distributed.

● Every household has access to at least one cooking pot, enough fuel for food preparation, water containers to store 40 litres; and 250g soap per person per month. (See Shelter and Site Planning standards for household items, in chapter 4; and Water Supply and Sanitation water supply standards, in chapter 1.)

● Where the food basket contains unfamiliar commodities, instructions on preparation are provided to households to maximise acceptance and minimise nutrient loss.

● Individuals who cannot prepare food or cannot feed themselves have access to a carer who can prepare appropriate food in a timely manner and administer feeding where necessary.

● Where food is distributed in cooked form, staff demonstrate knowledge about potential health hazards caused by improper storage, handling and preparation of commodities. (See human resource capacity standard 1.)

● Adequate milling or other processing facilities are available reasonably close to home if required, for example if whole grain is distributed.

Guidance notes

1. *Sources of information:* sources of information for these indicators might include programme monitoring systems and rapid household surveys.

2. *If access to cooking fuel is inadequate:* foods requiring less cooking time should be distributed (eg cereal flour rather than whole grain, parboiled pulses or rice). Where these foods are unfamiliar to the population, advice and support will need to be provided to ensure their proper use. If it is not possible to change the food commodities, then external sources of fuel supply should be established to fill the gap. (See Shelter and Site Planning, chapter 4.)

3. *Safe use of infant formula:* in the unusual situation of infants being fed formula milk, bottles should not be used as they are difficult to keep clean. Open cups (as opposed to feeding cups with a 'lip'), may be used instead. There should be capacity for boiling water and for

the thorough sterilisation of the cup (and spoon or saucer). Individuals administering infant formula to babies should have an excellent knowledge of its proper and safe use. (See general nutritional support standard 1.)

4. *Food hygiene:* people's changed circumstances may disrupt their normal hygiene practices. It may therefore be necessary to promote food hygiene messages and measures compatible with local conditions and disease patterns (see Water Supply and Sanitation hygiene promotion standards, in chapter 1). It is also important to provide information to caregivers on the optimal use of household resources for child feeding and safe methods for food preparation.

5. *Food processing facilities:* access to grinding mills, as well as other facilities such as clean water, is very important not only for food processing but also to enable people to use their time in the best way. Caregivers spending excessive amounts of time waiting for these services could otherwise be preparing food, feeding children and engaging in other care-related tasks that have a positive effect on nutritional outcomes.

6. *Whole grains require longer cooking and more fuel than milled cereals:* firewood is usually gathered by women and girls, who may have to venture out of protected areas; this often increases the risk of physical attack and rape. Security measures may be needed to minimise the risk of this happening. (See Shelter and Site Planning, site standard 4, security and planning, in chapter 4; and Health Services, health care services standard 2, reduction of morbidity and mortality, in chapter 5.)

3 Nutritional Support to Those Suffering from Malnutrition

This section presents minimum standards for programmes aiming to correct existing malnutrition, including deficiencies in vitamins and minerals.

Malnutrition is associated with increased risk of death. The strength of this association largely depends on the patterns of disease and infection which, in turn, are influenced by the local environment. There is a strong relationship between malnutrition and infection, and their impact on mortality. In other words, the combined impact of malnutrition and infection is greater than would be expected from their total individual contributions to mortality. Understanding the underlying causes of malnutrition is vital in defining the appropriate form of assistance, whether in nutrition or in the other sectors.

Before reading the standards, please see the definitions for *Body Mass Index (BMI)*, *defaulter from a therapeutic feeding programme*, *exits from a feeding programme* and *malnutrition* in Appendix 1.

Targeted nutritional support standard 1: moderate malnutrition

The public health risks associated with moderate malnutrition are reduced.

Key indicators

● There is no increase in levels of severe malnutrition and/or there is no increase in numbers registered for therapeutic care.

● Surveillance systems are established to monitor malnutrition trends.

● Programme objectives reflect understanding of the causes of malnutrition and clear identification of the target group(s).

● All staff who have regular contact with mothers of young children are trained in the principles of infant and young child feeding in the emergency context. (See human resource capacity standards.)

● From the outset feeding programmes have clearly defined and agreed criteria for closure of the programme.

Guidance notes

1. *Sources of information:* information for monitoring adherence to this standard can be gathered from a wide variety of sources, including: programme monitoring data (including data from outside the nutrition sector); anthropometric surveys; feeding centre records (including rates of coverage); staff training protocols (particularly in anthropometric measurements); and/or project proposals.

2. *Demonstrating change in prevalence:* demonstrating a change in the indicator for the level of severe malnutrition may be difficult when the prevalence of severe malnutrition is low. Given the confidence intervals around the prevalence estimate, it may not be possible to demonstrate a statistically significant change.

3. *Programme design:* in contrast to the correction of severe malnutrition (see targeted nutritional support standard 2),

moderate malnutrition can be addressed in many different ways. Programme design must be based on an understanding of the complexity and dynamics of the nutrition situation, and the factors contributing to and affecting it.

4. *Surveillance:* surveillance is an important component of information gathering and monitoring of the situation. The information gathered must be analysed in the light of seasonal and disease patterns and used to initiate appropriate responses and inform other programmes.

5. *Supplementary feeding programmes:* supplementary feeding programmes may be implemented in the short term before general nutritional support standard 1 and targeted nutritional support standard 2 are met. An assessment of the situation must justify a decision to close a programme, but if the other standards have been achieved a supplementary feeding programme should not last longer than six months.

Targeted nutritional support standard 2: severe malnutrition

Mortality, morbidity and suffering associated with severe malnutrition are reduced.

Key indicators

● Proportion of exits from a therapeutic feeding programme who have died is <10%.

● Proportion of exits from therapeutic feeding programme recovered is >75%.

● Proportion of exits from therapeutic feeding programme defaulted <15%.

● There is a mean weight gain of ≥8g per kg per person per day.

● Nutritional and medical care is provided to people who are severely malnourished, according to clinically proven therapeutic care protocols.

● Discharge criteria include non-anthropometric indices such as: good appetite; no diarrhoea, fever, parasitic infestation or other untreated illness; and no micronutrient deficiencies.

● Nutrition worker to patient ratio is at least 1:10.

● All carers of severely malnourished individuals are able to feed and care for them.

Guidance notes

1. *Programme duration:* the time needed to achieve the indicators for a therapeutic feeding programme is between one and two months.

2. *Links with other sectors:* achieving the indicators for therapeutic feeding depends on the achievement of the indicators and of the standards in other sectors (eg the existence of a functioning water and sanitation system). All information required to assess achievement of the standard will be available from records kept at the site of the therapeutic feeding and also reports from follow-up home visits.

3. *Coverage:* adherence to this standard and targeted nutritional support standard 1 will have a positive impact on the levels of severe malnutrition in a population, if coverage of therapeutic feeding is maintained at a high level. An indicator for coverage has not been stipulated as it is influenced by many context specific factors. Individuals cannot be forced to take up a service, but its use can be promoted and encouraged. Nevertheless it must be remembered that very low coverage (such as less than 30-40%) may be indicative of a poorly designed programme.

4. *Weight gain:* mean weight gain on exits $\geq$ 8g per kg per person per day applies to adults and children who receive therapeutic care. Similar rates of weight gain can be achieved in adults as in children when they are given similar diets. This indicator however may mask situations where patients are not improving and are not being discharged.

Part 2:2

5. ***Recovery:*** as a rule of thumb, most cases of severe malnutrition should recover and be discharged after 30 to 40 days in a programme. HIV and TB may result in some malnourished individuals failing to recover. Such cases need to be documented and consideration of longer-term treatment or care should be made in conjunction with the health programme.

6. ***See also:*** WHO (1998b).

Targeted nutritional support standard 3: micronutrient deficiencies

Micronutrient deficiencies are corrected.

Key indicators

- There are no cases of scurvy, pellagra or beri-beri.

- Rates of xerophthalmia are not of public health significance (see general nutritional support standard 1).

- Rates of iodine deficiency disorders are not of public health significance (see general nutritional support standard 1).

- Appropriate WHO micronutrient supplementation protocols are implemented for individuals admitted to feeding programmes.

- All clinical cases of deficiency diseases presenting at health centres are treated using WHO micronutrient supplementation protocols.

- All children under five years old presenting at health centres with diarrhoeal disease receive Vitamin A supplements. (See Health Services measles control standards, in chapter 5.)

- All children under five years old presenting at health centres with hookworm, and who are not severely malnourished, receive iron supplements in conjunction with treatment for disease.

- Procedures to respond efficiently to micronutrient deficiency to which the population may be vulnerable are established. These might include active searching for cases, tracing and campaigning to raise public awareness.

Guidance notes

1. *Sources of information to measure the indicators might include:* health centre records, feeding programme records, nutrition surveys and case definitions for deficiency diseases.

2. *There is a range of possible options for the prevention of micronutrient deficiencies:* see general nutritional support standard 1, guidance note 2.

3. *Identifying micronutrient deficiencies:* recognition of some micronutrient deficiencies (eg iodine and vitamin A) is possible through simple clinical examination. Such indicators can then be incorporated into health or nutritional surveillance systems, although careful training of staff is required to ensure that assessment is accurate. Other micronutrient deficiencies cannot be identified without bio-chemical examination (eg iron deficiency anaemia). For these reasons, case definition of micronutrient deficiencies in emergencies is problematic and can often only be determined through the response to supplementation by individuals who present themselves to health staff.

4. *Supplements for pregnant and breastfeeding women:* pregnant and breastfeeding women should receive daily supplements of iron and folic acid (60mg iron per day, with 0.4mg folic acid, starting as soon as possible after the third month of gestation). This is to address nutritional anaemias and to prevent neural tube defects in babies. In emergencies, however, the provision of supplementation is problematic as women's compliance with the daily supplementation protocols has been shown to be very difficult to maintain. Community health workers will need to address this issue.

Part 2:2

4 Human Resource Capacity and Training

All aspects of humanitarian assistance rely on the skills, knowledge and commitment of staff and volunteers working in difficult and sometimes insecure conditions. The demands placed on them can be considerable, and if they are to conduct their work to a level where minimum standards are assured, it is essential that they are suitably experienced and trained and that they are adequately managed and supported by their agency.

Capacity standard 1: competence

Nutrition interventions are implemented by staff who have appropriate qualifications and experience for the duties involved, and who are adequately managed and supported.

Key indicators

- All staff working on a nutrition programme are informed of the purpose and methods of activities they are asked to carry out.

- Assessments, programme design and key technical decision-making are carried out by staff with relevant technical qualifications and previous emergency experience.

- Staff and volunteers are aware of gender issues relating to the affected population. They know how to report incidents of sexual violence.

- Staff with technical and management responsibilities have access to support for informing and verifying key decisions.

● Staff responsible for assessing the nutritional status of individuals are trained and regularly supervised in the necessary techniques (weight, height/length, MUAC and use of appropriate indices) for children, adolescents and/or adults.

● Introduction of new equipment (for assessment of nutritional status, preparation of foods, testing of food quality etc) is accompanied by training and testing in their use.

● Food aid programme staff have the demonstrated ability to advise members of the affected population on safe and appropriate use and preparation of blended foods, if these are included in a general ration.

● Targeted feeding interventions have clear written guidelines and protocols.

● All staff involved in targeted feeding have been thoroughly trained and tested on application of the protocols.

● The treatment of severely malnourished people is supervised by a medically qualified, experienced practitioner with specific training in this area.

● Health, nutrition and/or outreach workers who have contact with moderately malnourished individuals or their carers (at home, in feeding centres, in clinics etc), have the demonstrated ability to provide appropriate advice and support as appropriate.

● Health staff have the demonstrated ability to advise mothers and carers on appropriate infant and young child feeding practices.

● Health staff have the demonstrated ability to identify key micronutrient deficiencies correctly – through clinical examination and/or biochemical analysis if available.

Part 2:2

Capacity standard 2: support

Members of the disaster-affected population receive support to enable them to adjust to their new environment and to make optimal use of the assistance provided to them.

Key indicators

- Carers are trained in how to care for severely malnourished individuals after recovery and discharge to the home environment.

- Households are advised on preparation methods for blended foods, and their contribution to the family diet, particularly for young children.

- Mothers and caregivers identified for relactation receive support, advice and encouragement on a regular basis by experienced and trained women.

- Pregnant women and mothers of new-borns are advised on the benefits of breastfeeding and are provided with the necessary support.

- All members of the emergency affected population are informed about the range, location and timing of facilities and services.

Capacity standard 3: local capacity

Local capacity and skills are used and enhanced by emergency nutrition programmes.

Key indicators

- Women and men from the disaster-affected population are included in the planning, implementation, monitoring and evaluation of nutrition programmes.

- Staff understand the importance of strengthening local capacities for long-term benefit.

● The skills base within existing local partners and institutions and in the affected population is tapped and strengthened during the course of the humanitarian assistance programme.

Guidance notes

1. *See:* ODI/People In Aid (1998), *Code of Best Practice in the Management and Support of Aid Personnel.*

2. *Staffing:* staff and volunteers should demonstrate capabilities equal to their respective assignments. They should also be aware of key aspects of human rights conventions, international humanitarian law and the *Guiding Principles on Internal Displacement* (see the Humanitarian Charter).

   Providing training and support as a part of emergency preparedness is important to ensure that skilled personnel are available to deliver quality services. Given that emergency preparedness cannot be assured in many countries, humanitarian agencies should ensure that qualified and competent staff are identified and properly prepared before eventual assignment to an emergency situation.

   When deploying staff and volunteers, agencies should seek to ensure that there is a balance in the number of women and men on emergency teams.

Part 2:2

Appendix 1

Definitions

Access

This term describes the availability of enough food (eg through production, markets, gathering in the wild, gift etc), and people's ability to acquire it (through their own labour, purchase, exchange etc). Access is central to the concept of food security (defined below) and should take account of seasonal dynamics and supply mechanisms.

ACC/SCN

United Nations Administrative Committee on Coordination / Subcommittee on Nutrition.

BMI

Body Mass Index: $\dfrac{\text{weight (kg)}}{\text{height (m)}^2}$ (a nutritional index for adults)

Defaulter from a therapeutic feeding programme

An individual who has not attended the feeding programme for more than 48 hours.

Exits from a feeding programme

Exits from a feeding programme are those no longer registered. The population of exited individuals is made up those who have defaulted, recovered (those who are referred) and died.

Food security

The World Bank's definition is used: access by all people at all times to enough food for an active, healthy life.

IU

The International Unit measures Vitamin A: 1 IU=0.3 µg Retinol Equivalent.

Malnutrition

Malnutrition is wasting (thinness) and/or nutritional oedema. Although micronutrient deficiencies are also forms of malnutrition, these are referred to specifically. Stunting is also a form of malnutrition but in disaster-affected populations is an indication of longer-term nutritional problems which preceded the disaster event. Correction of wasting and oedema reduces the risk of death. For these reasons, the nutrition standards only apply to nutrition activities which correct wasting and oedema (as well as micronutrient deficiencies).

Part 2:2

Definitions of malnutrition

	Total malnutrition	Moderate malnutrition	Severe malnutrition
Children 6.0-59.9 months	• <-2Z scores WFH or • 80% median WFH or • <12.5cm MUAC +/or • nutritional oedema	• -3 to <-2 Z scores WFH or • 70% to <80% median WFH or • 11.0 to <12.5 cm MUAC	• <-3Z scores WFH or • <70% median WFH or • <11.0 cm MUAC +/or • nutritional oedema
Children 5-9.9 years	• <-2Z scores WFH or • <80% median WFH +/or • nutritional oedema	• -3Z to <-2 Z scores WFH or • 70% to <80% median WFH	• <-3Z scores WFH or • <70% median WFH +/or • nutritional oedema
Adults 20.0-59.9 years	• BMI <17 +/or • nutritional oedema	• 16 to <17 BMI	see *Critical Issues* below

Children

Guidance notes:

Weight-for-height indicators use the NCHS/CDC reference data.

MUAC is one of the best predictors of death, partly as it is biased towards younger children. MUAC is often used for screening to select those most at risk.

WFH is the most commonly used indicator for assessing the severity of a nutritional problem. It is the preferred tool for assessments and surveys.

Critical issue:

There are no agreed anthropometric cut-offs for malnutrition in infants below six months, apart from the presence of nutritional oedema. The NCHS/CDC growth references are not useful since they are drawn from a population of artificially-fed babies – whereas breastfed babies grow at a different rate. For this reason, it is important to assess infant feeding practices, particularly access to breastmilk, and the implications for support of the lactating woman, in order to determine whether malnutrition in this age group is a potential problem.

Adolescents

Critical issue:

There is no clear, tested, agreed definition of malnutrition in adolescents (defined as 10.0-19.9 years by WHO). Indicators currently used include:

BMI-for-age, which is not applicable in contexts where growth retardation is prevalent and age is difficult to determine. In these circumstances, BMI-for-height could be used. Provisional cut-offs for both these indicators are given below. Maturational indicators, specifically menarche and adult voice, improve interpretation of BMI reference data as the peak in the adolescent growth spurt occurs prior to these milestones. However, the BMI cut-offs have NOT been validated yet and should be used with caution. It is imperative that any assessment of nutritional status in adolescents is accompanied by clinical assessment.

Provisional definitions of malnutrition in adolescents[1]

Total malnutrition	Moderate malnutrition	Severe malnutrition
• <-2Z scores BMI-for-age or • <-2Z scores BMI-for-ht +/or nutritional oedema	• -3 to <-2 Z scores BMI-for-age or • -3 to <-2Z scores BMI-for-ht	• <-3Z scores BMI-for-age or • <-3Z scores BMI-for-ht +/or nutritional oedema

These indicators use the NCHS/CDC reference standards.

It may also be possible to assess adolescents with respect to stage of maturation (rather than age or height), making it possible to use local patterns of maturation and thus negating the need for reference data. However, this is as yet at the concept stage and requires further investigation and validation.

Adults

Guidance note:

Any assessment of severe malnutrition in adults should always be accompanied by clinical examination since, as with children, malnutrition associated with infection carries higher risks of death.

Critical issues:

The cut-offs for adult malnutrition are indicators of chronic energy deficiency. There are no agreed cut-offs for rapid-onset malnutrition in adults, but evidence suggests that cut-offs for severe malnutrition could be lower than a BMI of 16. The cut-off must distinguish between those who require specialised food to recover (ie rapid-onset, severe malnutrition) and those who do not (ie those chronically energy deficient). This needs verification. Furthermore, a universal cut-off for BMI has limited application since there are large variations in BMI between populations, occurring independently of nutritional status. Such variations would have to be corrected for.

Part 2:2

There are also dangers in using BMI as a tool for screening, since there are large variations in BMI within populations caused by body shape and not nutritional status. For this reason, adults should also be assessed with MUAC and appropriate cut-offs created.

MUAC may be used as a screening tool for pregnant women (eg as a criterion for entry into a feeding programme). Given their additional nutritional needs, pregnant women may be at greater risk than other groups in the population (see Nutrition Analysis standard 2). MUAC does not change significantly through pregnancy. MUAC <20.7 cm (severe risk) and <23.0cm (moderate risk) has been shown to carry a risk of growth retardation of the foetus.[2] The risk is likely to vary according to the population.

Elderly people

Critical issue:

There is currently no agreed criterion of malnutrition in the elderly and yet this group may be at risk of malnutrition in emergencies. WHO suggests that BMI thresholds for adults may be appropriate for elderly people aged 60-69 years. Measurement accuracy is problematic because of spinal curvature (stooping) and compressing of the vertebrae. Arm span (the measurement from the tip of the middle finger on one hand to the tip of the middle finger on the other when arms are extended) can be used instead of height, but the multiplication factor to calculate height varies according to the population. BMI could be used on those elderly people able to stand up straight. MUAC may be a useful tool for measuring malnutrition in the elderly but research on appropriate cut-offs is currently in progress.

Mean weight gain (g/kg/d)

Calculated as follows: (weight on exit (g) minus lowest weight recorded during recovery (g)) ÷ (lowest weight recorded during recovery(kg)) x number of days between lowest weight recorded and exit.

MUAC

Mid Upper Arm Circumference

NCHS/CDC

National Center for Health Statistics / Centers for Disease Control, USA 1975

Nutritional oedema

Bilateral, symmetrical pitting oedema which cannot be accounted for by heart failure, gross proteinuria, renal or cardiac failure, liver disease or pre-eclampsia.

Proportion of exits defaulted

$$\frac{\text{number of defaulters in the programme}}{\text{number of exits}} \text{ X } 100\%$$

Proportion of exits died

$$\frac{\text{number of deaths in the programme}}{\text{number of exits}} \text{ X } 100\%$$

Proportion of exits recovered

$$\frac{\text{number of individuals successfully discharged in the programme}}{\text{number of exits}} \text{ X } 100\%$$

Recovered

To classify an individual as recovered from severe malnutrition he/she must be free from medical complications and have achieved and maintained sufficient weight gain (eg for two consecutive weighings). Cut-offs for weight gain (expressed as a nutritional index) at discharge from therapeutic care will depend on whether the patient is being referred to another feeding programme for the moderately malnourished (ie 'recovered' here includes those

Part 2:2

individuals who are referred to supplementary feeding); the type of programme; and the nature of the nutritional problem. Established protocols suggest appropriate discharge criteria for therapeutic care. These discharge criteria should be strictly adhered to, in order to avoid the risks associated with premature exit from the programme. Similarly, protocols define limits for the mean length of stay for patients in therapeutic feeding, aimed at avoiding prolonged recovery periods (eg typical lengths of stay may be 30-40 days).

Social and care environment

The provision in the household and community of time, attention and support to meet the physical, mental and social needs of household members.[3] Social norms and support mechanisms are important in considering the potential role and impact of individuals as carers in their household. There are six types of activities practised by caregivers: 1) care for women; 2) breastfeeding and feeding of young children; 3) stimulation of children and adolescents and support for their development; 4) food preparation and food storage practices; 5) hygiene practices; and 6) home health practices.

WFH

Weight for height (a nutritional index for children). In children below 85cm (or under two years of age), recumbent length is taken instead of standing height.

Notes

1. WHO (1997, draft), *The Management of Nutrition in Major Emergencies*. WHO. Geneva.
2. WHO (1995), *Physical Status: The Use and Interpretation of Anthropometry*. WHO. Geneva.
3. Based on definitions in UNICEF (1997a).

Appendix 2

Nutritional Requirements

The following figures can be used for planning purposes in the initial stage of an emergency:

Nutrient	Mean population requirements
Energy	2,100 kcals
Protein	10-12% total energy (52-63g), but < 15%
Fat	17% of total energy (40g)
Vitamin A	1,666 IU (or 0.5mg Retinol Equivalents)
Thiamine (B[1])	0.9mg (or 0.4mg per 1,000 kcal intake)
Riboflavin (B[2])	1.4mg (or 0.6mg per 1,000 kcal intake)
Niacin (B[3])	12.0mg (or 6.6mg per 1,000 kcal intake)
Vitamin C	28.0mg
Vitamin D	3.2 - 3.8 µg calciferol
Iron	22mg (low bioavailability (ie 5-9%))
Iodine	150 µg

Adapted from: WHO (1997, draft) and WFP/UNHCR (December 1997).

Appendix 3

Provisional Nutrient Densities

In the absence of population requirements for these essential nutrients, the following nutrient densities are proposed as a provisional tool for planning purposes.

The Desirable Nutrient Densities relate to a refugee diet. The Lower Threshold Density is suggested as the minimum value below which the nutrient density of the whole diet should not fall.

	Unit	Desirable Nutrient Density	Lower Threshold Density
Minerals: all values are per 100 kcal			
POTASSIUM (K)	mg	190	74
SODIUM (Na)	mg	60	26
MAGNESIUM (Mg)	mg	30	10
CALCIUM (Ca)	mg	84	28
PHOSPHORUS (P)	mg	70	21
ZINC (Zn)	mg	0.9	0.4
COPPER (Cu)	µg	95	28
SELENIUM (Se)	µg	3.6	1.85
MANGANESE (Mn)	µmol	0.3	
CHROMIUM (Cr)	nmol	2.0	
MOLYBDENUM (Mo)	nmol	5.0	
FLOURINE (Fl)	µmol	<1	

Source: Golden M H N, Briend A, Grellety Y (1995), *Report of Meeting on Supplementary Feeding Programmes with Particular Reference to Refugee Populations.* European Journal of Clinical Nutrition. No 49, pp137-145.

Appendix 4

Select Bibliography

FAO/WHO (mixed years), *Joint FAO/WHO Food Standards Programme. Codex Alimentarius Commission*, Volumes 1 to 14. Further information is available from codex@FAO.org.

Jaspars, S and Young, H (1995), Good Practice Review 3: *General Food Distribution in Emergencies: from Nutritional Needs to Political Priorities*. Relief and Rehabilitation Network/Overseas Development Institute. London.

MSF (1995), *Nutrition Guidelines*. Médecins Sans Frontières. Paris.

Overseas Development Institute/People In Aid (1998), *Code of Best Practice in the Management and Support of Aid Personnel*. ODI/People In Aid. London.

Oxfam (1997 draft), *Food Security: an Oxfam Perspective. Theory and Practice of Assessment and Analysis in Emergencies*. Oxfam. Oxford.

Save the Children (1995), *Toolkits. A Practical Guide to Assessment, Monitoring, Review and Evaluation*. Development Manual 5. Save the Children Fund (UK), London.

Shoham, J (1994), Good Practice Review 2: *Emergency Supplementary Feeding Programmes*. Relief and Rehabilitation Network/Overseas Development Institute. London.

Sommer, A (1995), *Vitamin A Deficiency and its Consequences: a Field Guide to Detection and Control*. WHO. Geneva.

UNHCR/WFP (1999), *Guidelines for Selective Feeding Programmes in Emergency Situations*. United Nations High Commissioner for Refugees. Geneva.

UNICEF (1997a), *The Care Initiative. Assessment Analysis and Action to Improve Care for Nutrition*. Nutrition Section, UNICEF. New York.

UNICEF (1997b), *Progress of Nations*.

Walker, D J (ed) (1992), *Food Storage Manual*. World Food Programme/Natural Resources Institute.

WCRWC/UNICEF (1998), *The Gender Dimensions of Internal Displacement*. Women's Commission for Refugee Women and Children. New York.

Weatherall, D J, Ledington, J G G, Warrell, D A, (eds) (1996), *Oxford Textbook of Medicine*, 3rd ed. Oxford University Press, Oxford. See section on severe malnutrition, pp 1278-1296.

WFP/UNHCR (December 1997), *Joint WFP/UNHCR Guidelines for Estimating Food and Nutritional Needs in Emergencies*. Rome/Geneva.

WFP/UNHCR (March 1997), *Memorandum of Understanding on the Joint Working Arrangements for Refugee, Returnee and Internally Displaced Persons Feeding Programmes*. World Food Programme. Rome.

WFP/UNICEF (February 1998), *Memorandum of Understanding between World Food Programme (WFP) and United Nations Children's Fund (UNICEF)*. New York.

WHO (1998a), *Complementary Feeding of Young Children in Developing Countries: A Review of Current Scientific Knowledge*. UNICEF, University of California Davis, WHO and ORSTROM. WHO, Geneva.

WHO (1998b), *Management of Severe Malnutrition - a Manual for Physicians and Other Senior Health Workers*. World Health Organization, Geneva.

WHO (1981), *International Code of Marketing of Breastmilk Substitutes*. World Health Organization. Geneva.

WHO (1995), *Physical Status: The Use and Interpretation of Anthropometry*. Report of a WHO Expert Committee. WHO Technical Report Series 854. World Health Organization. Geneva.

WHO (1997, draft), *The Management of Malnutrition in Major Emergencies*. World Health Organization. Geneva. This is an update of an earlier WHO publication: De Ville de Goyet, C, Seaman, J, and Geijer, U (1978), *The Management of Nutritional Emergencies in Large Populations*. World Health Organization, Geneva.

WHO (1996), *Trace Elements in Human Nutrition and Health*. World Health Organization. Geneva.

WHO (1997), *Vitamin A Supplements: A Guide to their Use in the Treatment and Prevention of Vitamin A Deficiency and Xerophthalmia*. Second Edition. WHO/UNICEF/IVACG Task Force.

Young, H (1992), *Food Scarcity and Famine: Assessment and Response*. Oxfam Practical Health Guide No 7. Oxfam. Oxford.

Other resources

Nutcalc is a simple software package for analysis of food rations run on MS DOS and developed by Action Contre la Faim (ACF).

Part 2:2

Minimum Standards in Food Aid

Minimum Standards in Food Aid

Contents

For the general glossary and acronyms, see Annexes 1 and 2 at the end of the book.

Part 2:3

Minimum Standards
in Food Aid

Introduction

The minimum standards for Food Aid are a practical expression of the principles and rights embodied in the Humanitarian Charter. The Charter is concerned with the most basic requirements for sustaining the lives and dignity of those affected by calamity or conflict, as reflected in the body of international human rights, humanitarian, and refugee law. It is on this basis that agencies offer their services. They undertake to act in accordance with the principles of humanity and impartiality, and with the other principles set out in the *Code of Conduct for the International Red Cross and Red Crescent Movement and NGOs in Disaster Relief.* The Humanitarian Charter reaffirms the fundamental importance of three key principles:

- the right to life with dignity

- the distinction between combatants and non-combatants

- the principle of non-refoulement

The minimum standards fall into two broad categories: those that relate directly to people's rights; and those that relate to agency processes which help ensure people acquire these rights. Some of the minimum standards combine both of these categories.

1 The importance of food in emergencies

All people need to consume adequate quantities of food of sufficient quality for their health and well-being. If a community's normal means of accessing food is compromised by disaster, a food aid intervention may be required. When people are unable to gain access to enough food, they are more likely to engage in short-term survival strategies, such as excessive disposal of household assets, which can lead to destitution, ill health and other long-term negative consequences. Food aid can thus act as an important mechanism to help develop people's self-reliance and restore their capacity to respond to future shocks.

Without enough food, other humanitarian assistance interventions are likely to be less effective. Cases of observable malnutrition will increase, despite the existence of nutrition programmes; health interventions alone will not be enough to prevent illnesses that are compounded by lack of adequate nutritional intake; and even if there are adequate hygiene facilities, people will continue to be susceptible to risk of disease because of weakened immune systems and diminished bodily reserves.

The purpose of food aid is to:

● Sustain life by ensuring adequate availability and access to food by people affected by disaster. (See also Minimum Standards in Nutrition, chapter 2.)

● Provide sufficient food resources to eliminate the need for survival strategies which may result in long-term negative consequences to human dignity, household viability, livelihood security and the environment.

● Provide a short-term income transfer or substitution to people to allow household resources to be invested in recovery and longer-term development.

Women usually assume overall responsibility for food in the household and, because they and their children are the major recipients of food aid, they have an important role to play in helping to ensure that food aid programmes are equitable, appropriate and accessible. Gender roles and the cultural practices that are likely to affect how women and men access food aid will need to be taken into consideration; and measures to monitor, prevent and respond to gender-based violence or sexual exploitation at food distribution points will be needed. It is important therefore that women's participation in the design and implementation of food aid programmes is encouraged wherever possible.

2 Finding your way around this chapter

This chapter is divided into nine sections (analysis, participation, coordination etc), each of which includes the following:

● **The minimum standards:** these specify the minimum levels to be attained in each area.

● **Key indicators:** these are 'signals' that show whether the standard has been attained. They provide a way of measuring and communicating both the impact, or result, of programmes as well as the process, or methods, used. The indicators may be qualitative or quantitative.

● **Guidance notes:** these include specific points to consider when applying the standard and indicators in different situations, guidance on tackling practical difficulties, and advice on priority issues. They may also include critical issues relating to the standard or indicators, and describe dilemmas, controversies or gaps in current knowledge. Filling these gaps will help improve the minimum standards for food aid in the future.

Additional critical issues are highlighted in Appendix 1 and a select bibliography is provided in Appendix 2.

The standards have been developed and arranged in a deliberate sequence. The first section deals with the analysis of the problem and participation of the people affected by the disaster. The remaining sections (requirements, targeting, resource management, logistics and distribution) follow in a logical progression and cover the main aspects of the food aid programme. Section 7 applies to all work and deals with issues related to the human capacity required to implement effective food aid programmes.

Reference to other sectors' technical standards is made where relevant. The purpose of this is to highlight how work in one sector is closely linked to work in other sectors, and that progress in one is dependent on progress in other areas.

In particular, there are close connections between the food aid and nutrition standards. The two sectors overlap in terms of the types of information required for assessment of the situation and identification

Part 2:3

of needs. There is also commonality with respect to defining nutritional (and hence food) requirements.

The two have been kept as separate chapters for three reasons. First, nutrition in emergencies is concerned with more than simply making decisions about food aid needs. Second, food aid programming carries with it specific requirements regarding financial and logistical management procedures; merging the two sectors would have made the chapter too long and too broad. Third, nutrition is associated with broader issues of food security rather than simply food aid. Food aid might be one component of a food security response but further standards are needed to cover this area.

The Minimum Standards

1 Analysis

Programmes that meet the needs of disaster-affected populations must be based on a clear understanding of the current situation, including political and security factors, and anticipated developments. The people affected by the disaster, agencies, donors and local authorities need to know that interventions are appropriate and effective. Analysis of the effects of the disaster and of the impact of the food aid programme itself are therefore critical. If the problem is not correctly identified and understood then it will be difficult, if not impossible, to make the right response.

Analysis of the need to provide food aid to a disaster-affected population presents special difficulties. Disaster may reduce people's access to food directly, by affecting production or household food stocks; or it may reduce access indirectly, by preventing access to markets, for example. In some situations, food aid may be only one of a number of ways of restoring people's access to food; alternatives might include road repair after an earthquake or the sale of food to stabilise market prices.

With the exception of specific cases of population displacement where people probably have no access to food at all, disaster-affected populations are often able to find part of their own food supply from their own resources. No practical assessment technique exists which can discriminate precisely between the different food aid needs of households within a population. It is therefore impossible to determine exactly the food aid needs of a population, except when people are wholly dependent on food aid for survival. Nevertheless, an agreed population estimate must be established. There are also practical limitations to the accuracy with which food aid can be targeted to those in need. It is important to be aware of these practical difficulties when using the analysis standards.

These standards apply before any programme takes place and throughout the programme cycle. Analysis should start with an immediate initial assessment that identifies the impact of the disaster and whether and how to respond. It continues with monitoring, which identifies how well the programme is meeting needs and determines whether changes are required; and with evaluation, which determines the overall effectiveness of the programme and identifies lessons for the future.

Given that techniques for assessing food needs in a disaster are limited, the sharing of information and knowledge among all those involved is fundamental to achieving a full understanding of the problem and coordinated assistance. Documenting and disseminating information from the analysis process contributes to a broad understanding of the adverse public health and other livelihood consequences of disasters, and can assist in the development of improved disaster prevention and mitigation strategies.

Analysis standard 1: initial assessment

Before any programme decisions are made, there is a demonstrated understanding of the basic conditions that create risk of food insecurity and the need for food aid.

Key indicators

- An immediate initial assessment that follows internationally accepted procedures is carried out by appropriately experienced personnel.

- The assessment is conducted in cooperation with a multi-sectoral team (water and sanitation, nutrition, food, shelter, health), local authorities, women and men from the affected population and humanitarian agencies intending to respond to the situation.

- The information is gathered and presented in a way that allows for transparent and consistent decision-making.

● Data are disaggregated by sex and age.

● The information collected should include:

– The extent and nature of any population displacement.

– Information on people's access to food before the disaster including:

The affected population's normal means of access to food prior to the disaster, including any seasonal considerations.

Social, economic and political factors that influenced the affected population's access to food prior to the disaster, including variations within and between populations in the area concerned.

– Information on, and analysis of, the effects of the disaster on people's access to food including:

Morbidity and malnutrition.

Direct effects of the disaster on households of different economic types.

Indirect effects on the wider economy and political economy including changes in market supply, demand and price; changes in political control of food supply.

Factors affecting the safety and security of the population and constraints on freedom of movement and access.

Evidence that households are unable to meet food deficits.

The relative needs of different groups within the population (eg with respect to age, gender).

The extent to which intervention is required to prevent impoverishment through the loss of productive assets or adoption of extreme measures to earn income.

The possible negative impact of food aid.

● Recommendations are made about the need for external assistance and the options available. If assistance is required, recommendations

Part 2:3

are made on priorities, a strategy for intervention and resources needed. There is reference to:

- The size, scope and duration of a food aid programme.

- The estimated number of people affected and demographic characteristics.

- The social and political structure of the population.

- Local capacity and resources.

- The needs of groups at risk.

- Access to the affected population and the best methods for making food available.

- The length of time food aid may be required.

- The necessary logistical requirements and resources to support the effective delivery of food aid; local infrastructure and existing facilities and services.

- Factors affecting the personal safety and security of the affected population: the specific security threats faced by vulnerable groups, especially women and girls, are taken into account in the design of food aid programmes.

- The possible immediate negative effects of food aid including: population movements to food distribution sites; increased insecurity around food aid sites; depopulation of agricultural production sites; disruption of local markets; decreased agricultural production.

- The possible long-term implications and environmental impact of the interventions proposed.

● An assessment report is produced that covers key areas and appropriate recommendations.

● Assessment findings are made available to other sectors, local authorities, participating agencies and male and female representatives from the affected population.

Guidance notes

1. *Internationally accepted procedures for initial assessment:* see MSF (1995), Young (1992) and WFP/UNHCR (December 1997).

2. *Timeliness:* timeliness is of the essence for the initial assessment, which should be carried out as soon as possible after the disaster. As a general rule, a report should be generated within a week of arrival at the site of the disaster, though this depends on the particular event and the wider situation.

3. *People conducting the assessment:* people who are able to collect information from all groups in the affected population in a culturally acceptable manner should be included, especially with regard to gender analysis and language skills. Ideally, there should be a balance in the numbers of men and women taking part.

4. *Assessment procedure:* the procedure for conducting the assessment should be agreed upon by all participants before field work begins and specific tasks contributing to the assessment should be assigned accordingly.

5. *Gathering information:* there are many different techniques for information gathering and these should be chosen carefully to match the situation and the type of information required. As a general rule, information should be gathered more frequently when the situation is changing more rapidly, and when there are critical developments such as new population movements or an epidemic outbreak of diarrhoea. Initial assessments may be quick and unrefined but analysis improves as more time and data are available. Checklists are a useful way of ensuring that all the key questions have been examined.

6. *Sources of information:* it is important to access information that is already available. This includes existing literature, relevant historical material and pre-emergency data. Discussions with appropriate, knowledgeable people including donors, agency staff, government personnel, local specialists, male and female community leaders, elders, health staff, teachers, traders, and so on are also useful. Group discussions with members of the affected population can yield useful

Part 2:3

information on beliefs and practices. Other sources of information include early warning systems and vulnerability assessments, and national or regional level preparedness plans.

The methods used for collecting information and the limits of its reliability must be clearly communicated. Information should never be presented in such a way as to provide a misleading picture of the true situation.

7. *Underlying issues:* an awareness of the rights of those affected by disasters, under international law, should underpin the assessment. Initial assessment and subsequent analysis should demonstrate an awareness of underlying structural, political, security, economic, demographic and environmental issues operating in the area. It is imperative that prior experience and the views of the people affected by the disaster are taken into consideration when analysing the dynamics and impact of the new emergency. This requires inclusion of local expertise and knowledge in data collection and analysis of resources, capacities, vulnerabilities and needs. The current and pre-emergency living conditions of displaced and non-displaced people in the area must also be considered.

8. *Livestock:* where livestock husbandry is a key livelihood strategy assessment and analysis should determine the nature and scale of the threat to livestock health and mortality. Consideration should be given to terms of trade between livestock and grain, distress sale of livestock, right to pasture and water, and access to veterinary services as indicators of the impact of the threat.

9. *Groups at risk:* the needs of groups that are at risk of additional harm such as women, adolescents, unaccompanied minors, children, elderly people and people with disabilities must be considered. Gender roles within the social system need to be identified.

10. *Recovery:* thinking and analysis concerning the post-disaster recovery period should be part of the initial assessment, so that interventions to meet immediate emergency requirements can serve to foster recovery among the affected population.

Analysis standard 2: monitoring and evaluation

The performance and effectiveness of the food aid programme and changes in the context are monitored and evaluated.

Key indicators

- The information collected for monitoring and evaluation is timely and useful; it is recorded and analysed in an accurate, logical, consistent and transparent manner.

- Systems are in place that enable stock levels, movements and distributions to be monitored.

- Supply chain monitoring is established, and identifies problems that require corrective action.

- The quality of the food distribution system is monitored.

- End-user monitoring through household-level visits and interviews ensures people can provide feedback on the effectiveness of the food aid intervention.

- There is regular analytical reporting on the impact of the emergency and of the programme on the nutrition situation. There is also reporting of any contextual changes and other factors that may necessitate adjustment to the programme.

- Systems are in place that enable an information flow between the progamme, other sectors, the affected population, the relevant local authorities, donors and others as needed.

- Monitoring activities provide information on the effectiveness of the programme in meeting the needs of different groups within the affected population.

- Women, men and children from the affected population are regularly consulted, and are involved in monitoring activities.

- The programme is evaluated with reference to stated objectives and agreed minimum standards to measure its overall effectiveness and impact on the affected population.

Part 2:3

Guidance notes

1. *Duty:* agencies carrying out food aid programmes are entrusted with a considerable resource for the benefit of people whose ability to access food has been severely compromised. As with other resources, agencies have a duty to monitor how food aid and programme funds are used.

2. *Use of monitoring information:* emergencies are volatile and dynamic by definition. Regular and current information is therefore vital in ensuring that programmes remain relevant. Information derived from continual monitoring of programmes should be fed into reviews and evaluations. In some circumstances, a shift in strategy may be required to respond to major changes in the context or needs.

3. *Use of assessment information:* information generated by the assessment process is used for monitoring and evaluation activities for the food aid programme.

4. *Monitoring activities may include:* regular audit review of inventory documents and reporting on commodity movements; independent checks on the quantity and equity of the distribution; review of distribution records and random checks on rations received; and random visits to households receiving food aid to ascertain the acceptability and usefulness of the ration.

5. *Household visits:* monitoring through sample household visits provides information concerning the acceptability of the ration and how people use it. Household visits also enable identification of people who meet the selection criteria but who are not receiving food aid.

6. *Wider effects:* monitoring should consider the effect of the food distribution system on: the agricultural cycle, market conditions, availability of agricultural inputs and agricultural activities.

7. *Safety:* monitoring of food distribution points is critical to ensure that food distribution is safe and equitable, particularly for women and children.

8. *Using and disseminating information:* information collected should be directly relevant to the programme, in other words it should be useful and should be used. It should also be made available as needed to other sectors and agencies, and to the affected populations. The means of communication used (dissemination methods, language and so on) must be appropriate for the intended audience.

9. *People involved in monitoring:* when monitoring requires consultation, people who are able to collect information from all groups in the affected population in a culturally acceptable manner should be included, especially with regard to gender and language skills. Women's involvement should be encouraged.

10. *Evaluation:* evaluation is important because it measures effectiveness, identifies lessons for future preparedness, mitigation and humanitarian assistance, and promotes accountability. Evaluation refers here to two, linked processes:

   a) Internal programme evaluation is normally carried out by staff as part of the regular analysis and review of monitoring information. The agency must also evaluate the effectiveness of all its programmes in a given disaster situation or compare its programmes across different situations.

   b) External evaluation may by contrast be part of a wider evaluation exercise by agencies and donors, and may take place, for example, after the acute phase of the emergency. When evaluations are carried out it is important that the techniques and resources used are consistent with the scale and nature of the programme, and that the report describes the methodology employed and the processes followed in reaching conclusions. Outcomes of evaluations should be disseminated to all the humanitarian actors, including the affected population.

Part 2:3

Analysis standard 3: participation

The disaster-affected population has the opportunity to participate in the design and implementation of the assistance programme.

Key indicators

● Women and men from the disaster-affected population are consulted, and are involved in decision-making that relates to needs assessment, programme design and implementation.

● Women and men from the disaster-affected population receive information about the assistance programme, and have the opportunity to comment back to the assistance agency about the programme.

Guidance notes

1. *Equity:* the participation of disaster-affected people in decision-making, programme design and implementation helps to ensure that programmes are equitable and effective. Special effort should be made to ensure the participation of women and balanced male and female representation within the assistance programme. Participation in the food aid programme may also serve to reinforce people's sense of dignity and worth in times of crisis. It generates a sense of community and ownership which can help ensure the safety and security of those who are receiving the aid, as well as those who are responsible for its distribution.

2. *People can be involved in the food aid programme in different ways:* for example through provision of paid and volunteer labour for handling and distribution; through participation on distribution committees; through involvement in decision-making on ration levels and selection criteria; by disseminating information about food distributions; by supplying household lists; by assisting in crowd control and security.

3. *Coordination committees:* coordination committees help ensure people's involvement in the assistance programme. Gender, age, ethnicity and socio-economic status should be taken into consideration in order to ensure that committees adequately represent the affected population. Acknowledged political leaders, female and male community leaders and religious leaders should also be represented. The roles and functions of a coordination committee should be agreed upon when it is set up.

4. *Seeking views and opinions:* participation can also be achieved through regular polling and discussions. This can take place during distribution, through home visits or when addressing individual concerns. Group discussions with members of the affected community can yield useful information on cultural beliefs and practices.

Part 2:3

2 Requirements

The initial assessment and analysis of the emergency situation should identify people's own food and income sources, and indicate the quantity and type of food assistance required to maintain adequate nutritional status for the general population.

The standard for food aid requirements is based on WHO's planning estimate for a typical population (for further details see Nutrition, Appendix 2, in chapter 2).

Food aid requirements may be established for:

> A general ration: to provide a complete basket of food commodities in quantities sufficient to meet requirements (see indicators below).

> A complementary ration: to provide one or two food commodities to complement existing foods available and accessible to the affected population (for example, pulses and oil might be provided to complement locally accessible cereals).

> A supplementary ration: to provide specific foods as a supplement to the general ration, in order to cover the needs of particular groups. Typically such groups would include malnourished individuals, young children and/or pregnant or nursing mothers.

Requirements standard

The food basket and rations are designed to bridge the gap between the affected population's requirements and their own food sources.

Key indicators

● Requirements are based on the following WHO initial planning estimates:

  – 2,100 kcals per person per day.

  – 10-12% of total energy is provided by protein.

  – 17% of total energy is provided from fat.

  – Adequate micronutrient intake through fresh or fortified foods.

● Estimates of people's food and income sources include consideration of:

  – Market and income opportunities.

  – Foraging and wild food potential.

  – Agricultural seasons and access to productive assets.

  – Sources of income and coping strategies.

● Ration scales include consideration of:

  – General nutritional requirements.

  – Specific needs of vulnerable groups.

  – Access to alternative sources of food and/or income.

● Commodity selection includes consideration of:

  – Local availability and market impact.

  – Local acceptability and preparation.

  – Fitness and nutritional composition.

  – Fuel requirements for cooking.

  – Other nutritional factors (see general nutritional support standard, in chapter 2).

Part 2:3

Guidance notes

1. *Initial reference value:* it is recommended that the initial reference value of 2,100 kcal per person per day is used as a planning figure when the adjustment factors are not yet known. The ICRC uses a ration requirement of 2,400 kcals per person per day as their reference point. The additional 300 kcal allows the needs of specific groups under the care of supplementary feeding programmes to be met. (See Nutrition standards in chapter 2. See also WFP/UNHCR (1997) *Guidelines for Estimating Food and Nutritional Needs in Emergencies.*)

2. *Coordination:* all organisations involved in providing food aid should be committed to coordinated assistance. Improperly coordinated food aid programmes can exacerbate existing problems or create new ones. Some groups may be over-served, while others are unfairly deprived. Different ration scales, food baskets and/or selection criteria may result in people moving to where they think they can receive the most benefit. It is also important to coordinate significant local purchases of food commodities. Failure to do so can create problems such as agencies bidding against each other and increasing prices. Excess purchases may create shortages and generate price increases for the non-recipient population. Working together to agree on food aid policies and activities helps ensure that interventions are effective and may also serve to stabilise a volatile situation.

3. *Adjusting the ration level:* populations affected by natural disasters may adopt strategies that enable them to provide for a significant part of their food requirements (eg early harvesting/salvage of crops, livestock sales, cash labour). In this case the ration level may be adjusted down from the initial reference value.

4. *Other cases of food deficit:* periodic food security assessments should target female- and adolescent-headed households to identify cases of food deficit which do not fall into normal assessment categories.

5. *Early use of food aid:* using food aid early on to meet expected shortfalls in response to slow-onset disasters can result in a need for

less food aid later on and less household decapitalisation, making recovery easier.

6. *Fuel assessment:* when assessing food requirements, a fuel assessment should be undertaken so that recipients can cook their food in ways that avoid adverse effects to their health or degradation of the environment. Agencies should provide appropriate fuel or establish a wood harvesting programme that is supervised for the safety of women and children who collect firewood. Grain mills should be provided to reduce cooking time and the amount of fuel required. (See Nutrition, general nutritional support standard 4: food handling and safety, in chapter 2.)

7. *Unfamiliar foods:* where the food basket contains unfamiliar food, cooking instructions should be provided to women and other food preparers to maximise acceptance and minimise nutrient loss.

8. *Essential non-food items:* it is important to ensure that there is adequate provision of essential non-food items, such as soap. A lack of these may result in recipients of food aid trading food commodities to meet their needs. (See Shelter and Site Planning, household items standards, in chapter 4.)

9. *Additional food commodities:* additional food commodities may be provided during selected times of the year (eg planting season) or for specific periods of increased activity to meet caloric requirements. In cases of food insecurity, it may be advisable to distribute food commodities at the same time as seed distribution. This serves to ensure that seed is not eaten, bartered or sold to obtain food, and provides additional energy for clearing and planting fields.

10. *Supporting recovery:* see Appendix 1.

Part 2:3

3 Targeting

Targeting standard

Recipients of food aid are selected on the basis of food need and/or vulnerability to food insecurity.

Key indicators

- Targeting objectives are agreed between the coordinating authorities, female and male representatives from the affected population and implementing agencies.

- Targeting criteria are clearly documented, whether in terms of population group(s) or geographical location.

- The distribution system is monitored to ensure that the targeting criteria are respected.

Guidance notes

1. **The objectives of targeting food aid may include any of the following:**

    - Saving lives, if nutritional status is of immediate concern.

    - Strengthening food security and/or the local economy.

    - Protecting the nutritional/health status of specific sub-groups within a population who are physiologically vulnerable (such as young children, adolescents, breastfeeding mothers, pregnant women, elderly people and people with disabilities).

    - Preserving households' assets (if these are being sold to cover food needs).

– Providing food supplements to those whose food need is caused by social/political vulnerability (eg separated minors, refugees or displaced persons, female-headed households, people with disabilities and ethnic or religious minority groups).

– Effectively using limited available resources (whether this is available food, logistical infrastructure, experienced personnel, transportation and so forth).

2. ***Costs:*** targeting sub-groups or individuals within a population is more costly to administer than a general distribution. Thus, if the objective of the targeting is to manage limited resources, the cost of the targeting should be weighed against potential savings.

3. ***Responding to change:*** the objectives and criteria for targeting may need to be changed to respond to contextual changes. Any modifications should be clearly communicated to all stakeholders.

4 Resource Management

Food commodities, like all resources entrusted to humanitarian agencies, must be managed in an effective and accountable way. Many agencies have standardised commodity or inventory management procedures and accounting systems that are based on principles of sound, transparent resource stewardship. Inventory systems are essential for producing reports for donors. More importantly, they provide programme planners and managers with information to make decisions about service priorities for the people receiving food aid.

Agencies are expected to take all reasonable measures to safeguard the food commodities in their care. The theft or diversion of food aid cannot be tolerated, so third party contractors acting on behalf of agencies, such as transporters and forwarding agents, must accept liability for commodities in their care.

Resource management standard

Food aid commodities and programme funds are managed, tracked, and accounted for using a transparent and auditable system.

Key indicators

- Safe stewardship practices are maintained to ensure that all commodities are safeguarded until distribution to recipient households:

    - Storage is safe and clean, and protects food commodities from damage and loss.

    - Third party service providers assume total liability for food commodities in their care and agree to reimburse any losses.

- Food commodities are inspected and unfit commodities are certified and disposed of in accordance with standard procedures.

- Damaged commodities are inspected and salvaged to the best possible extent.

- Physical inventory counts are periodically reconciled with stock balances.

● Contracting for goods and services is transparent and fair.

● Inventory accounting and reporting systems are established:

- Waybills document commodity transactions.

- Stock ledgers provide summaries of receipts, issues and balances.

- All losses are identified and accounted for.

- Summary inventory reports are compiled and made available.

Guidance notes

1. *Reporting requirements:* most bilateral and multilateral donors of food aid specify reporting requirements for food aid. Agencies should be aware of these requirements and establish the means to meet them.

2. *Accounting system: Generally Accepted Commodity Accountability Principles*, published by Food Aid Management (1993), provides guidance in establishing a food aid accounting system.

3. *Certification:* where possible, commodities purchased for distribution should be accompanied by phytosanitary certificates or other inspection certificates that confirm fitness for human consumption.

4. *Disposal of commodities unfit for human consumption:* if commodities are shown by qualified inspection to be unfit for human consumption, every effort must be made to ensure that they do not enter local markets. Methods of disposal may include sale for animal feed, burial or incineration.

Part 2:3

5. *Transparency:* fair and open contracting procedures are essential to avoid the impression of favouritism or personal financial reward and should be followed. Most agencies have contracting and procurement guidelines that meet requirements for non-profit or charitable status.

6. *Expertise:* experienced food aid managers should be recruited to all food aid programmes in order to manage and train permanent staff, and/or to establish inventory management systems.

7. *Documentation:* a sufficient stock of inventory management documentation and forms (waybills, stock ledgers, reporting forms) must be available at locations where food aid is received, stored, and/or dispatched in order to maintain a documented audit trail of commodity transactions.

8. *Providing information:* the use of local media or traditional methods for disseminating news should be considered as a way of keeping people informed about food aid supplies and operations. This reinforces transparency. Women's groups in the affected population may be enlisted to help provide information to the community about food aid programmes.

5 Logistics

Agencies must have sufficient capacity to manage the logistics of food aid programmes. If food aid is available, but agencies do not have adequate resources and systems to deliver it to the affected population, the programme will have failed. The goal of logistics management is to deliver the right goods, to the right location, in the right condition, at the right time and for the right price.

The weight and volume of food aid required to sustain a large population severely affected by disaster may measure thousands of tonnes. The physical movement of food commodities to point of distribution may involve an extensive network of purchasers, forwarding agents, transporters and receivers, and multiple handling and transfers from one mode of transport to another. These networks, or supply chains, are put together using a series of contracts and agreements which define roles and responsibilities and establish liability and compensation among the contracting parties.

Establishing the supply chain entails cooperation between donors, humanitarian agencies and local authorities. Each party has specifically defined roles and responsibilities, serving as a link, or series of links, in the supply chain. As a chain is only as strong as its weakest link, all parties involved in food aid logistics share equal responsibility for maintaining the flow of sufficient commodities to meet distribution targets and schedules established by the food aid programme.

Logistics standard

Agencies have the necessary organisational and technical capacity to manage the procurement, receipt, transport, storage and distribution of food commodities safely, efficiently and effectively.

Key indicators

● The supply chain is established and includes procurement, documentation, transport, storage and handling from point(s) of origin to final destination(s) or distribution site(s).

● Local purchases of food commodities and contracting for logistics resources and services are coordinated; impact on the local market is taken into consideration.

● Information on food aid stock levels, expected arrivals, distributions and any other information relevant to planning, forecasting and managing the flow and availability of food aid is shared between agencies.

● Special staff are assigned responsibility for logistics management (eg planning and control, importation and clearance, primary and secondary logistics, warehouse and inventory management, transport planning and management, contract management and supervision).

● Delays in distribution arising from a commodity shortfall are no longer than than two weeks.

Guidance notes

1. *Sources of food aid commodities may include:* diversion (loan or reallocation) from existing programmes using food aid (agency programmes or government grain reserves); loans from, or swaps with, commercial suppliers; commercial purchases (locally, regionally, internationally); direct supply of food from bilateral and multilateral donor agencies.

2. *Agency roles:* in large scale disasters, WFP usually plays a key role in the mobilisation of food aid and in primary logistics. WFP may

be responsible for all food aid logistics up to the Extended Delivery Point (EDP), an inland destination close to the affected area. Implementing partners (humanitarian agencies or government) assume responsibility for transportation from the EDP to the distribution site and distribution to recipient households.

3. *Using local services:* local or regional freight forwarders and/or transport brokers can provide general logistics services to a client under contract and are a valuable source of knowledge on local regulations and procedures.

4. *Stock levels:* tracking and forecasting of stock levels along the supply chain highlights anticipated shortfalls or problems with the supply of food commodities. Alternatives and solutions need to be sought to avoid or reduce problems in the supply chain.

5. *Measuring performance:* logistics accounting and inventory systems generate valuable information for measuring performance. For example:

   – Food distribution plans can be compared with actual food deliveries. Extreme deviations from the plan can direct managers' attention to problems or bottle-necks in the logistics system.

   – Budgeted and actual costs for each activity in the logistics system (eg handling, clearance, storage, transportation and distribution) can be compared to assess cost control within the logistics system. Extreme deviations from the budget can direct managers' attention to inefficiencies and/or economies of scale within the logistics system.

   – Tonne-kilometres are frequently used to measure performance and productivity in trucking fleets. Extreme deviations from an acceptable range of activity can direct managers' attention to problems in truck tasking and/or transit and turn-around times.

   – 'Throughput' measures the volume of goods handled and moved through the warehouse. It is useful for identifying the number of staff needed for a specific level of activity, and can be used to produce cost-savings and to increase productivity.

Part 2:3

- 'Pipeline analysis' views the logistics network, from origin(s) to destination(s), as a network of pipelines through which food commodities move. It is useful for producing an estimation of the expected duration of existing food aid stocks, and a schedule of delivery dates for shipments (to avoid stocks dropping below requirement). Pipeline analysis is key to forecasting potential problems and to planning procurement and delivery schedules.

6. *Links with other sectors:* the principles of good logistics management, accountability and transparency apply equally to the planning and delivery of materials and supplies for water and sanitation programmes, shelter and household support and health services. The logistics of food aid operations differ only from the other services in being quantitatively larger.

7. *Theft:* at all stages of the supply chain, there is the potential for loss of goods through theft. Stock control and storage systems must be designed and run in such a way as to minimise the risk of theft. This is particularly an issue in situations of armed conflict, where food may be at risk from banditry or could be commandeered by armed forces. Where large quantities are involved, this can be a significant factor in the war economy.

6 Distribution

An appropriate distribution method is central to the effectiveness of food aid. Distribution must therefore be considered during the initial assessment. Food aid may be distributed freely to the general population, or to specific segments or groups within a population. It may also be distributed as payment for work, or may be sold on the commercial market to address problems of supply.

Equity in the distribution process is of primary importance and the involvement of people from the disaster-affected population in decision-making and implementation should be encouraged. People should be informed about the quantity and type of food rations to be distributed, and they should feel assured that the distribution process is fair and that they receive what has been promised. Any differences between rations, for example adjusted rations provided to groups at risk, must be explained and understood.

Distribution standard

The method of food distribution is equitable, and appropriate to local conditions. Recipients are informed of their ration entitlement and its rationale.

Key indicators

- People are aware of the quantity and type of ration to be distributed for each distribution cycle, and reasons for any differences from established norms are provided.

- People receive the quantities and types of commodities planned.

- The method of distribution is readily accessible and scheduled at convenient times to minimise disruption to everyday activity.

● Recipients are involved in deciding the most efficient and equitable method of distribution; women are consulted and have an equal input into decision-making.

● When deciding the frequency of distributions (monthly or more frequently) there is consideration of:

– The cost of transporting commodities from the distribution centre.

– The time spent travelling to and from the distribution centre.

– The security of recipients and commodities once distributed.

Guidance notes

1. *Participation:* the extent to which people feel able to be involved in the distribution depends on the effect of the disaster on their social structures. Communities affected by slow-onset drought or other natural disasters may remain intact and continue to function well, enabling them to participate fully in the distribution process. By contrast, communities that are severely affected by war and civil strife may not at first be able to assume a significant role in the distribution process; they are more likely to do so as the situation stabilises and civil structures emerge. Participation in distribution committees may also serve to stimulate civil society. The participation of women should be actively sought.

2. *Registration:* formal registration of households receiving food aid should be carried out in the initial stages. Independent registration should be carried out wherever possible by the agency concerned. Women have the right to be registered in their own names if requested. Lists developed by local authorities and community-generated family lists may also be used. Corruption and/or control by powerful individuals may mean that female- and adolescent-headed households and people with exceptional vulnerabilities are omitted from distribution lists. The involvement of women from various segments of the population should improve representation of the community. In situations where registration is impossible at the initial stage, it should nonetheless be completed after three months when the

population has stabilised and if there is an expectation that food aid will be required for longer periods.

3. *Random weighing:* random weighing of rations collected by households leaving the distribution site measures the accuracy and competence of distribution management. It also helps to ensure equity.

4. *Distribution of food aid should be equitable:* variation of 20% between distribution targets (households or communities) is within the acceptable range.

5. *Distribution methods:* the method of distribution should evolve over time. In the early stages, community managed distribution based on family lists or population estimates provided by local communities may be the only way possible to get food aid distributed among the affected population. Community managed distributions should be monitored closely by the responsible agency to ensure that norms are met.

6. *Recipients should be informed about changes:* changes in the food basket or ration level caused by insufficient availability of food aid must be discussed with the recipients through the distribution committee, or female and male community leaders, and a course of action should be jointly developed. The distribution committee can inform the population of the change and why this has come about.

7. *Substitution ratios:* WFP/UNHCR distribution guidelines recommend that the following substitution ratios are used for periods of less than one month when all commodities in the food basket are not available:

Blended food and beans	1:1
Sugar and oil	2:1
Cereals and beans	2:1
Cereal and oil	3:1

Part 2:3

8. *Minimising security risks:* as with the distribution of any valuable commodity, food distribution can create security risks, including both the risk of diversion and the potential for violence. When delivery of desperately needed food is made, tensions can run high. Women, children, elderly people and people with disabilities may be especially vulnerable, and may be unable to obtain their entitlement, or have it taken from them by force. The risks must be assessed in advance and steps taken to minimise them. Steps should include adequate supervision of distributions and appropriate guarding of distribution points. One essential safeguard is to communicate clearly what people should receive. For example, ration quantities should be displayed prominently at distribution sites, written in the local language and/or drawn pictorially so that people can know their entitlements.

7 Human Resource Capacity and Training

All aspects of humanitarian assistance rely on the skills, knowledge and commitment of staff and volunteers working in difficult and sometimes insecure conditions. The demands placed on them can be considerable, and if they are to conduct their work to a level where minimum standards are assured, it is essential that they are suitably experienced and trained and that they are adequately managed and supported by their agency.

Capacity standard 1: competence

Food aid programmes are implemented by staff who have appropriate qualifications and experience for the duties involved, and who are adequately managed and supported.

Key indicators

- All staff working on a food aid programme are informed of the purpose and methods of activities they are asked to carry out.

- Assessments, programme design and key technical decision-making are carried out by staff with relevant technical qualifications and emergency experience.

- Staff and volunteers are aware of gender issues relating to the affected population. They know how to report incidents of sexual violence.

- Staff with technical and management responsibilities have access to support for informing and verifying key decisions.

- Food programme managers and supervisors have experience in resource management, safe stewardship, logistics and/or using food as a resource in humanitarian assistance or development programmes.

- Staff and volunteers involved in information gathering are thoroughly briefed and regularly supervised.

- Food aid programme staff have the demonstrated ability to advise members of the affected population on safe and appropriate use and preparation of foods if these are included in a general ration.

- Targeted feeding interventions have clear written guidelines and protocols.

- All staff involved in targeted feeding have been thoroughly trained and tested on application of the protocols.

- Female food monitors and distributors are equally represented on staff teams.

- Training and supervision mechanisms are in place.~

Capacity standard 2: local capacity

Local capacity and skills are used and enhanced by food aid programmes.

Key indicators

- Women and men from the disaster-affected population are included in the planning, implementation, monitoring and evaluation of food programmes.

- Selection criteria for international staff recruitment include a commitment to building local capacities for long-term benefit.

- The skills base within existing local partners and institutions and the affected population is tapped and strengthened during the course of the humanitarian assistance programme.

Guidance notes

1. *See:* ODI/People In Aid (1998), *Code of Best Practice in the Management and Support of Aid Personnel.*

2. *Staffing:* staff and volunteers should demonstrate capabilities equal to their respective assignments. They should also be aware of key aspects of human rights conventions, international humanitarian law and the *Guiding Principles on Internal Displacement* (see the Humanitarian Charter).

   Providing training and support as a part of emergency preparedness is important to ensure that skilled personnel are available to deliver quality services. Given that emergency preparedness cannot be assured in many countries, humanitarian agencies should ensure that qualified and competent staff are identified and properly prepared before eventual assignment to an emergency situation.

   When deploying staff and volunteers, agencies should seek to ensure that there is a balance in the number of women and men on emergency teams.

Part 2:3

Appendix 1

Other Critical Issues

This section refers in brief to a number of issues that need consideration when food aid is provided. In practice they will be addressed in different ways, according to the specific context and the needs of the people affected by the disaster.

1 Preparedness and early warning

Monitoring of early warning information and a continual state of preparedness are critical. Early warning information should be used to guide programming and to advocate for action and resources on behalf of the affected population. Information about increased levels of food insecurity should be communicated as a matter of course to the relevant bodies.

Agencies working in disaster-prone areas should identify and make use of appropriate early warning systems. These may include locally based agricultural and meteorological monitoring systems and extension networks, national monitoring systems or regional or international early warning systems such as VAM, GIEWS and FEWS. They may monitor specific phenomena such as hurricane development or more general issues such as food security or crop production.

2 Supporting recovery

Food aid can provide the affected population with time to recover from an event that has threatened life and livelihood, to consolidate resources and to start to re-establish the conditions for a normal life.

Programming that aims to improve the availability, access and utilisation of food resources should be put in place at the same time as food aid distributions in order to support recovery of food production capability, initiation of income generating activities and/or recovery of health status.

People congregate at distribution sites, so these provide a natural focus for communication and dissemination of information – such as health and safety awareness, or ration entitlements – adding value to that provided by food distribution activities.

The food distribution infrastructure can be used to support rehabilitation of local trade and markets, and to distribute other material resources, thereby avoiding duplication of costs and effort. Seeds, agricultural tools, other productive materials and non-food assistance items (jerry cans, kitchen sets, soap, shelter materials and blankets) can be distributed in this way.

3 Transition and exit strategies

Agencies that respond to an emergency should define in advance their area of operation, the duration of their involvement and the desired outcomes of the intervention. They should also define a strategy for ending the programme, or making a transition to activities that provide support for further recovery, should this be required, when acute needs have been met.

When local people know the extent of an agency's commitment, they can make better decisions about how to employ household resources. By discussing with them the objectives of the programme, indicators of success and outcomes, problems that would otherwise result from differing expectations can be avoided.

Agencies have a vital role in helping to identify and support appropriate community and household investments that strengthen self-reliance and interdependence.

4 Interpreting nutritional data

Indicators of improved nutritional status must be interpreted with great care and should be used in conjunction with information relating to the population's food security status. Figures showing significantly improved levels of nutrition may mean that the ration mix, the quantities provided and the distribution of food have been

Part 2:3

effective. They should not be interpreted to mean that people's independent access to food has improved. If people are still unable to provide for their own minimum household food requirements, terminating the aid programme may result in an erosion of the nutritional gains that have been made and precipitate a return to emergency conditions.

Appendix 2

Select Bibliography

Boudreau, T (1998), *The Food Economy Approach: a Framework for Understanding Rural Livelihoods*. RRN Network Paper 26. Relief and Rehabilitation Network/Overseas Development Institute. London.

Buchanan Smith, M and Davies, S (1995), *Famine Early Warning and Early Response – the Missing Link*. Intermediate Technology Publications. London.

EuronAid and Liaison Committee of Development NGOs to the European Union (1995), *Code of Conduct on Food Aid and Food Security*. The Hague/Brussels.

FAM (1993), *Generally Accepted Commodity Accountability Principles*. Food Aid Management. Washington DC.

FAO/WHO (mixed years), *Joint FAO/WHO Food Standards Programme. Codex Alimentarius Commission*, Volumes 1 to 14. Further information is available from codex@FAO.org.

Jaspars, S and Young, H (1995), Good Practice Review 3: *General Food Distribution in Emergencies*: *From Nutritional Needs to Political Priorities*. Relief and Rehabilitation Network/Overseas Development Institute. London.

MSF (1995), *Nutrition Guidelines*. Médecins Sans Frontières. Paris.

ODI Seeds and Biodiversity Programme (1996), Good Practice Review 4: *Seed Provision During and After Emergencies*. Relief and Rehabilitation Network/Overseas Development Institute. London.

OFDA, *Field Operations Guide*. Office for Disaster Assistance, USAID. Available from OFDA's web site.

Overseas Development Institute/People In Aid (1998), *Code of Best Practice in the Management and Support of Aid Personnel*. ODI/People In Aid. London.

Riley, F, et al (1995), *IMPACT Food Security Indicators and Framework for Use in the Monitoring and Evaluation of Food Aid Programs.* A USAID supported project. Contract no. DAN-5110-Q-00-0013-00, Delivery Order 16. Task Order 803. (Available through USAID/Food for Peace).

Telford, J (1997), Good Practice Review 5: *Counting and Identification of Beneficiary Populations in Emergency Operations: Registration and its Alternatives.* Relief and Rehabilitation Network/Overseas Development Institute. London.

UNHCR (1997), *Commodity Distribution, a Practical Guide for Field Staff.* UNHCR Division of Operational Support. Geneva.

UNHCR (1996), *Partnership: A Programme Management Handbook for UNHCR's Partners.* UNHCR. Geneva.

WCRWC/UNICEF (1998), *The Gender Dimensions of Internal Displacement.* Women's Commission for Refugee Women and Children. New York.

WFP/UNHCR (December 1997), *Joint WFP/UNHCR Guidelines for Estimating Food and Nutritional Needs in Emergencies.* WFP/UNHCR. Rome/Geneva.

WFP/UNHCR (1997), *Memorandum of Understanding.* WFP and UNHCR. Geneva.

Young, H (1992), *Food Scarcity and Famine. Assessment and Response.* Oxfam Practical Health Guide No 7. Oxfam. Oxford.

Other Resources

The WFP *Catalogue of Institutions With Expertise in Food Assistance* is available on the WFP web site:
http://wfp.org/studies/catalog_fa/index.htm

WFP *Vulnerability and Analysis Mapping* web site:
http://www.wfp.it/vam/vahmhome/htm

Minimum Standards in Shelter and Site Planning

Minimum Standards in Shelter and Site Planning

Contents

For the general glossary and acronyms, see Annexes 1 and 2 at the end of the book.

Part 2.4

Minimum Standards in Shelter and Site Planning

Introduction

The minimum standards for Shelter and Site Planning are a practical expression of the principles and rights embodied in the Humanitarian Charter. The Charter is concerned with the most basic requirements for sustaining the lives and dignity of those affected by calamity or conflict, as reflected in the body of international human rights, humanitarian, and refugee law. It is on this basis that agencies offer their services. They undertake to act in accordance with the principles of humanity and impartiality, and with the other principles set out in the *Code of Conduct for the International Red Cross and Red Crescent Movement and NGOs in Disaster Relief*. The Humanitarian Charter reaffirms the fundamental importance of three key principles:

- the right to life with dignity
- the distinction between combatants and non-combatants
- the principle of non-refoulement

The minimum standards fall into two broad categories: those that relate directly to people's rights; and those that relate to agency processes which help ensure people acquire these rights. Some of the minimum standards combine both of these categories.

1 The importance of shelter and site planning in emergencies

Along with water supply, sanitation, nutrition, food and health care, shelter is a critical determinant of survival in the initial stage of an emergency. Beyond survival, shelter is necessary to enhance resistance to disease and provides protection from the environment. It is also important for human dignity and to sustain family and community life in difficult circumstances.

The purpose of shelter, site selection and physical planning interventions is to meet the physical and primary social needs of individuals, families and communities for safe, secure and comfortable living space, incorporating as much self-sufficiency and self-management into the process as possible.

Interventions should be designed and delivered in such a way as to minimise any negative impact on the host population or on the environment.

Three possible scenarios dictate the basic shelter needs of people directly affected by a disaster. These scenarios are determined by the type of disaster, the number of people involved, the political context and the ability of the community to cope.

Scenario A: people stay at home

It is not always the case that people are displaced from their homes in a disaster. People in communities directly affected by a natural disaster almost always want to stay in or near their homes if possible. In such situations, even if homes are destroyed or damaged, assistance to people 'where they are' is more sustainable, and helps restore normality more quickly than assistance which causes them to move away in search of temporary shelter. Inputs directed into the area where people live and know each other help them to maintain social structures and allow them to continue life as normally as possible.

Scenario B: people are displaced and stay in host communities

During military conflict, and after some natural disasters such as extensive flooding, entire communities may be forced to flee their homes and home area. In such situations, displaced people may stay with the local host community, other family members or people who share historical, religious or other ties. Assistance in such situations includes responding to the rights and needs of the disaster-affected population as well as those who are secondarily affected by the disaster.

Scenario C: people are displaced and stay in clusters

Temporary settlement for refugees or displaced populations becomes necessary when circumstances of natural disaster or conflict make it necessary for people to leave their homes and local regions, and settle elsewhere. In these situations populations live as groups, often very large, for undetermined lengths of time. Assistance requires response to the needs of people in both self-settled and selected sites.

This chapter first addresses the standards needed for the provision of shelter, clothing and household items, which are common to all three scenarios. It then addresses standards for site selection and planning, which are relevant to the third scenario.

Involving women in shelter and site programmes can help ensure that they and all members of the population affected by the disaster have equitable and safe access to shelter, clothing, construction materials, food production equipment and other essential supplies. Women should be consulted about a range of issues such as security and privacy, sources and means of collecting fuel for cooking and heating, and how to make sure that there is equitable access to housing and supplies. Particular attention will be needed to prevent and respond to gender-based violence and sexual exploitation. For example, improved lighting and security patrols can help make the site safe and accessible for all the population, but particularly groups who are likely to be at risk of violence. It is therefore important to encourage women's participation in the design and implementation of shelter and site planning programmes wherever possible.

Part 2:4

2 Finding your way around this chapter

The chapter is divided into six sections (analysis, housing, clothing etc) each of which includes the following:

● **The minimum standards:** these specify the minimum levels to be attained in each area.

● **Key indicators:** these are 'signals' that show whether the standard has been attained. They provide a way of measuring and communicating both the impact, or result, of programmes as well as the process, or methods, used. The indicators may be qualitative or quantitative.

● **Guidance notes:** these include specific points to consider when applying the standard and indicators in different situations, guidance on tackling practical difficulties, and advice on priority issues. They may also include critical issues relating to the standard or indicators, and describe dilemmas, controversies or gaps in current knowledge. Filling these gaps will help improve the minimum standards for shelter and site planning in the future.

A select bibliography is provided in Appendix 1.

Reference to other sectors' technical standards are made where relevant. The purpose of this is to highlight how work in one sector is closely linked to work in other sectors, and that progress in one is dependent on progress in other areas.

The Minimum Standards

1 Analysis

Programmes that meet the needs of disaster-affected populations must be based on a clear understanding of the current situation, including political and security factors, and anticipated developments. The people affected by the disaster, agencies, donors and local authorities need to know that interventions are appropriate and effective. Analysis of the effects of the disaster and of the impact of the shelter and site programme itself are therefore critical. If the problem is not correctly identified and understood then it will be difficult to make the right response.

Standardised methods of analysis that are used across the sectors have great potential to rapidly identify acute humanitarian needs and to ensure that resources are directed accordingly. This section sets out agreed standards and indicators for collecting and analysing information to identify needs, to design programmes, to monitor and evaluate their effectiveness, and to ensure the participation of the affected population.

The standards for analysis apply before any programme takes place and throughout the programme cycle. Analysis starts with an immediate initial assessment that identifies the impact of the disaster and whether and how to respond. It continues with monitoring, which identifies how well the programme is meeting needs and determines whether changes are required; and with evaluation, which determines the overall effectiveness of the programme and identifies lessons for the future.

The sharing of information and knowledge among all those involved is fundamental to achieving a full understanding of the problem and coordinated assistance. Documenting and disseminating information from the analysis process contributes to a broad understanding of the adverse public health and other consequences of disasters, and can assist in the development of improved disaster prevention and mitigation strategies.

The standards for analysis apply to the various types of shelter needs described in the introduction to this chapter, and to the standards for shelter, clothing, household items, site selection and site planning which follow.

Analysis standard 1: initial assessment

Programme decisions are based on a demonstrated understanding of the emergency situation and on a clear analysis of people's needs for shelter, clothing and household items.

Key indicators

● An immediate initial assessment that follows internationally accepted procedures is carried out by appropriately experienced personnel.

● The assessment is conducted in cooperation with a multi-sectoral team (water and sanitation, nutrition, food, shelter, health), local authorities, women and men from the affected population and humanitarian agencies intending to respond to the situation.

● The information is gathered and presented in a way that allows for transparent and consistent decision making.

● Data are disaggregated by sex, and by age where feasible.

● The information gathered identifies needs for shelter, clothing and household items, and baseline data for monitoring and evaluation. The initial assessment considers the profile and situation of the displaced population; physical information; local infrastructural, natural and material resources; and land use.

● The assessment considers the national standards for shelter in the country where the disaster has occurred, or in the country where humanitarian assistance is provided, if different.

● Recommendations are made about the need for external assistance. If assistance is required, recommendations are made on priorities, a strategy for intervention and resources needed. An assessment report is produced that covers key areas and appropriate recommendations.

● General threats to people's security and specific threats faced by vulnerable groups, especially women and girls, are taken into account in the design of shelter and site interventions.

● Assessment findings are made available to other sectors, national and local authorities, participating agencies and female and male representatives from the affected population.

Guidance notes

1. *Internationally accepted procedures for initial assessment:* see, for example, Davis, J and Lambert, R (1995), Telford, J (1997), UNHCR (1982), and USAID (1994).

2. *For further details of assessment requirements for site selection and planning:* see Site standard 1, site selection. The guidance notes for this standard provide details of the information needed for physical and environmental assessments.

3. *The profile of the affected population should include:*

   – Demographic profile (by gender, age, social grouping).

   – Traditional means of support, and whether people are rural or urban in origin.

   – Traditional lifestyle in terms of public/private use of space, cooking and food storage, child care and hygiene practices.

   – Traditional building skills and construction methods.

   – Assets people have brought with them.

   – The type of shelter adopted by the displaced population, where relevant.

   – The needs of groups that are at risk of additional harm.

Part 2:4

– Actual or potential threats to the security of the displaced population both externally and from within. This should include specific threats faced by vulnerable groups, especially women and girls.

4. *Assessments of infrastructure and local resources should include:*

   – Level and condition of access including roads, potential supply airstrips, railheads and ports.

   – Quantities of wood required for fuel and construction, and of water that can be extracted in a sustainable way.

   – Heavy equipment already in the area, such as bulldozers and graders, for road-building and site preparation.

5. *Physical information should include:*

   – Topography of the area of land available, and suitable for, settlement and agriculture.

   – Variety and protection of potential water sources. (See Water Supply and Sanitation, chapter 1.)

   – Areas in the environment that are particularly vulnerable.

   – Seasonal variations including rainfall, snowfall, temperature variation, high winds, flooding.

   – Endemic diseases, vectors and pests. (See Water Supply and Sanitation, chapter 1 and Health Services, chapter 5.)

6. *Use of early warning information and emergency preparedness:* these should be supported wherever possible as they can contribute to the assessment. Preparedness includes personnel training and stockpiling of supplies, such as shelter materials, in strategic positions. If there is an early warning that a population movement is likely to take place, relevant information needs to be collected immediately and analysed: an inventory of the response capacity of local authorities, the UN system and agencies on the ground should be made; there should be awareness of available experienced personnel, of development plans and of supplies and equipment that can be diverted until replacements are available.

7. **Timeliness:** timeliness is of the essence for the initial assessment, which should be carried out as soon as possible after the disaster. If required, there should be an immediate response to critical needs at the same time. As a general rule, a report should be generated within a week of arrival at the site of the disaster, though this depends on the particular event and the wider situation.

8. **People conducting the assessment:** people who are able to collect information from all groups in the affected population in a culturally acceptable manner should be included, especially with regard to gender analysis and language skills. Ideally, there should be a balance in the numbers of men and women taking part. A shelter and construction specialist should be included in the team if possible.

9. **Assessment procedure:** the procedure for conducting the assessment should be agreed upon by all participants before field work begins and specific tasks contributing to the assessment should be assigned accordingly.

10. **Gathering information:** there are many different techniques for information gathering and these should be chosen carefully to match the situation and the type of information required. As a general rule, information should be gathered more frequently when the situation is changing more rapidly, and when there are critical developments such as new population movements or an epidemic outbreak of diarrhoea. Initial assessments may be quick and unrefined but analysis improves as more time and data are available. Checklists are a useful way of ensuring that all the key questions have been examined.

11. **Sources of information:** information for the assessment report can be compiled from existing literature, relevant historical material, pre-emergency data and from discussions with appropriate, knowledgeable people including donors, agency staff, government personnel, local specialists, female and male community leaders, elders, participating health staff, teachers, traders and so on. National or regional level preparedness plans may also be an important source of information. The methods used for collecting information and the limits of its reliability must be clearly communicated.

12. *Underlying issues:* an awareness of the rights of those affected by disasters, under international law, should underpin the assessment. Initial assessment and subsequent analysis should demonstrate an awareness of underlying structural, political, security, economic, demographic and environmental issues operating in the area. It is imperative that prior experience and the views of the people affected by the disaster are taken into consideration when analysing the dynamics and impact of the new emergency. This requires inclusion of local expertise and knowledge in data collection and analysis of resources, capacities, vulnerabilities and needs. The current and pre-emergency living conditions of displaced and non-displaced people in the area must also be considered.

13. *Groups at risk:* the needs of groups that are at risk of additional harm such as women, adolescents, unaccompanied minors, children, elderly people and people with disabilities must be considered. For example, when communal support systems for protection of widows, single women and unaccompanied adolescent girls are no longer present, it is important to be aware of actual or potential threats to women's security in closed living quarters. Gender roles within the social system also need to be identified.

14. *Recovery:* thinking and analysis concerning the post-disaster recovery period should be part of the initial assessment, so that interventions to meet immediate emergency requirements can serve to foster recovery among the affected population.

Analysis standard 2: monitoring and evaluation

The performance and effectiveness of the shelter and site programme and changes in the context are monitored and evaluated.

Key indicators

● The information collected for monitoring and evaluation is timely and useful; it is recorded and analysed in a logical, consistent and transparent manner.

● Systems are in place that ensure systematic collection of information on the impact (positive or negative) of the intervention on shelter, clothing and household needs, and on the environment.

● The use of household items and goods, particularly by women, is monitored.

● Women, men and children from the affected population are involved in monitoring activities.

● There is regular analytical reporting on the impact of the shelter and site programme on the affected population. There is also reporting of any contextual changes and other factors that may necessitate adjustment to the programme.

● Monitoring activities provide information on the effectiveness of the programme in meeting the needs of different groups within the affected population.

● Systems are in place that enable an information flow between the programme and other sectors, the affected population, the relevant local authorities, donors and others as needed.

● The programme is evaluated with reference to stated objectives and agreed minimum standards to measure its overall effectiveness and impact on the affected population.

Guidance notes

1. *Use of monitoring information:* emergencies are volatile and dynamic by definition. Regular and current information is therefore vital in ensuring that programmes remain relevant. Information derived from continual monitoring of programmes should be fed into reviews and evaluations. In some circumstances, a shift in strategy may be required to respond to major changes in the context or needs. Evaluation of the shelter situation after a period of around six months allows for decisions to be made as to whether and how the programme should continue. On the basis of this information it becomes possible to plan for sustainable activities, long-term involvement of agencies, and to address issues of return and reintegration.

Part 2.4

2. ***Cooperating with other sectors:*** information generated by the assessment process is used for monitoring and evaluation of the shelter and site programme. It may also contribute to an initial baseline for the health information system. Monitoring and evaluation activities require close cooperation with other sectors.

3. ***Using and disseminating information:*** information collected should be directly relevant to the programme, in other words it should be useful and should be used. It should also be made available as needed to other sectors and agencies, and to the affected populations. The means of communication used (dissemination methods, language and so on) must be appropriate for the intended audience.

4. ***Safety:*** monitoring of shelter and site programmes is critical to ensure the safety of groups at risk of harm, and to identify and address areas where violence occurs.

5. ***People involved in monitoring:*** when monitoring requires consultation, people who are able to collect information from all groups in the affected population in a culturally acceptable manner should be included, especially with regard to gender and language skills. Women's involvement should be encouraged.

6. ***Evaluation:*** evaluation is important because it measures effectiveness, identifies lessons for future preparedness and humanitarian assistance, and promotes accountability. Evaluation refers here to two, linked processes:

   a) Internal programme evaluation is normally carried out by staff as part of the regular analysis and review of monitoring information. The agency must also evaluate the effectiveness of all its programmes in a given disaster situation or compare its programmes across different situations.

   b) External evaluation may by contrast be part of a wider evaluation exercise by agencies and donors, and may take place, for example, after the acute phase of the emergency. When evaluations are carried out it is important that the techniques and resources used are consistent with the scale and nature of the programme, and that the report describes the methodology employed and the processes followed in reaching conclusions. Outcomes of evaluations should be disseminated to all the humanitarian actors, including the affected population.

Analysis standard 3: participation

The disaster-affected population has the opportunity to participate in the design and implementation of the assistance programme.

Key indicators

● Women and men from the disaster-affected population are consulted, and are involved in decision-making that relates to needs assessment, programme design and implementation.

● Women and men from the disaster-affected population receive information about the assistance programme, and have the opportunity to comment back to the assistance agency about the programme.

Guidance notes

1. *Equity:* the participation of disaster-affected people in decision-making, programme design and implementation helps to ensure that programmes are equitable and effective. Special effort should be made to ensure the participation of women and balanced male and female representation within the assistance programme. Participation in shelter and site planning programmes may also serve to reinforce people's sense of dignity and worth in times of crisis. It generates a sense of community and ownership which can help ensure the safety and security of those who are receiving assistance, as well as those who are responsible for its implementation.

2. *People can be involved in shelter, clothing and household item provision in different ways:* for example through participation in assessment teams; involvement in decision-making (eg public/private use of space); disseminating information about food storage,

traditional building and construction; assisting in identifying threats to security and special threats to women and vulnerable groups; supplying household lists.

3. *Coordination committees:* coordination committees help ensure people's involvement in the assistance programme. Gender, age, ethnicity and socio-economic status should be taken into consideration in order to ensure that committees adequately represent the affected population. Acknowledged political leaders, female and male community leaders and religious leaders should also be represented. The roles and functions of a coordination committee should be agreed upon when it is set up.

4. *Seeking views and opinions:* participation can also be achieved through regular polling and discussions. This can take place during distribution, through home visits or when addressing individual concerns. Group discussions with members of the affected community can yield useful information on cultural beliefs and practices.

2 Housing (Shelter)

The purpose of shelter interventions is to help the repair of homes, the construction of temporary shelters or the settlement of displaced people within existing communities, depending on the situation.

Housing standard 1: living quarters

People have sufficient covered space to provide protection from adverse effects of the climate. They have sufficient warmth, fresh air, security and privacy to ensure their dignity, health and well-being.

Key indicators

● The covered area available per person averages 3.5-4.5m².

● In warm, humid climates, shelters allow optimal ventilation and provide protection from direct sunlight.

● In hot, dry climates, shelter material is heavy enough to ensure high thermal capacity. If only plastic sheeting or tents are available, provision of a double-skinned roof or an insulating layer is considered.

● In cold climates, shelter material and construction ensures optimal insulation. A temperature that is comfortable to the occupants is achieved by means of insulated shelter combined with sufficient clothing, blankets, bedding, space heating and calorific intake.

● If plastic sheeting is provided for shelter, it meets the specifications defined by UNHCR.

Part 2:4

Guidance notes

1. *Link with Water Supply and Sanitation:* for indicators on minimum and maximum distances to, and number of, water points and toilets, see Water Supply and Sanitation, excreta disposal standards, in chapter 1.

2. *Shelter standards depend on the climate and the size of the household:* in a cold climate people need more interior space, as they spend more time inside than in a hot climate. Older people, women and young children generally spend more time inside the covered area.

3. *In warm, humid climates:* shelters must be oriented and designed to maximise ventilation and prevent entry of direct sunlight, so the door and windows should preferably face north and south. The roof should have a good slope for rainwater drainage and have large overhangs. The construction of the shelter should be light, as low thermal capacity is required. Appropriate orientation is important to maximise airflow; it should not be obstructed, for example, by neighbouring shelters. Shaded space outside the shelter is recommended for cooking and air-drying cooking utensils. Frequent monsoon seasons should be taken into account and surface water drainage is extremely important. (See Water Supply and Sanitation, drainage standards, in chapter 1.)

4. *In hot, dry climates:* construction must be heavy enough to ensure high thermal capacity, allowing changes in night and day temperatures to cool and heat the interior alternately. Windows should be small. If only plastic sheeting or tents are available, a double-skinned roof with ventilation between the layers to prevent radiant heat transfer should be considered. Alternatively, use of insulation materials should be supported. In a light structure, maximum ventilation is not an objective but should be easily controlled (eg by opening opposite doors) to prevent heating by hot winds and radiation from the surrounding ground, and to prevent sand coming into the shelter. Shade can be gained from surrounding shelters or trees.

5. *In cold climates:* it is essential to provide well-insulated shelters. However, good quality shelters alone are not sufficient to ensure adequate body warmth, which depends on a combination of factors. Key factors are: the external temperature; wind; insulation of the shelter; heating arrangements; available clothes and blankets; and calorific intake.

The chill factor can be minimised by ensuring that air flow through the shelter is kept to the minimum necessary for personal comfort and safety, and to prevent respiratory problems caused by space heaters or fires for cooking. However, a minimum level of ventilation must be ensured. Doors should be designed to minimise drafts.

Space heaters are essential and must be appropriate to the shelter. Ideally, air intake and exhaust from cookers or space heaters should be contained in flues.

Conduction through the floor is a major issue and needs attention to ensure that people do not lose a lot of body heat during the night. This can be addressed by ensuring that the floor is insulated, as well as the shelter itself, and/or by providing bed mats or mattresses.

6. *Supply of sheeting and other materials:* reinforced sheets of polyethylene are generally supplied in the early stage of the emergency, occasionally with rope and support materials such as local bush poles, galvanised steel, aluminium or high density paper. Assistance in harvesting materials should be considered, as should local purchase of materials. The provision of shelter systems should be considered if harvesting of materials is expected to damage the local economy or the environment.

The average household of five people should receive at least one 4 metres x 6 metres sheet of plastic. This is best imported in rolls for easy transportation, storage and distribution (4 metres x 60 metres for 10 families). However, sheets of 4 metres x 7 metres per family would give more head clearance. (See Davis, J and Lambert, R (1995), UNDP (1995) and MSF (1997).

Part 2.4

7. ***Plastic sheeting:*** plastic sheeting provided for shelter should meet specifications defined by UNHCR. Plastic sheeting for weather-proofing damaged buildings should follow different performance specifications.

8. ***Shared accommodation:*** shared accommodation is not a desirable solution to shelter problems. Where it has to be used, particular attention needs to be paid to maximising people's privacy.

9. ***Damaged homes:*** displaced people returning to homes damaged by war or natural disasters must be adequately supported. In cold climates it is preferable to help people to make one room habitable, rather than providing collective accommodation. Victims of earthquakes should be discouraged from inhabiting damaged buildings if there is a significant risk of aftershocks or further earthquakes.

10. ***Vector control:*** control measures may be required in shelters in both hot and cold climates to prevent infestation by vectors such as mosquitoes, rats and flies, and pests such as snakes and scorpions (see Water Supply and Sanitation, vector control standards in chapter 1). An understanding of local building practices, the patterns of shelter use by displaced people, and material selection should inform shelter programmes and subsequent control measures.

11. ***Environmental impact:*** appropriate measures need to be taken to minimise the environmental impact of shelter programmes. These include:

    – Provision of construction material to avoid depletion of local environmental resources.

    – Protection of vegetation essential for control of erosion and/or flooding.

    – Safeguarding agricultural and productive forest.

3 Clothing

Clothing standard

The people affected by the disaster have sufficient blankets and clothing to provide protection from the climate and to ensure their dignity, safety and well-being.

Key indicators

● People have access to sufficient blankets.

● Children up to 2 years old have at least one full set of clothing and hygiene materials appropriate to the culture, season and climate.

● Women, girls, men and boys have at least one full set of clothing in roughly the correct size, appropriate to the culture, season and climate. In addition, women and girls have a regular supply of sanitary protection.

● Culturally appropriate burial cloth is available as required.

Guidance notes

1. *Appropriateness:* the initial assessment report should indicate climatic and cultural factors in order to ensure that blankets and clothing are appropriate to men, women and children, and to age. They should be supplied separately, not in mixed bales.

2. **Women's needs:** women need specialised clothing for reasons of hygiene and personal dignity. They must also receive appropriate material for their monthly sanitary needs. It is important that these materials are appropriate and discrete, or women will not use them. Given the sensitivity of this issue, women must be involved in making decisions about what is provided. (See Water Supply and Sanitation, excreta disposal standards, in chapter 1.)

3. *Insulation:* the insulation capacity of blankets and clothes decreases significantly when they are wet (10 to 15 times) and bodies lose more thermal energy. Using many layers of clothing or blankets does not necessarily keep people warmer because with more fabric weight there is less warmth. It is therefore more cost-effective to invest in better quality blankets that will keep people warm rather than larger numbers of cheaper, poorer quality blankets.

4. *Issues relating to thermal resistance and climate:* for further guidance see UNDP (1995).

4 Household Items

People who have been displaced from their homes often arrive with only the things they can carry. When setting up a household at a new site, families need basic supplies and these should be identified by the initial assessment.

Household items standard 1: items for households and livelihood support

Families have access to household utensils, soap for personal hygiene and tools for their dignity and well-being.

Key indicators

● People have appropriate household items: 1 cooking pot with well-fitting lid, 1 basin, 1 kitchen knife, 2 wooden spoons; and 2 water collection vessels of 1-20 litres plus water storage vessels of 20 litres.

● Each person has: 1 eating plate, 1 metal spoon and 1 mug.

● Each person has access to 250g of soap per month.

● There is planning for durable items to be replaced when necessary.

● As soon as possible, each household has access to appropriate tools and materials to support livelihood activity.

● Tools and materials supplied are appropriate and familiar to the population, and are of a similar technological level to that which people were used to before the disaster. Items are appropriate to the conditions in which they are to be used.

● Those affected are aware of their entitlements under assistance programmes.

Guidance notes

1. *Link with Water Supply and Sanitation:* see also Water Supply and Sanitation, water supply standard 3: water use facilities and goods, for indicators relating to water storage, soap and washing containers; and solid waste management standard 2: solid waste containers/pits, for requirements for refuse containers.

2. *Opportunities for self-reliance:* as soon as feasible, women and men should be given the opportunity to develop current and future self-reliance by means of food production, training or other activities that contribute to their general health and well-being. This needs to be considered when planning household space requirements.

3. *Supply and procurement:* technical items can be paid for in cash, by means of labour supplied, or on the basis of a loan. Wherever possible materials should be supplied and procured locally, preferably by the people themselves on a household-to-household basis. It is important to ensure that female- and adolescent-headed households, single women and widows enjoy fair access to supplies, allowances, cash-for-work programmes and training. More durable items supplied to the population should be technologically simple, and be maintained by the people themselves or locally.

Household items standard 2: environmental concerns

Fuel-economic cooking implements and stoves are made avilable, and their use is promoted.

Key indicators

● People have access to, and make use of, fuel-economic and low smoke wood stoves (produced locally if possible), gas or kerosene stoves and cooking pots with well-fitting lids.

● The use and benefit of fuel-economic devices is promoted through community education programmes, if needed, and their production is planned as early as possible.

● People are aware of the benefits of using fuel-economic devices.

● Women are consulted about the location and means of collecting fuel for cooking and heating.

5 Site Selection and Planning

This section applies to the third scenario described at the beginning of this chapter, where the only available means of providing shelter for a displaced population is a planned temporary settlement.

A well-situated and well-planned temporary settlement provides a healthy environment where people can live in dignity and at peace, and where they can lead as sustainable a family life as possible. In meeting minimum standards, site selection and planning should aim to produce the best living conditions possible under the circumstances, with minimal damage to the environment.

The site selection and planning standards are structured around the assessment process and subsequent steps that should be taken to establish the type and form of settlement appropriate to the needs of the displaced population. Site selection is determined with reference to four types of temporary settlement (reception or transit centres, self-settled camps, planned temporary settlements, extensions to temporary settlements). Once the preferred option has been identified, information from the physical assessment is then used to decide whether this can be achieved and, if not, what compromises should be made.

Site standard 1: site selection

The site is suitable to host the number of people involved.

Key indicators

These indicators combine to describe a process which is expanded upon in the guidance notes.

● The appropriate population size of a temporary settlement is defined following socio-economic assessments of both displaced and host populations, and assessments of the carrying capacity of the region and site.

● The appropriate type of temporary settlement required is determined: reception or transit centre; self-settled camp; planned temporary settlement or extension to a temporary settlement.

● Requirements for the form the settlement is to take are determined with reference to:

– Information generated by the physical assessment.

– Actual or potential threats to the security of the affected population. This is particularly important for refugee populations and is always critical for single women, widows and unaccompanied adolescent girls.

– The maximum estimated duration of the settlement.

– The preferred population density of the settlement.

– The level of integration of the displaced population with the host population.

● The requirements for the form of the settlement are tested against the physical constraints of each potential site. The site meets the following requirements, regardless of seasonal variations:

– It is located at a safe distance from possible external threats to physical security, usually not less than 50km.

– It is accessible by heavy trucks from an all-weather road. If it is necessary to construct a road, the soil type and terrain should support this activity. Communal facilities are accessible by light vehicles.

– It is near to existing social and economic facilities where appropriate.

– There are adequate quantities of water (for drinking, cooking, hygiene and sanitation).

Part 2:4

- It is not less than 3 metres above the anticipated water table in the rainy season.

- Water rights, and the right to use other natural resources such as wood, stone and sand are arranged before, or at the same time as, the site is selected.

- Land rights are firmly established prior to occupation and permitted use is negotiated as necessary.

- The soil type is suitable for digging and water infiltration.

- There are sufficient grasses, shrubs and trees for shade and to avoid soil erosion.

- Sufficient sustainable resources of fuel wood and construction materials are available.

- Sufficient and appropriate land is available for the required levels of agriculture and animal husbandry. The impacts of these are understood, and land use is negotiated as necessary.

- The site is not prone to endemic diseases that might affect inhabitants or their livestock, to standing water or to flooding; it is not situated on land at risk from landslides and is not close to an active volcano.

Guidance notes

These notes combine to describe a process by which the requirements of a settlement are identified, and which explore the critical characteristics of a site.

1. *Identifying the type of settlement:* the assessments provide information that guide selection of the type of settlement (this note) and the form it takes (note 2). There are four basic types of temporary settlement:

   a) **Reception or transit centres:** where displaced people or refugees stay for short periods. A reception and transit centre should be treated in the same way as a planned settlement (c below) if it is: (1) large, having a population over 2,000 or (2) expected to last a long time. Environmental resources will have to be carefully managed to make sure that both displaced and local populations have enough water, fuel, and construction material, and that the local economy and environment are not adversely affected. If a transit camp receives many groups for short periods over a long period of time, this will have similar social and economic impacts on the local population as for a planned settlement.

b) **Self-settled camps:** where people have settled spontaneously, yet require partial relocation, provision of infrastructure and sustainable environmental resources.

c) **Planned temporary settlements:** where settlements are constructed and serviced by physical planners in advance of the arrival of people (eg from reception or transit centres).

d) **Extensions to temporary settlements:** where extension to the settlement is required to accommodate new arrivals (eg from reception or transit centres).

2. *Deciding the form of settlement:* having identified the type of settlement, the next step is to decide the form it should take. This should take into account information from the socio-economic assessment and the following:

a) **Security of the displaced population:** whether there are threats from within the displaced population, from the host population or from other parties.

b) **The maximum envisaged duration of the settlement.**

c) **Interaction with the local population, economy and environment.**

3. *Assessing the physical site:* once the preferred type and form of settlement have been identified, information from the physical assessment should be used to decide whether the preferred option can be achieved and, if not, what compromises should be made. Specialist advice may be required at this stage. The physical site assessment should address the following:

Part 2:4

a) **Access**

– Proximity and condition of local road infrastructure.

– Proximity to host service infrastructure and whether siting will affect this positively or negatively.

– Proximity to airstrips, railheads or ports.

– Seasonal constraints on access, and vulnerability of access.

b) **Site conditions**

– Topography and site gradients should be sufficient for drainage while being habitable for the expected density of occupation. The appropriate maximum site gradient depends on soil conditions, vegetation and possible drainage and erosion control measures, which need to be taken into consideration in order to prevent flooding and mudslides. The ideal gradient is between 2% and 4%.

– Natural hazards including earthquakes, volcanic activity, landslides or flooding.

– Permeability of the ground. For example, fissured rock will disperse latrine waste widely; volcanic rock makes latrine construction difficult. (See Water Supply and Sanitation, excreta disposal standards, in chapter 1.)

– Micro-climatic conditions.

c) **Water (see Water Supply and Sanitation, chapter 1)**

– Availability of sufficient water within a suitable distance throughout the year for displaced people, the host community, agriculture and livestock.

– Separation of animal and water points.

– Whether there is more than one source of water, in order to reduce the vulnerability of the water supply.

– Height of the water table, whether it risks pollution by sanitation and flooding, and seasonal variations.

d) **Space**

– Whether there is sufficient space for the desired density of the population and dispersal of that population into the number of settlements required.

– Whether there is space for extension of the settlement(s), should the population increase.

– Current land use and expected impact of the settlement on the land.

– The levels and types of agriculture and livestock that can be supported.

e) **Environment**

– Expected temperature, wind and rainfall in terms of their influence on planning, agriculture and livestock.

– Existence of environmentally vulnerable or valuable areas nearby.

– Availability of sufficient, sustainable quantities of wood for fuel and construction for both the displaced and host populations.

– Type and quantity of ground cover in terms of their influence on micro-climatic conditions, wind speeds and soil erosion.

– Endemic diseases, pests, risk of disease. (See Health Services, standards for control of communicable diseases, in chapter 5; Water Supply and Sanitation, vector control standards, in chapter 1.)

Throughout this process it is essential that site selection is guided first and foremost by the needs of the affected population(s) rather than by purely technical considerations or the establishment of assistance mechanisms.

4. *For an alternative method for site selection, from an engineering perspective:* see the site selection matrix in Davis and Lambert (1995).

Part 2·4

5. ***Minimising negative impacts:*** when a displaced population settles close to a larger host community, it can benefit from access to locally available infrastructure services and livelihood opportunities. The displaced population may outnumber the host communities. This can place demands on the local infrastructure, economy and environment, which may create animosity between the two communities. Careful site selection and planning are thus critical in determining the effectiveness of the wider humanitarian assistance programme and the security of women, men and children from the affected populations.

6. ***See also:*** Analysis standard 1, assessment.

Site standard 2: site planning

Site planning ensures sufficient space for household areas and supports people's security and well-being. It provides for effective and efficient provision of services and internal access.

Key indicators

- The site provides 45m² space for each person. This includes infrastructure (eg roads, sanitation, schools, offices, water systems, security/fire breaks, markets, storage facilities, shelter locations), but excludes land for agriculture (crops and livestock).

- Clusters of living areas or village groups are established.

- Empty land for possible future expansion is identified.

- There is provision for social facilities such as markets, places of worship, graveyards, health facilities, solid waste disposal, water points, community and nutrition centres, workshops, wood lots and recreational areas.

- There is provision for facilities required by humanitarian agencies such as administrative offices, warehousing and staff accommodation.

- There are adequate firebreaks of at least: 2 metres between dwellings, 6 metres between clusters of dwellings, and 15 metres between blocks of clusters.

- There is a graveyard for each population group and graveyards are appropriately located.

- Quarantine camps are established, or sites are identified and prepared, in isolation from general residential areas, in order to minimise the spread of an epidemic.

- The site gradient is not more than 7% unless extensive drainage and erosion control measures are taken.

Guidance note

1. *Social factors:* wherever possible, the social structure and gender roles of the displaced population should be reflected in the planning of the settlement, which should take into account needs for markets, meeting places, recreational areas and so on. These facilities are essential in supporting the re-establishment of the displaced communities. Existing forms of social representation should also be supported, given the importance of consultation with displaced people, particularly women, and their involvement in humanitarian interventions.

Site standard 3: security

Site selection and planning ensure sufficient personal liberty and security for the entire affected population.

Key indicators

- The site is located at a safe distance from possible external threats to physical security.

- Site planning ensures that safe integrated living areas are provided for groups at risk.

- Social, health, sanitation and other essential facilities are safely accessible for everyone, and are lit at night if necessary.

- Cluster planning is used in order to support self-policing by the displaced population.

● The overall size of the settlement population does not exceed a level that makes internal and external security and protection measures ineffective.

● Internal and external security and protection activities are carried out by the host authorities and/or the relevant UN agency.

● The agency assigned responsibility for overall coordination assists with internal security for groups at risk.

● Systems to prevent and manage the consequences of sexual and gender-based violence are in place.

● Women and adolescents know about the availability of health services for victims of sexual violence.

● Reasonable steps are taken to ensure that staff are not at risk. In insecure areas an evacuation plan is agreed between agencies.

Guidance notes

1. *Security for all people affected by the disaster, and for field staff, is of crucial importance:* careful site planning that takes into account internal and external risks, is of particular importance when providing for refugee populations or internally displaced populations who feel similarly threatened. Identifying the security needs of particular groups, especially women, will help reinforce security measures taken by host authorities and UN agencies. It is important that women and other groups considered at risk of harm are not housed in isolated areas where they can be easily targeted for physical attack or rape.

2. *Security measures:* the coordinating agency should ensure that there is lighting in strategic areas at night and that female- and adolescent-headed households and single women are housed in secure areas near facilities, but not in such a way that 'ghettos' are created. It is important to work with the affected population to establish security measures including, for example, safe haven facilities and neighbourhood watch groups. Measures to prevent sexual violence may include: site planning in consultation with women and men from the affected population; ensuring the

presence of female protection and health staff and interpreters; reviewing issues of sexual violence in coordination meetings.

Site standard 4: environmental concerns

The site is planned and managed in such as way as to minimise damage to the environment.

Key indicators

● Planning of temporary settlements takes into consideration density and dispersal of the displaced population:

 – In fragile environments, the displaced population is concentrated in order to contain non-sustainable demand on the environment.

 – In more robust environments, the displaced population is dispersed into a number of small settlements since these are less likely to cause environmental damage than large settlements.

● During site planning, trees and other vegetation are spared as far as possible. Roads and drainage patterns are planned in such a way as to make use of natural contours in order to avoid erosion and flooding.

Guidance notes

1. *Space requirement:* UNHCR guidelines (unpublished at time of writing) recommend a total space requirement of $45m^2$ per person, which includes a small space for kitchen gardening. The ideal is for the displaced population to live at the same density as in their home region/country, or at the same density as the host population, whichever is most appropriate for the situation. Planning should take into account the dynamic evolution and growth of a camp. Population growth and the arrival of more people may see the camp expand by up to 4.5% annually, as has been the case in the past. Early repatriation or reintegration should be planned for as well.

Part 2:4

2. **Firebreaks:** care should be taken to prevent firebreaks acting as 'wind tunnels'. Fire control teams should be trained, equipped and regularly tested.

3. **Graveyards:** graveyards and mass graves must be located at least 30 metres from groundwater sources used for drinking water (in soil, and more in fractured rock formations), with the bottom of any grave 1.5 metres above the groundwater table. Surface water from graveyards must not enter the settlement. Customs of the local and displaced population should be considered.

4. **Fuel wood consumption:** no matter how much agricultural and habitation land is allocated to each family, people will return to communal areas to collect wood if there are no alternative sources of fuel. On a sustainable basis, it is assumed that 500 people need 1km^2 of undisturbed forest to cater for their annual fuel wood consumption need of 600-900 kg per person. Assuming however that only 20% of forest is undisturbed, only 100 people would be able to access the land.

6 Human Resource Capacity and Training

All aspects of humanitarian assistance rely on the skills, knowledge and commitment of staff and volunteers working in difficult and sometimes insecure conditions. The demands placed on them can be considerable, and if they are to conduct their work to a level where minimum standards are assured, it is essential that they are suitably experienced and trained and that they are adequately managed and supported by their agency.

Capacity standard 1: competence

Shelter and site interventions are implemented by staff who have appropriate qualifications and experience for the duties involved, and who are adequately managed and supported.

Key indicators

- All staff working on a shelter and site programme are informed of the purpose and method of the activities they are asked to carry out.

- Assessments, programme design and key technical decision-making are carried out by staff with relevant technical qualifications and previous emergency experience.

- Staff and volunteers are aware of gender issues relating to the affected population. They know how to report incidents of sexual violence.

- Staff with technical and management responsibilities have access to support for informing and verifying key decisions.

- Staff responsible for site planning are trained and regularly supervised.

- Staff and volunteers involved in information gathering are thoroughly briefed and regularly supervised.

- Staff and volunteers involved in construction and other manual activities are trained, supervised and equipped adequately to ensure their work is carried out efficiently and safely.

Capacity standard 2: local capacity

Local skills and capacity are used and enhanced by shelter and site programmes.

Key indicators

- Women and men from the disaster-affected population are included in the planning, implementation, monitoring and evaluation of shelter programmes.

- Staff understand the importance of strengthening local capacities for long-term benefit.

- The skills base within existing local partners and institutions, and in the local population, is tapped and strengthened during the course of the humanitarian assistance programme.

Guidance notes

1. *See:* ODI/People In Aid (1998), *Code of Best Practice in the Management and Support of Aid Personnel.*

2. *Staffing:* staff and volunteers should demonstrate capabilities equal to their respective assignments. They should also be aware of key aspects of human rights conventions, international humanitarian law and the *Guiding Principles on Internal Displacement* (see the Humanitarian Charter).

Providing training and support as a part of emergency preparedness is important to ensure that skilled personnel are available to deliver quality services. Given that emergency preparedness cannot be assured in many countries, humanitarian agencies should ensure that qualified and competent staff are identified and properly prepared before eventual assignment to an emergency situation.

When deploying staff and volunteers, agencies should seek to ensure that there is a balance in the number of women and men on emergency teams.

Appendix 1

Select Bibliography

Chalinder, A (1998), Good Practice Review 6: *Temporary Human Settlement Planning for Displaced Populations in Emergencies*. Overseas Development Institute/Relief and Rehabilitation Network. London.

Davis, J and Lambert, R (1995), *Engineering in Emergencies: A Practical Guide for Relief Workers*. RedR/IT Publications. London.

Jendritzky, G, Kalkstein, L S, and Maunder, W J (1996), *Climate and Human Health*. (WMO-No. 843). World Meteorological Organisation. Geneva.

LWF (1997), *Environmental Guidelines for Programme Implementation*. Lutheran World Federation and Department of World Service. Geneva.

MSF (1997), *Guide of Kits and Emergency Items. Decision-Maker Guide*. 4th English Edition. Médecins Sans Frontières. Belgium.

Overseas Development Institute/People In Aid (1998), *Code of Best Practice in the Management and Support of Aid Personnel*. ODI/People In Aid. London.

Telford, J (1997), Good Practice Review 5: *Counting and Identification of Beneficiary Populations: Registration and its Alternatives*. Overseas Development Institute/Relief and Rehabilitation Network. London.

UNDP (1995), *Emergency Relief Items, Compendium of Generic Specifications*. Vol 1, Telecommunications, Shelter and Housing, Water Supply, Food, Sanitation and Hygiene, Materials Handling, Power Supply. Inter-Agency Procurement Services Office, UNDP. Copenhagen.

UNHCR (1997), *Environmental Guidelines. Domestic Energy Needs in Refugee Situations*. UNHCR. Geneva.

UNHCR (1993), *First International Workshop on Improved Shelter Response and Environment for Refugees*. UNHCR. Geneva.

UNHCR (1991), *Guidelines on the Protection of Refugee Women*. UNHCR. Geneva.

UNHCR (1982), *Handbook for Emergencies. Part One: Field Operations*. UNHCR. Geneva.

UNHCR, *Handbook for Social Services*. UNHCR. Geneva.

UNHCR (1996), *Partnership: A Programme Management Handbook for UNHCR's Partners*. UNHCR. Geneva.

UNHCR (1994), *People-Oriented Planning at Work: Using POP to Improve UNHCR Programming*. UNHCR. Geneva.

UNHCR, *Planning Rural Settlements for Refugees*. UNHCR. Geneva.

UNHCR (1998), *Refugee Operations and Environmental Management: Key Principles of Decision-Making*. UNHCR. Geneva.

UNHCR (1995), *Sexual Violence Against Refugees*. UNHCR. Geneva.

UNHCR (1994), *Shelter and Infrastructure - Camp Planning*. Programme and Technical Support Section, UNHCR. Geneva.

USAID (1994), *Field Operations Guide for Disaster Assessment and Response*. Office of Foreign Disaster Assistance, USAID.

WCRWC/UNICEF (1998), *The Gender Dimensions of Internal Displacement*. Women's Commission for Refugee Women and Children. New York.

Part 2:4

Minimum
Standards
in
Health
Services

Minimum Standards in Health Services

Contents

For the general glossary and acronyms, see Annexes 1 and 2 at the end of the book.

Part 2:5

Minimum Standards
in Health Services

Introduction

The minimum standards for Health Services are a practical expression of the principles and rights embodied in the Humanitarian Charter. The Charter is concerned with the most basic requirements for sustaining the lives and dignity of those affected by calamity or conflict, as reflected in the body of international human rights, humanitarian, and refugee law. It is on this basis that agencies offer their services. They undertake to act in accordance with the principles of humanity and impartiality, and with the other principles set out in the *Code of Conduct for the International Red Cross and Red Crescent Movement and NGOs in Disaster Relief*. The Humanitarian Charter reaffirms the fundamental importance of three key principles:

- the right to life with dignity

- the distinction between combatants and non-combatants

- the principle of non-refoulement

The minimum standards fall into two broad categories: those that relate directly to people's rights; and those that relate to agency processes which help ensure people acquire these rights. Some of the minimum standards combine both of these categories.

1 The importance of health services in emergencies

In emergencies, major loss of lives due to increased incidence of diseases and injuries has been documented. Natural disasters (earthquakes, floods, volcanoes etc), warfare and conflicts, and technological disasters tend to result in excess mortality and morbidity.[1] Diseases responsible for such increases have also been identified: measles, diarrhoeas (including dysentery and cholera), acute respiratory infections, malnutrition and malaria (where prevalent). The high incidence of diseases is due to the environmental factors to which populations are exposed, namely overcrowding, inadequate quantities and quality of water, poor sanitation, inadequate shelter and inadequate food supply.

The main purpose of providing health services to a disaster-affected population is to prevent excess mortality and morbidity. Essential to this is the identification of priorities through rapid assessment, ongoing monitoring and surveillance; interventions must respond to priorities identified by the initial assessment and must be technically sound. Planning, implementation and monitoring should be coordinated among the agencies involved.

Priority should be given to primary health care (PHC) measures including multi-sectoral assistance in key areas (water, sanitation, nutrition, food, shelter). The participation of local health authorities and that of qualified members of the affected population including community workers and home visitors is paramount in carrying out primary health care measures.

In most emergency situations, women and children are the main users of health care services, and it is important to seek women's views as a means of ensuring that services are equitable, appropriate and accessible for the affected population as a whole. Women can contribute to an understanding of cultural factors and customs that impact on health, as well as the specific needs of vulnerable people within the affected population. They should therefore participate in the planning and implementation of health care services wherever possible.

2 Finding your way around this chapter

The chapter is divided into five sections (analysis, measles control etc), each of which includes the following:

● **The minimum standards:** these specify the minimum levels to be attained in each area.

● **Key indicators:** these are 'signals' that show whether the standard has been attained. They provide a way of measuring and communicating both the impact, or result, of programmes as well as the process, or methods, used. The indicators may be qualitative or quantitative.

● **Guidance notes:** these include specific points to consider when applying the standard and indicators in different situations, guidance on tackling practical difficulties, and advice on priority issues. They may also include critical issues relating to the standard or indicators, and describe dilemmas, controversies or gaps in current knowledge. Filling these gaps will help improve the minimum standards for health services in the future.

Further relevant information, including a select bibliography, is supplied in the Appendices.

The organisation of the chapter reflects the division of activities and responsibilities that commonly occurs in emergency situations. Action in each of these areas contributes to the overall purpose of addressing priority health needs.

Each of the sections is inter-related. The initial health assessment identifies needs, establishes priorities and provides the data to start priority interventions. Data from the ongoing health information system provides trends in morbidity and mortality which serve to detect new problems or to redirect resources. Both the initial assessment and the health information system serve to identify health problems such as malnutrition, communicable diseases or injuries that are addressed and controlled using standards outlined in the control of communicable diseases and the health care services sections. Section 5, human resource capacity and training, applies to all work and deals with issues related to the human capacity required to implement effective health interventions.

Part 2.5

Progress in achieving standards in one area determines the importance of progress in other areas. For instance, a good health information system identifies problems and then leads to appropriate control, preventative and curative activities.

Reference to other sectors' technical standards are made where relevant. The purpose of this is to highlight how work in one sector is closely linked to work in other sectors, and that progress in one is dependent on progress in other areas. For example, provision of clean water will reduce diarrhoea, provision of sufficient and appropriate foods will reduce nutritional problems.

Note

1. Excess mortality exists when the crude mortality rate (CMR) is higher than the prevailing mortality level of the surrounding population in an emergency setting. In developing countries a CMR higher than 1 death per 10,000 persons per day has been the traditional definition of excess mortality. This threshold is derived from the reported annual CMR in most developing countries, approximately 25 deaths per 1,000 persons, which corresponds to a daily rate of 0.6 per 10,000. The prevailing mortality rate in developed countries may vary from that of developing countries and this needs to be considered during the initial assessment. Calculating the CMR may not be applicable or relevant to a sudden-impact disaster unless there is a long-standing or significant population displacement.

The Minimum Standards

1 Analysis

Interventions that meet the needs of disaster-affected populations must be based on a clear understanding of the current situation, including political and security factors, and anticipated developments. The people affected by the disaster, agencies, donors and local authorities need to know that interventions are appropriate and effective. Analysis of the effects of the disaster and of the impact of the proposed health interventions is therefore critical. If the problem is not correctly identified and understood then it will be difficult, if not impossible, to make the right response.

Standardised methods of analysis that are used across the sectors have great potential to identify rapidly acute humanitarian needs and to ensure that resources are directed accordingly. This section sets out agreed standards and indicators for collecting and analysing information to identify needs, to design interventions, to monitor and evaluate their effectiveness, and to ensure the participation of the affected population.

Analysis starts with an immediate initial assessment. This provides baseline data that measures the impact of the disaster and determines whether and how to respond. It continues through the health information system with monitoring, which identifies how well interventions are meeting needs and whether changes are required. The health information system eventually provides data that can be used to evaluate the overall effectiveness of interventions and to identify lessons for the future.

The sharing of information and knowledge among all those involved, including the affected populations, is fundamental to achieving a full understanding of the problem and coordinated assistance. Documenting and disseminating information from the analysis process contributes to a broad understanding of the adverse public health and other consequences of disasters, and can assist in the development of improved disaster prevention and mitigation strategies.

Analysis standard 1: initial assessment

The initial assessment determines as accurately as possible the health effects of a disaster, identifies the health needs and establishes priorities for health programming.

Key indicators

● An immediate initial assessment that follows internationally accepted procedures is carried out by appropriately experienced personnel, including if possible at least one epidemiologist. Data collection starts before the field assessment using available maps, country profiles etc.

● The initial assessment is conducted in cooperation with a multi-sectoral team (water and sanitation, nutrition, food, shelter, health), national health authorities, men and women from the affected population and humanitarian agencies intending to respond to the situation.

● The information is gathered and presented in a way that allows for transparent and consistent decision making. Appendix 2 provides a sample Checklist for Initial Health Assessment. Information gathered usually includes:

– Geographic extent of the impact of the disaster.

– Demographics of the disaster-affected area:

The total disaster-affected population (population denominator is estimated if census is impossible or not available).

Sex and age breakdown of the affected population is collected for two age groups at least (<5 years age group) and (5 and >5 years age group); if it is feasible to collect more detailed age data, the following breakdown is used: <1, 1-4, 5-14, 15-44, 45+.

Average family or household size including estimates of female- and child-headed households and pregnant and lactating women.

– Information on communicable diseases, injuries and deaths.

– Presence of continuing hazards.

– Nutritional status of affected population.

– Crude mortality rate (CMR) for total population expressed as deaths per 10,000 population per day.

– Under-5 mortality rate (U-5MR) (age specific mortality rate for under five year old age group) expressed as deaths/10,000/population/day.

– Age and sex specific incidence rates of major problems and diseases.

– Environmental conditions (access to potable water, current level of sanitation, availability and adequacy of shelter, disease vectors etc).

– Availability of food.

– Status and quality of local health infrastructure (services and staffing) and medical supplies.

– Status of transportation system.

– Level of communications network.

– Estimates of external assistance based on preliminary findings.

● The daily crude mortality rate (CMR) for the total population and the U-5MR are calculated regularly (daily in the early stages of an emergency if necessary, and less frequently thereafter) to allow for detection of sudden changes.

Part 2:5

● In situations of prevailing insecurity, the assessment includes an analysis of factors affecting the personal safety and security of affected populations.

● The initial assessment team's programming and recommendations aim from the start to prevent excess mortality and morbidity as well as anticipate future public health problems resulting from the ongoing emergency conditions. Recommendations are made on whether or not external assistance is needed to supplement in-country resources. If assistance is required, recommendations are made on priorities and a strategy is outlined for providing needed human and material resources. There is also consideration of:

– The social and political structure of the population including the potential influx of refugees.

– Special attention for groups at risk.

– Access to the affected population.

– Insecurity and violence.

– Distribution systems.

– The possible long-term implications and environmental impact of the interventions proposed.

● The specific security threats faced by vulnerable groups, especially women and girls, are taken into account in the design of health interventions.

● An assessment report is produced that covers key areas and appropriate recommendations which are immediately shared with national and local authorities, representatives from the affected population and participating agencies.

Guidance notes

1. *Internationally accepted procedures for initial assessment:* see WHO (1999).

2. *Indicators of overall health status:* during the acute phase of an emergency, the crude mortality rate (CMR) for the whole

population and the under-5 mortality rate (U-5MR) for children under five years of age are very important indicators of the overall status of the affected population.

3. *Crude mortality rates:* the following method is used to calculate crude mortality rates over short periods of time (<1 month).

   a) Total the deaths for a given number of days.

   b) Divide the total by the number of days over which data were gathered – this gives the average number of deaths per day.

   c) Divide this number by the size of the affected population.

   d) Multiply by 10,000 for a daily crude mortality rate.

4. *Timeliness:* timeliness is of the essence for the initial assessment, which should be carried out as soon as possible after the disaster. If required there should be an immediate response to critical needs at the same time. A report should be generated as soon as possible after arrival at the site of the disaster, though this depends on the particular event and the wider situation.

5. *People conducting the assessment:* people who are able to collect information from all groups in the affected population in a culturally acceptable manner should be included, especially with regard to gender analysis and language skills. Ideally there should be a balance in the numbers of men and women taking part.

6. *Assessment procedure:* the logistics of conducting the assessment and the use of internationally recognised standards should be agreed upon by all participants before field work begins and specific tasks contributing to the assessment should be assigned accordingly.

7. *Information gathering:* while there are some emergencies where advance knowledge will determine what actions are necessary, most humanitarian assistance must be based on some assessment data, even if incomplete. There are many different techniques for information gathering and these should be chosen carefully to match the situation and the type of information required. As a general rule, information should be gathered more frequently when the situation

Part 2:5

is changing more rapidly, and when there are critical developments such as new population movements or an epidemic outbreak of diarrhoea. Initial assessments may be quick and unrefined but analysis improves as more time and data are available through the health information system. As the emergency stabilises, better health information data on pregnant and lactating women, disabled people, elderly people and unaccompanied minors and other groups at risk should become available. However, efforts should be made to gather health information data on the reproductive health needs of the affected population from the start of the emergency response.

8. *Sources of information:* further information for the assessment report can be compiled from other existing literature, relevant historical material, pre-emergency data and from discussions with appropriate, knowledgeable people including donors, agency staff, government personnel, local specialists, female and male community leaders, elders, participating health staff, teachers, traders and so on. National or regional level preparedness plans may also be an important source of information. Group discussions with members of the affected population can yield useful information on beliefs and practices.

The methods used for collecting information and the limits of its reliability must be clearly communicated. Information should never be presented in such a way as to provide a misleading picture of the actual situation.

9. *Underlying issues:* an awareness of the rights of those affected by disasters, under international law, should underpin the assessment. Initial assessment and subsequent health information analyses should demonstrate an awareness of underlying structural, political, security, economic, demographic and environmental issues operating in the area. It is imperative that prior experience and local understanding are taken into consideration when analysing the dynamics and impact of the new emergency. This requires inclusion of local expertise and knowledge in data collection and analysis of resources, capacities, vulnerabilities and needs. The current and pre-emergency living conditions of displaced and non-displaced people in the area and local resources must also be considered.

10. *Groups at risk:* the needs of groups that are at risk of additional harm such as women, adolescents, unaccompanied minors, children, elderly people and people with disabilities must be considered. Gender roles within the social system need to be identified.

11. *Areas of activity:* although each emergency generates particular health needs and problems, the following broad areas of activity are likely to be needed: surveillance of diseases and injuries, control of communicable diseases, measles immunisation, food and nutrition, water, sanitation and shelter. In addition, the initial assessment should indicate the extent of need for: prevention services, curative health care, the referral system, reproductive health, women's and children's health, community services, health education, medical supplies, personnel and the organisational resources required to establish and operate these services in an interrelated and coordinated manner.

Analysis standard 2: health information system - data collection

The health information system regularly collects relevant data on population, diseases, injuries, environmental conditions and health services in a standardised format in order to detect major health problems.

Key indicators

● Surveillance starts at the same time as the initial assessment and ideally uses the existing ongoing local health information system. In some emergencies, a new or parallel system may be necessary and this is determined by the initial assessment team.

● Responsibility for organising and supervising the surveillance system is clearly assigned to an individual agency to assure coordination between all partners if the local health authorities cannot serve in this function.

Part 2.5

- The health information system in the initial stages of the emergency concentrates on demography, mortality and its causes, morbidity and priority programme activities (water, sanitation, food, nutrition, shelter) as specified by the initial assessment.

- Mortality data is collected from: health facilities and the community including cemetery staff, shroud distributors and other key informants to assess the daily CMR for the total population and U-5MR (age specific mortality rate for under five year olds). Cause-specific mortality data is also collected.

- Morbidity data on diseases, injuries and health conditions is collected from: health facilities providing outpatient services, nutrition centres, feeding programmes and community health workers, in order to calculate: incidence rates for primary causes of injury or illness; age and sex specific incidence rates; and to detect changes or new health problems.

- Each health facility providing outpatient services completes the standard surveillance forms for mortality and morbidity providing age, sex, and cause-specific data.

- Health service data is collected from participating agencies, local health facilities and community health workers in most emergency situations. Since the kind of data to be collected varies with each emergency, the initial assessment team determines the priority areas for which data is collected, such as feeding programme coverage, measles immunisation coverage, sexual violence etc.

- The local health authority or agency designated with responsibility for the health information system regularly summarises and shares data received from health facilities and the community using standard forms and standard data compilation, entry and analysis methods.

- Standard case definitions and standard reporting forms are available and used for every disease to be monitored. Definitions are simple, clear and adapted to available diagnostic means.

- People working at reporting sites are trained in the use of standard reporting forms and case definitions. The frequency of reporting is specified and is adapted to the type and phase of the emergency situation.

- Communications and logistics systems for disseminating and receiving surveillance reports and feedback are in place or are created.

- The health information system is periodically assessed to determine its accuracy, completeness, simplicity, flexibility and timeliness.

Guidance notes

1. *The health information system serves to:*

   a) Rapidly detect and respond to health problems and epidemics.

   b) Monitor trends in health status and continually address health-care priorities.

   c) Evaluate the effectiveness of interventions and service coverage.

   d) Ensure that resources are correctly targeted to the areas and groups of greatest need.

   e) Evaluate the quality of health interventions.

2. *Reporting:* see Appendix 3 for a sample mortality surveillance form; Appendix 4 for an example of presentation of mortality data; Appendix 6 for sample water, sanitation and environment forms, and Appendix 7 for a sample sexual violence report form. Please refer as well to Water Supply and Sanitation, chapter 1, and Nutrition, chapter 2.

3. *Clinical case definitions:* examples of clinical case definitions for use in some emergency and post-emergency situations are provided below.

   – **Measles:** generalised rash lasting >3 days and temperature >38 C and one of the following: cough, runny nose, red eyes.

Part 2.5

- **Dysentery:** 3 or more liquid stools per day and presence of visible blood in stools.

- **Common diarrhoea:** 3 or more liquid watery stools per day.

- **Cholera:** severe, profuse, watery diarrhoea with or without vomiting.

- **Acute Respiratory Infection (ARI):** cough or difficult breathing >50/minute for infant aged 2 months to <1 year; breathing >40/minute of child aged 1-4 years; and no chest indrawing, stridor or danger signs.

- **Malnutrition:** for detailed definitions, see Nutrition, chapter 2, Appendix 1.

- **Malaria:** temperature >38.5C and absence of other infection.

- **Meningitis:** sudden onset of fever >38.9 C and neck stiffness or purpura.

4. *Sexual violence:* the number of cases of sexual and domestic violence reported to health services and to protection and security officers should be regularly monitored.

Analysis standard 3: health information system - data review

Health information system data and changes in the disaster-affected population are regularly reviewed and analysed for decision-making and appropriate response.

Key indicators

● During the emergency phase, the crude mortality rate (CMR) and incidence rates of major health problems (diseases and injuries) are monitored and analysed regularly for decision-making. However, for some emergencies, the initial assessment team may recommend a less frequent cycle of analysis.

● Reports of health problems (malnutrition, injuries etc) are rapidly identified, further investigated and appropriate measures immediately instituted to prevent excess mortality from the identified problem(s).

● Individual cases of diseases of epidemic potential (cholera, measles etc) and/or outbreaks of communicable diseases are investigated as soon as possible and confirmed. Outbreak control measures are instituted if indicated and cases receive appropriate treatment. (See control of communicable diseases standards.)

Analysis standard 4: health information system - monitoring and evaluation

Data collected is used to evaluate the effectiveness of interventions in controlling disease and in preserving health.

Key indicators

● Measures of effectiveness used for evaluation include:

– Decreasing death rate aiming towards less than 1/10,000/day.

– The under-5 mortality rate (U-5MR) is reduced to no more than 2/10,000/day.

– Epidemics/diseases are controlled.

– Injuries and impact of violence are reduced or eliminated.

– Measles vaccination coverage reaches more than 95%.

– There is access to adequate food (see Nutrition, chapter 2 and Food Aid, chapter 3).

– There is access to adequate water (see Water Supply and Sanitation, chapter 1).

– Adequate sanitation facilities are available (see Water Supply and Sanitation, chapter 1).

Part 2:5

Guidance notes

1. *Objective:* the objective of an emergency intervention should be to achieve a CMR of <1/10,000/day and an U-5MR of <2/10,000/day as soon as possible.

2. *Integration:* the health information system should be integrated into the host community system and include health facility and community health workers. Both the affected population and the host community participate in the health information system.

3. *Use of monitoring information:* emergencies are volatile and dynamic by definition. Regular and current information is therefore vital in ensuring that interventions remain relevant. Information derived from continual monitoring of interventions should be fed into reviews and evaluations. In some circumstances, a shift in strategy may be required to respond to major changes in the context or needs of the disaster-affected population.

4. *People involved in monitoring:* when monitoring requires consultation, people who are able to collect information from all groups in the affected population in a culturally acceptable manner should be included, especially with regard to gender and language skills. Women's involvement should be encouraged.

5. *Evaluation:* evaluation is important because it measures effectiveness, identifies lessons for future preparedness, mitigation and humanitarian assistance, and promotes accountability. Evaluation refers here to two, linked processes:

   a) Internal programme evaluation is normally carried out by staff as part of the regular analysis and review of monitoring information. The agency must also evaluate the effectiveness of all its interventions in a given disaster situation or compare its interventions across different situations.

   b) External evaluation may by contrast be part of a wider evaluation exercise by agencies and donors, and may take place, for example, after the acute phase of the emergency. When evaluations are carried out it is important that the techniques and resources used are consistent with the scale and nature of the intervention or programme, and that the report describes the methodology employed and the processes followed in reaching conclusions.

6. *Links with other sectors:* monitoring and evaluation activities require close cooperation with other sectors (see chapters on Water Supply and Sanitation, Nutrition, Food Aid, Shelter and Site Planning), host authorities and agencies.

Analysis standard 5: participation

The disaster-affected population has the opportunity to participate in the design and implementation of the assistance programme.

Key indicators

● Women and men from the disaster-affected population are consulted, and are involved in decision-making that relates to needs assessment, programme design and implementation.

● Women and men from the disaster-affected population receive information about the assistance programme, and have the opportunity to comment back to the assistance agency about the programme.

Guidance notes

1. *Equity:* the participation of disaster-affected people in decision-making, programme design and implementation helps to ensure that programmes are equitable and effective. Special effort should be made to ensure the participation of women and balanced male and female representation within the assistance programme. Participation in the health programme may also serve to reinforce people's sense of dignity and worth in times of crisis. It generates a sense of community and ownership which can help ensure the safety and security of those who are receiving the assistance, as well as those who are responsible for its implementation.

Part 2:5

2. *People can be involved in health services in different ways:* for example through participation in social mobilisation; providing key health information messages to the affected population; early reporting of suspect cases of illness; house-to-house case detection and surveys; registration and support at health events (vaccinations, vitamin A supplementation, ORT at household level or designated community centres, condom distribution, etc.); assisting at health facilities with logistics (crowd control and security) and by assisting in matters relating to language and culture.

3. *Coordination committees:* coordination committees help ensure people's involvement in the assistance programme. Gender, age, ethnicity and socio-economic status should be taken into consideration in order to ensure that committees adequately represent the affected population. Acknowledged political leaders, female and male community leaders and religious leaders should also be represented. The roles and functions of a coordination committee should be agreed upon when it is set up.

4. *Seeking views and opinions:* participation can also be achieved through regular polling and discussions. This can take place during distribution, through home visits or when addressing individual concerns. Group discussions with members of the affected community can yield useful information on cultural beliefs and practices.

2 Measles Control

Measles is one of the most contagious and lethal viruses known. Crowded emergency settings and unexpected population movements provide an ideal environment for the rapid and intense transmission of this virus, which can result in high levels of morbidity and mortality, especially among young children.

Measles vaccination campaigns should be assigned the highest priority at the earliest possible time in emergency situations. The necessary personnel, vaccine, cold chain equipment and other supplies to conduct a mass campaign should be assembled at the site of the emergency as quickly as possible. The decision of when to begin the vaccination campaign should be based on epidemiological factors such as whether a mass campaign in the population has taken place recently, level of measles vaccination coverage, and the estimated number of susceptible persons in the affected population. In some instances the initial assessment team may recommend that persons up to 15 years of age or higher be included if there is evidence of high susceptibility in this age group.

Measles control standard 1: vaccination

In disaster-affected populations, all children 6 months to 12 years old receive a dose of measles vaccine and an appropriate dose of vitamin A as soon as possible.

Measles control standard 2: vaccination of newcomers

Newcomers to displaced settlements are vaccinated systematically. All children 6 months to 12 old years receive a dose of measles vaccine and an appropriate dose of vitamin A.

Key indicators

● Coordination with local health authorities (Expanded Programme on Immunisations – EPI) and involved agencies is established and ongoing.

● More than 95% of all children in the target group (including newcomers) are vaccinated. (See Appendix 5 for sample measles vaccination form.)

● On-site supply of measles vaccine equals 140% of the target group including 15% for wastage and a 25% reserve stock; projections of vaccine needs for subsequent newcomers are made and vaccine is procured if not already available.

● Only vaccines and autodestruct syringes meeting WHO specifications are used.

● The cold chain is continuously maintained and monitored from vaccine manufacture to vaccination site.

● On-site supply of autodestruct syringes equals 125% of expected target groups including a 25% reserve stock. Sufficient 5ml syringes for diluting multiple dose vials are available. One syringe is required for each vial diluted.

● Sufficient WHO-recommended 'safety boxes' are used to store autodestruct and dilution syringes before their disposal. Boxes are disposed of according to WHO recommendations.

● On-site supply of vitamin A equals 125% of the target group including a 25% reserve stock if vitamin A is to be provided as part of a mass vaccination campaign.

● The date of measles vaccination is entered in each child's health record.

Health records for recording vaccinations are provided if possible.

● Infants vaccinated prior to 9 months require re-vaccination upon reaching that age.

● Health facilities have the capacity to ensure routine ongoing measles vaccination of new arrivals if this is a displaced situation, and to identify infants needing to be re-vaccinated at 9 months.

● Relevant messages in the local language are provided to groups of waiting mothers or caregivers on the benefits of measles vaccination, possible side effects, when to return if re-vaccination is indicated and the importance of retaining the health record.

● A public information campaign is conducted by community workers before conducting a mass vaccination campaign.

Guidance notes

1. *Temperature:* vaccines must be maintained at the manufacturer's recommended temperature of <8 C to maintain vaccine potency.

2. *Records:* individual health records for recording measles vaccinations should be provided but may not always be available or issued in an emergency situation; the lack of records should not delay the implementation of measles vaccination activities.

3. *Target group:* it may be necessary to raise the measles target group from 12 to 15 years of age or higher in some areas if there is epidemiological evidence that this higher age group is susceptible. In other instances, the initial assessment may recommend a target group below 12 years of age.

4. *During a mass campaign:* WHO recommends the integration of vitamin A supplementation as follows:

    – Infants 6-12 months: 100,000 International Units (IU) (repeat every 4-6 months).

    – Children > 12 months: 200,000 IUs (repeat every 4-6 months).

5. *Staffing:* previous experience indicates that staffing for vaccination activities (including administration of vitamin A) should consist of at

Part 2:5

least one supervisor and one logistics officer who can supervise one or more teams. The following team should be able to vaccinate up to 500-700 persons in approximately one hour, though the number of vaccinators needed will depend on the target population to be immunised: four staff members to prepare the vaccines; two staff members to administer the vaccines; six staff members to register and tally; six staff members to maintain order (crowd control).

Measles control standard 3: outbreak control

A systematic response is mounted for each outbreak of measles within the disaster-affected population and the host community population.

Key indicators

● A single case (suspected or confirmed) warrants immediate on-site investigation which includes looking at the age and vaccination status of the suspect or confirmed case.

● Control measures include the vaccination of all children 6 months to 12 years of age (or higher if older ages are affected) and the provision of an appropriate dose of vitamin A.

Measles control standard 4: case management

All children who contract measles receive adequate care in order to avoid serious sequellae or death.

Key indicators

● A community-wide system for active case detection using the standard case definition and referral of suspected or confirmed measles cases is operational.

● Each measles case receives vitamin A and appropriate treatment for complications such as pneumonia, diarrhoea, severe malnutrition and meningoencephalitis which cause the most mortality.

● The nutritional status of children with measles is monitored, and if necessary children are enrolled in a supplementary feeding programme.

Guidance notes

1. *EPI vaccines:* because measles vaccination is so important in the early stages of an emergency in many countries, vaccination should not be delayed. In some emergencies other EPI vaccines may be introduced along with measles vaccination, provided measles vaccination is not delayed until other EPI vaccines are available. If only measles vaccination is provided, other EPI vaccines are introduced only when the immediate needs of the disaster-affected population have been met.

2. *In conflict* situations: UNICEF and others have sometimes been successful in getting agreement from the warring parties to a temporary cease-fire, in order to allow a vaccination campaign to be safely conducted.

3. *Re-vaccination:* when mass measles vaccination is indicated and individual records are not available, the immunisation of children who may have previously received vaccine is not harmful. It is more important to re-vaccinate than to leave a child unvaccinated and susceptible.

4. *For measles case management or for treatment of vitamin A deficiency:* administration of vitamin A contributes to a decrease in mortality and measles sequellae. WHO recommends:

   – Infants <6 months: 50,000 IU on day one; 50,000 IU on day two.

   – Infants 6-12 months: 100,000 IU on day one; 100,000 IU on day two.

   – Children >12 months: 200,000 IU on day one; 200,000 IU on day two.

5. *If measles disease is in the affected population:* it is possible that children who are vaccinated during their incubation period may still develop the disease.

Part 2:5

241

3 Control of Communicable Diseases

The primary causes of morbidity and mortality in a disaster-affected population are measles, diarrhoeal diseases, acute respiratory infections, malnutrition and, in areas where it is endemic, malaria. Other communicable diseases, such as meningococcal meningitis, hepatitis, typhoid fever, typhus and relapsing fever, may cause outbreaks in some settings. Diarrhoeal diseases and communicable diseases such as tuberculosis commonly appear at the onset of an emergency and may also be the first manifest symptoms of HIV/AIDS.

Local health authorities, including community health workers and home visitors, are likely to be in the front line of the control effort, where resources allow, and work in conjunction with health facilities and participating agencies. The affected population plays an important part in disease prevention and control through the application of, and adherence to, good public health practices.

Prevention is a key priority in communicable disease control and therefore successful implementation of other sector activities such as water, sanitation, nutrition, food and shelter is of vital importance. Crowded populations, contamination of water supply, poor sanitation and low quality housing all contribute to the rapid spread of disease. Poor nutrition, particularly among young children, increases susceptibility to disease and contributes to high rates of mortality.

It is also important to consider what measures may be needed for the control and prevention of STDs and HIV. Any measures taken will depend on available epidemiological information concerning the affected population and the nature of the disaster.

Control of communicable diseases standard 1: monitoring

The occurrence of communicable diseases is monitored.

Key indicators

- The responsible surveillance and disease control unit or agency is clearly identified and all participants in the emergency know where to send reports of suspect or confirmed communicable diseases.

- Staff experienced in epidemiology and disease control are part of the surveillance and disease control unit or agency.

- Surveillance is maintained at all times to rapidly detect communicable diseases and to trigger outbreak response.

Control of communicable diseases standard 2: investigation and control

Diseases of epidemic potential are investigated and controlled according to internationally accepted norms and standards.

Key indicators

- Diseases of epidemic potential are identified by the initial assessment; standard protocols for prevention, diagnosis and treatment are in place and appropriately shared with health facilities and community health workers/home visitors.

- Case reports and rumours of disease occurrence are investigated by qualified staff.

- There is confirmation of the diagnosis.

- Outbreak control measures are instituted and include:

    - Attacking the source, by reducing the sources of infection to prevent the disease spreading to other members of the

Part 2:5

community. Depending on the disease, this may involve the prompt diagnosis and treatment of cases (eg cholera), isolation of cases (eg viral haemorrhagic fevers, ebola) and controlling animal reservoirs (eg plague).

– Protecting susceptible groups in order to reduce the risk of infection: immunisation (eg meningitis and measles); better nutrition and, in some situations, chemoprophylaxis for high risk groups (eg malaria prophylaxis may be suggested for pregnant women in outbreaks); safe blood supply and condoms for prevention of sexually transmitted infections and HIV.

– Interrupting transmission in order to minimise the spread of the disease by improvements in environmental and personal hygiene (for all faeco-orally transmitted diseases), health education, vector control (eg yellow fever and dengue), and disinfection and sterilisation (eg hepatitis B, ebola).

● Qualified outreach personnel (community health workers, home visitors) participate in the control measures at community level by providing both prevention messages and proper case management (provision of ORT and drugs, compliance with prescribed treatment, follow-up at home etc) following agreed guidelines.

● Public information and health promotion messages on disease prevention are part of control activities.

● Community leaders and community health workers/home visitors facilitate access to population groups and disseminate key prevention messages.

● Only drugs from WHO's *Essential Drugs List* (1998) are used.

Guidance notes

1. *Internationally accepted norms and standards:* see WHO (1997), listed under Health Information System in the select bibliography.

2. *Rumours:* reports and rumours of outbreaks are common among disaster-affected populations, including refugees, and should always be followed up.

3. *Determining if there is an epidemic:* an epidemic is defined as an excessive number of cases of a given disease in relation to prior experience according to place, time and population. It can sometimes be difficult to decide whether there is an epidemic or not, and criteria for epidemic thresholds should be established (by the surveillance unit) for the diseases for which this is possible. Since many diseases do not have a defined threshold for declaring an epidemic, any suspected or confirmed epidemic must be reported to the responsible surveillance and disease control unit.

4. *Setting up a clinical laboratory is not a priority in most emergencies:* most cases will be diagnosed clinically and treatment will be presumptive or symptomatic. Some infectious agents will need to be identified and sample material will need to be collected for testing and sent to a reference lab. This can be determined by the responsible surveillance and disease control unit.

5. *Control of diarrhoeal diseases:* diarrhoeal diseases represent an important cause of death among disaster-affected populations, mainly because overcrowding, lack of water and poor hygiene and sanitation favour the transmission of this group of diseases. As treatment of common diarrhoea relies on the prevention of dehydration through oral rehydration therapy (ORT), the basic health services in a disaster-affected setting should include a network of ORT points. Since poor nutritional status further increases the case fatality rate of the disease, all children with diarrhoea must be checked for malnutrition and be managed accordingly. The provision of safe water in sufficient quantity, building of latrines, distribution of soap, and appropriate site planning to avoid overcrowding are the most effective ways of controlling diarrhoea-related morbidity and mortality.[1]

6. *Control of acute respiratory infections (ARI):* in developing countries, 25-30% of deaths among children under five are caused by ARI, and 90% of them are attributable to pneumonia alone. Proper case management is the cornerstone of the prevention of deaths from pneumonia. Clinical diagnosis, based on observation of the child's breathing, has been developed by WHO and UNICEF, and can be used for early recognition of cases in a refugee

Part 2.5

population. Cotrimoxazole remains the drug of choice because it is easy to administer and cost-effective in the ambulatory treatment of pneumonia.

7. **HIV prevention:** action must be taken in the acute stage following the disaster to minimise risk of infection. The nature of the disaster and the epidemiological situation of the people affected will dictate what HIV/AIDS interventions are called for and what is feasible. A basic response to any emergency must aim to maintain respect for the individual rights of people with HIV infection or AIDS, and to prevent nosocomial transmission of HIV (transmission that takes place in the health facility). The intervention must ensure: safe blood transfusion; access to condoms; availability of materials and equipment needed for universal precautions; and relevant information, education and communication.[2]

8. **Control of dysentery:** *S dysenteriae type 1* (Sd1) infection has been a major public health problem in Latin America, south Asia and central Africa. Unfortunately, Sd1 has proven its extraordinary ability to develop resistance to antibiotics. In some areas today, the only effective antimicrobial agent against Sd1 is ciprofloxacine (5 day regimen), further complicating patient management and increasing the cost of the treatment to a level which may prevent its use on a large scale.

9. **Control of cholera:** cholera outbreaks are frequently observed in settings in Asia and Africa. When properly managed, cholera case fatality rates can be kept below 1% during outbreaks occurring in refugee settings. Outbreak control is based on active case-finding and appropriate case-management. Severely dehydrated patients receive intravenous (IV) treatment. Mild cholera cases are treated with ORT. A short course of antibiotic therapy can reduce the duration of the disease and is still recommended by the WHO for severely dehydrated patients. Cholera transmission is reduced by appropriate waste management and water treatment (chlorination). Mass vaccination has never been used for controlling cholera outbreaks, and it is agreed that vaccination would have very little or no impact once the outbreak has started (reactive strategy) and would divert resources from other essential control activities.

10. *Measles control:* measles remains a major cause of childhood mortality throughout the world. While the Expanded Programme on Immunisation (EPI) has achieved satisfactory overall vaccine coverage levels in some countries, coverage levels vary widely among regions of the world. Outbreaks can occur in camp settings and other crowded environments where a concentration of susceptible individuals is an important risk factor for transmission of the virus. High mortality rates occur because of poor nutritional status, vitamin A deficiency and intensive exposure to virus due to overcrowding. High mortality due to measles is preventable and mass immunisation coupled with vitamin A distribution is a top priority in an emergency.

11. *Malaria control:* malaria caused by plasmodium falciparum remains the main health hazard in tropical areas all over the world. Even for populations displaced from a highly endemic area, prevention of malaria is based on individual protection with impregnated bednets and community protection through vector control. Mass distribution of mosquito nets impregnated with insecticide can have a significant impact on malaria transmission by reducing the mosquito population and creating a shield effect, thus benefiting even people who do not themselves use nets. Mass chemoprophylaxis has not been recommended because it is extremely difficult to implement and to monitor on a large scale and because it can accelerate the development of drug resistance. The ideal strategy in principle is to treat cases with confirmed parasitaemia, but this is rarely possible in practice. In the absence of laboratory facilities and in highly endemic areas, treatment is often administered on a purely clinical basis. Therapy should be in line with the national malaria programme of the host country but adapted to the epidemiological patterns in the affected population. This is best defined in the post-emergency phase, when epidemiological trends can be better assessed.

12. *For control of rarer or less severe diseases:* see the references provided in the bibliography in Appendix 1; see in particular Médecins Sans Frontières (1997).

Part 2:5

13. *Drug resistance:* in some instances, studies will need to be carried out to assess drug resistance.

14. *Burial of the dead:* see guidance note 5 on the dead, in solid waste management standard 2, Water Supply and Sanitation, chapter 1.

Notes

1. Notes on control of diarrhoeal disease including dysentery and cholera, ARI, measles and malaria are adapted and modified from *Control of Infectious Diseases in Refugee and Displaced Populations in Developing Countries* by C Paquet and G Hanquet, published in the Bulletin Institut Pasteur, 1998, 96, 3-14.

2. Adapted from *Guidelines for HIV Interventions in Emergency Settings*, published by UNAIDS 1996, reprinted 1998.

4 Health Care Services

Health care services standard 1: appropriate medical care

Emergency health care for disaster-affected populations is based on an initial assessment and data from an ongoing health information system, and serves to reduce excess mortality and morbidity through appropriate medical care.

Key indicators

● Interventions are designed to be responsive to the identified major causes of excess death, disease and injuries.

● If possible, the local health authorities lead the health care effort and local health facilities are used and strengthened by participating humanitarian agencies. If this is not possible, an external agency leads the effort, works with existing facilities which may require substantial support and coordinates efforts of participating agencies.

● All participating humanitarian agencies agree to coordinate with the lead health care authority which is designated at the time of the initial assessment.

● The health care system is able to cope with a high level of demand.

● The health care system is flexible enough to adapt to changes identified by the health information system.

Health care services standard 2: reduction of morbidity and mortality

Health care in emergencies follows primary health care (PHC) principles and targets health problems that cause excess morbidity and mortality.

Key indicators

● Emergency health care interventions are implemented through the existing PHC system if available. The PHC system includes the following levels of care:

- Household level.

- Community level including community health workers and home visitors.

- Peripheral health facilities (dispensary, health post or health clinic).

- Central health facilities (health centre).

- Referral hospital.

● Health care interventions are implemented at the appropriate level of the PHC system. Not every emergency will need all levels of care and the initial assessment can make this determination. If a local health care system does not exist, only those levels needed to prevent excess mortality and morbidity are introduced.

● Emergency health care, including treatment of disease and injuries, is provided to the population largely at community level. Some treatment occurs at health facilities and a smaller number of serious cases is sent to referral centres.

● Staffing at each level of the PHC system is appropriate to meet the needs of the population and only those levels required to reduce excess mortality and morbidity are used or introduced.

● Health professionals from the disaster-affected population are integrated into the health services as much as possible. Outreach workers are selected from the community and reflect the gender and cultural profile of the population as determined during the initial assessment.

● All health care providers agree on the common use of standardised procedures for diagnostic techniques and the treatment of the major priority diseases causing excess mortality and morbidity.

● The New Emergency Health Kits (1/10,000 population) are used to start the intervention but subsequent drug needs are ordered and follow the WHO recommended Essential Drug List.

● The Minimum Initial Service Package is used from the start of the intervention to respond to the reproductive health needs of the population.

● Unsolicited donations of drugs that do not follow guidelines for drug donations are not used and are disposed of safely.

● Universal precautions to prevent and limit the spread of infections are taught and practised.

● Suitable transportation is organised for patients to reach the referral facilities.

Guidance notes

1. *Availability of health care services:* emergency health care should be available to the disaster-affected population and, if displaced persons are involved, to the host population. The geography, ethnicity, language and gender characteristics of the affected populations need to be considered when implementing interventions.

2. *Services provided at the different levels of the PHC system usually include the following:*

   – **Family level:** some preventive and curative care is provided by the family itself, nearby relatives or by community health workers such as taking medications, administration of oral rehydration therapy (ORT).

   – **Community level:** data collection; ORT, compliance with treatments, home visits and case detection; referral of patients to facilities; health promotion/education, information.

   – **Peripheral level:** first level outpatient services; ORT; dressing; referral of patients to higher level; data collection; vaccinations.

   – **Central health facility level:** diagnoses; outpatient department (first level and referral); dressing and injections; ORT; emergency service; uncomplicated deliveries, reproductive health activities (including family planning, maternal and infant care, safe

Part 2.5

motherhood services, and treatment and counselling related to sexual and gender-based violence, sexually transmitted infections and HIV/AIDS); minor surgery; pharmacy; health surveillance; basic hospitalisation; referral to hospital; possibly: laboratory, transfusions; ongoing measles immunisations.

– **Referral hospital level:** surgery; major obstetric emergencies; referral laboratory.

3. *Neo-natal and maternal morbidity and mortality should be prevented by:* establishing ante-natal services for preparing to handle obstetric emergencies; making available and distributing clean delivery kits; ensuring that UNICEF midwife TBA kits or the UNFPA reproductive health emergency kits are available at health centres. Health care providers should plan for the provision of comprehensive reproductive health services by identifying sites for the future delivery of those services.

4. *Staffing:* staffing at each level of a PHC system can vary, but the following are based on general guidelines taken from Médecins Sans Frontières, *Refugee Health, an Approach to Emergency Situations:*

– **Community level:** 1 home visitor for 500-1,000 population; 1 traditional birth attendent for 2,000 population; 1 supervisor for 10 home visitors; 1 senior supervisor.

– **Peripheral health facility level** (for approximately 10,000 population): total of 2 to 5 workers with a minimum of 1 qualified health worker based on 1 person for 50 consultations per day; locally trained person for ORT, dressing, registering etc.

– **Central health facility level** (for approximately 50,000 population): 1 doctor for diagnoses, 1 health worker for 50 consultations/day; 1 health worker for 20-30 beds (8 hour shifts); 1 ORT; 1 to 2 for pharmacy; 1 to 2 for dressing/injection/sterilisation. Non-medical staff: 1 to 2 clerks; 1 to 3 guards (8 hour shifts); cleaners.

– **Referral hospital level:** variable: at least 1 doctor; 1 nurse for 20-30 beds (8 hour shifts).

5. ***The Minimum Initial Service Package (MISP):*** the MISP is designed to prevent and manage the consequences of sexual violence, reduce HIV transmission, prevent excess neonatal and maternal morbidity and mortality and plan for the provision of comprehensive reproductive health services. The MISP should be implemented by appropriately trained staff from the start of the emergency intervention. Implementation should be coordinated with other agencies and sectors and should include: reporting of cases of sexual violence to health services, supplies for universal precautions (gloves, protective clothing and disposal of sharp objects), sufficient quantities of condoms for the affected population, and clean delivery kits for births.

6. ***Universal precautions:*** universal precautions to prevent and limit spread of infections should include measures to reduce transmission of HIV. Health staff may need training or retraining in this area. (See also communicable disease control standard 2, investigation and control, guidance note 7, HIV prevention.)

7. ***Strengthening local health services:*** throughout the emergency and thereafter, humanitarian agencies should aim to strengthen local health services rather than to create separate services. (See human resource capacity and training standard 3, local capacity.)

8. ***Use of medical facilities:*** consideration should be given to factors affecting the use of, and attendance at, medical facilities. These may include cultural factors, and in conflict situations may also relate to security concerns. Although the impartial provision of health care should be seen as a neutral act, it is not always perceived as such by warring factions, and health facilities may become the target of attacks. The siting and staffing of facilities should take such concerns into account as far as possible.

Note

It should be noted that Caritas Internationalis members cannot endorse: guidance note 7 of the control of communicable diseases section, dealing with condoms; and guidance note 5 of the health care services section, dealing with the Minimum Initial Service Package (MISP).

Part 2:5

5 Human Resource Capacity and Training

All aspects of humanitarian assistance rely on the skills, knowledge and commitment of staff and volunteers working in difficult and sometimes insecure conditions. The demands placed on them can be considerable, and if they are to conduct their work to a level where minimum standards are assured, it is essential that they are suitably experienced and trained and that they are adequately managed and supported by their agency.

Capacity standard 1: competence

Health interventions are implemented by staff who have appropriate qualifications and experience for the duties involved, and who are adequately managed and supported.

Key indicators

- All staff working on a health intervention are informed of the purpose and method of the activities they are asked to carry out.

- Staff with technical and management responsibilities have access to support for informing and verifying key decisions.

- The initial assessment, the design of interventions and key technical decision-making are carried out by staff with relevant technical qualifications (epidemiology, water, sanitation, food, nutrition, shelter, health care expertise) and previous emergency experience.

- Staff and volunteers involved in surveillance (as part of assessment, monitoring or review processes) are thoroughly briefed and regularly supervised.

- Staff responsible for communicable disease control and for health care interventions in the affected population have previous experience or training and are regularly supervised in the use of recommended treatment protocols, guidelines and procedures.

- Staff and volunteers are aware of gender issues relating to the affected population. They know how to report incidents of sexual violence.

- Introduction of any new medical supplies or equipment is accompanied by thorough explanation and supervision.

- Vaccination programme staff have the demonstrated ability to implement the programme including advising people about the vaccine, side effects and other relevant messages.

- Targeted health care procedures have clear written guidelines and protocols.

- The treatment of severe disease or injury is supervised by a medically qualified, experienced practitioner with specific training in this area.

- Health, nutrition and/or outreach workers who have contact with moderately malnourished individuals or their carers (at home, in feeding centres, in clinics etc), have the demonstrated ability to provide appropriate advice and support.

- Health staff have the demonstrated ability to advise mothers and carers on appropriate infant and young child feeding and other priority practices.

Part 2:5

Capacity standard 2: support

Members of the disaster-affected population receive support to enable them to adjust to their new environment and to make optimal use of the assistance provided to them.

Key indicators

● Carers are informed about priority prevention activities such as need for vaccination, use of soap, bednets, latrines and good health seeking behaviours.

● All members of the emergency affected population are informed about the availability of community health workers, home visitors and the location of health facilities and services.

Capacity standard 3: local capacity

Local capacity and skills are used and enhanced by emergency health interventions.

Key indicators

● Local health professionals, health workers, leaders and women and men from the disaster-affected population are included in the implementation of health interventions.

● Staff understand the importance of strengthening the capacities of local health systems for long-term benefit.

● The skills base within existing local partners and institutions and in the affected population is tapped and strengthened during the course of the humanitarian assistance programme.

● Training is provided to community outreach workers.

Guidance notes

1. *See:* ODI/People In Aid (1998), *Code of Best Practice in the Management and Support of Aid Personnel.*

2. *Link with Nutrition:* see also Nutrition, human resource capacity and training standard 1, in chapter 2.

3. *Staffing:* staff and volunteers should demonstrate capabilities equal to their respective assignments. They should also be aware of key aspects of human rights conventions, international humanitarian law and the *Guiding Principles on Internal Displacement* (see the Humanitarian Charter).

   Providing training and support as a part of emergency preparedness is important to ensure that skilled personnel are available to deliver quality services. Given that emergency preparedness cannot be assured in many countries, humanitarian agencies should ensure that qualified and competent staff are identified and properly prepared before eventual assignment to an emergency situation.

   When deploying staff and volunteers, agencies should seek to ensure that there is a balance in the number of women and men on emergency teams.

Part 2:5

Appendix 1

Select Bibliography

Initial Health Assessment

IFRC (1997), *Handbook for Delegates. Needs Assessment, Targeting Beneficiaries*. International Federation of Red Cross and Red Crescent Societies. Geneva.

MSF (1996), *Evaluation Rapide de l'Etat de Santé d'une Population Déplacée ou Refugiée*. Médecins Sans Frontières. Paris.

RHR Consortium (1997), *Refugee Reproductive Health Needs Assessment Field Tools*. Reproductive Health for Refugees Consortium. New York.

WHO (1999), *Rapid Health Assessment Protocols for Emergencies*. World Health Organization. Geneva.

UNHCR (1994), *People-Oriented Planning at Work: Using POP to Improve UNHCR Programming*. UNHCR. Geneva.

Health Information System

WHO (1997), *Communicable Disease Surveillance Kit*. World Health Organization. Geneva.

WHO (1999), *Recommended Surveillance Standards* (WHO/CDS/ISR/99.2). World Health Organization. Geneva.

Measles Control

WHO (1997), *Immunization in Practice. A Guide for Health Workers Who Give Vaccines*. Macmillan. London.

WHO (1998), *Integration of Vitamin A Supplementation With Immunization: Policy and Programme Implications* (WHO/EPI/GEN/98.07). World Health Organization. Geneva.

WHO (1996), *Safety of Injections in Immunization Programs. WHO Recommended Policy.* (WHO/EPI/LHIS/96.05). World Health Organization. Geneva.

WHO (1997), *Surveillance of Adverse Events Following Immunization.* (WHO/EPI/TRAM/93.02 Rev.1). World Health Organization. Geneva.

Control of Communicable Diseases

Benenson, A S (1995), *Control of Communicable Diseases in Man.* American Public Health Association. Washington, DC. 16th edition.

UNAIDS (1998), *Guidelines for HIV Interventions in Emergency Settings.* UNAIDS. Geneva.

Health Care Services

MSF (1993), *Clinical Guidelines, Diagnostic and Treatment Manual.* Médecins Sans Frontières. Paris.

MSF (1997), *Refugee Health, An Approach to Emergency Situations.* Macmillan. London.

Perrin, P (1996), *War and Public Health. Handbook on War and Public Health.* International Committee of the Red Cross. Geneva.

UNDP/IAPSO (1999), *Emergency Relief Items, Compendium of Basic Specifications.* United Nations Development Programme. New York.

UNFPA (1998), *The Reproductive Health Kit for Emergency Situations.* United Nations Population Fund Emergency Relief Operations. Geneva.

UNHCR (1999), *Reproductive Health in Refugee Situations: An Inter-agency Field Manual.* United Nations High Commissioner for Refugees. Geneva.

UNCHR (1996), *Sexual Violence Against Refugees: Guidelines on Prevention and Response.* United Nations High Commissioner for Refugees. Geneva.

Part 2:5

WCRWC (1999), *Sexual Violence in the Kosovo Crisis: A Synopsis of UNHCR Guidelines for Prevention and Response*. Women's Commission for Refugee Women and Children. New York.

WHO (1999a), *Guidelines for Drug Donations* (WHO/EDM/PAR/99.4). World Health Organization. Geneva.

WHO (1999b), *Guidelines for Safe Disposal of Unwanted Pharmaceuticals in and after Emergencies* (WHO/EDM/PAR/99.2). World Health Organization. Geneva.

WHO (1998) *HIV/AIDS and Health Care Personnel: Policies and Practices*. World Health Organization. Geneva.

WHO (1998), *The New Emergency Health Kit 1998. Lists of Drugs and Medical Supplies for 10,000 people for approximately three months*. World Health Organization. Geneva.

UNHCR/WHO(1996), *Guidelines for Drug Donations*. World Health Organization and United Nations High Commissioner for Refugees. Geneva.

WHO (1998), *Essential Drugs. WHO Model List* (revised in December 1997), WHO Drug Information Vol 12, No 1. World Health Organization. Geneva.

WHO (1997), *WHO Drug Information. Recommended INN list. International Non-proprietary Names for Pharmaceutical Substances*. Vol I-III. World Health Organization. Geneva.

Human Resources

Overseas Development Institute/People In Aid (1998), *Code of Best Practice in the Management and Support of Aid Personnel*. ODI/People In Aid. London.

Gender Issues

WCRWC/UNICEF (1998), *The Gender Dimensions of Internal Displacement*. Women's Commission for Refugee Women and Children. New York.

Appendix 2

Sample Checklist for Initial Health Assessment

(Adapted from CDC (1992), *Famine-Affected, Refugee, and Displaced Populations: Recommendations for Public Health Issues*. MMWR (RR-13), July.)

Preparation

● Obtain available information on the disaster-affected population and resources from host country ministries and organisations.

● Obtain available maps or aerial photographs.

● Obtain demographic and health data from international organisations.

Field Assessment

● Determine the total disaster-affected population and proportion of children <5 years old.

● Determine the age and sex breakdown of population.

● Identify groups at increased risk.

● Determine the average household size and estimates of female- and child-headed households.

Health Information

● Identify primary health problems in country of origin if refugees are involved.

● Identify primary health problems in the disaster-affected area if no refugees are involved.

● Identify previous sources of health care.

● Ascertain important health beliefs, traditions and practices.

● Determine the existing social structure and the psycho-social dimensions of the situation.

● Determine the strengths and coverage of local public health programmes in people's country of origin.

Nutritional Status

● Determine the prevalence of protein-energy malnutrition (PEM) in population <5 years of age.

● Ascertain prior nutritional status.

● Determine hierarchical food allocation practices as they affect the nutritional status of women and different social and age groups.

● Determine the prevalence of micronutrient deficiences in the population <5 years of age.

Mortality Rates

● Calculate the overall mortality rate (crude mortality rate – CMR).

● Calculate the under-5 mortality rate (age specific mortality rate for children under five years old).

● Calculate cause-specific mortality rates.

Morbidity

● Determine age, and sex-specific incidence rates of major health problems and diseases that have public health importance, including sexual violence/rape.

Environmental conditions

● Determine climatic conditions; identify geographic features; ascertain local disease epidemiology; assess access to affected population; assess the level of insecurity and violence.

● Assess local, regional and national food supplies (quantity, quality, types), distribution systems, coordination and services of existing organisations, logistics of food transport and storage, feeding programmes and access to local supplies.

● Assess existing shelters and availability of local materials for shelter, access, amount of land and building sites, topography and drainage, blankets, clothing, domestic utensils, fuel, livestock, money.

- Identify and assess water sources, quantity, quality, transport and storage.

- Assess sanitation including excreta practices, soap, vectors and rats, burial sites.

Resources available

- Identify and assess local health services including: access to facilities, health personnel, interpreters, types of facilities/structures, water, refrigeration, generators at facilities, drug and vaccine supplies.

Logistics

- Assess transport, fuel, storage of food, vaccines and other supplies, communication.

Appendix 3

Sample Weekly Surveillance Reporting Forms

(Actual forms should be established and based on findings and recommendations of the initial assessment)

Site:_____ Date: from_____ to_____

1. Disaster-affected population

   A. Total population at the beginning of week:_____

   B. Births this week:_____ Deaths this week:_____

   C. Arrivals this week *(if applicable)*:_____ Departures this week:_____

   D. Total population at the end of the week: _____

   E. Total population < 5 years of age: _____

2. Mortality

Number of deaths	0-4 years		5+ years		Total
	Males	Females	Males	Females	
Diarrhoeal disease					
Respiratory disease					
Malnutrition					
Measles					
Malaria					
Maternal factors					
Other/Unknown					
Total by Age and Sex					
Total < 5 years					

Average total mortality rate: M_____ F_____ Total _____
(Deaths/10,000 total population/day averaged for week) by age + sex

Average under-five mortality rate: M_____ F_____ Total _____
(Deaths/10,000 under-fives/day averaged for week)

3. Morbidity

Primary symptoms/ diagnosis	0-4 years Males	Females	5+ years Males	Females	Total
Diarrhoea/dehydration					
Fever with cough					
Fever and chills/malaria					
Measles					
Trauma/accident					
Suspected meningitis					
Suspected cholera					
Other/Unknown					
Total					

4. Comments

_____
_____
_____
_____
_____
_____
_____

(Please note that these forms may include age specific morbidity and mortality for use by the health information system. The following age groups should be used: <1, 1-4, 5-14, 15-44, 45+.)

Appendix 4

Example of Mortality Dataset Presentation

Proportional mortality among
Mozambican refugees in Malawi, 1987-89

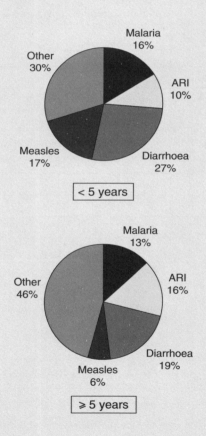

Source: MSF (1997), *Refugee Health, An Approach to Emergency Situations*. Macmillan. London.

Appendix 5

Sample Measles Vaccination Form

Place: .... **Reported by:** ....

From: ..../......./....... **To:** ..../......./.......
    day/month/year   day/month/year

• Mass measles vaccination campaign

Yes ☐   **No** ☐

• Routine measles vaccination in health facilities

Yes ☐   **No** ☐

• Measles vaccination coverage

Target population

< 5 years old: ......   ≥ 5 years old: ......

Total target population: ......

No. vaccinated	Mass campaign A		Routine vaccination B		Cumulative measles vaccination coverage*
	No. this week	Cumulative No.	No. this week	Cumulative No.	
< 5 years old					
≥ 5 years old					
TOTAL					

* Calculation of the cumulative coverage: A + B/target population

Comments: ....
....
....
....
....

N.B.: This form can also be used for another mass vaccination campaign; just change the name.

Source: MSF (1997), *Refugee Health, An Approach to Emergency Situations*. Macmillan. London.

Part 2:5

Appendix 6

Sample Water, Sanitation and Environment Forms

(Please note: these forms should be adapted to the particular situation and follow the initial assessment recommendations.)

Place: ....   **Reported by:** ....

From: ..../......./.......   **To:** ..../......./.......
        day/month/year   day/month/year

• Water

	No. of litres/day	Population	No. of litres/pers/day	Objective
Water supply				

	No. of water points	Population	No. of pers./water point	Objective
Water supply				

• Sanitation

	No. of latrines	Population	No. of persons /latrine	Objective
Latrines				

• Crowding (space/person)

	Surface area in m²	Population	M² per person	Objective
Crowding				

Comments: ....
....
....
....
....
....

Source: MSF (1997), *Refugee Health, An Approach to Emergency Situations*. Macmillan. London.

Appendix 7

Sample Sexual Violence Report Form

(Please note: this form should be adapted to the particular situation.)

CONFIDENTIAL

Sexual Violence Incident Report Form

Camp: _____ Reporting Officer: _____ Date: _____

1) Affected Person

Code*: _____ Date of Birth: _____ Sex: _____

Address:
_____

Civil Status: _____

If a Minor: Code/Name of Parents/Guardian: _____

2) Report of Incident:

Place: _____ Date: _____ Time: _____

Description of incident (specify type of sexual violence):

Persons involved:

3. Actions Taken

Medical examination done ❑ yes ❑ no ❑ By whom: _____

Major findings and treatment given: _____

Protection Staff Notified: ❑ yes ❑ no

If no, reasons given: _____

If yes, actions taken: _____

Psycho-social counselling given: ❑ yes ❑ no

By whom and actions taken: _____

4. Proposed Next Steps

5. Follow-up Plan

❑ Medical follow-up: _____

❑ Psycho-social counselling: _____

❑ Legal proceedings: _____

* Code numbers should be used rather than names to ensure confidentiality.

Part 3

Annexes

1 Glossary of Key Terms

The glossary defines key terms in the context of the Humanitarian Charter and Minimum Standards in Disaster Response.

Accountability

The responsibility to demonstrate to stakeholders, foremost of whom are disaster-affected people, that humanitarian assistance complies with agreed standards.

Disaster

A situation where people's normal means of support for life with dignity have failed as a result of natural or human-made catastrophe.

Disaster-affected people/population

All people whose life or health are threatened by disaster, whether displaced or in their home area.

Gender

Gender encompasses the socially defined sex roles, attitudes and values which communities and societies ascribe as appropriate for one sex or the other. Gender does not describe the biological sexual characteristics by which females and males are identified.

Groups at risk

People considered to be exceptionally vulnerable.

Host government

Government of the country in which humanitarian assistance takes place.

Humanitarian actor

An organisation that supports the provision of humanitarian assistance.

Humanitarian agency

A local or international non-governmental organisation, UN body or donor institution whose activities support the provision of humanitarian assistance.

Humanitarian assistance

The provision of basic requirements which meet people's needs for adequate water, sanitation, nutrition, food, shelter and health care.

Impartial assistance

Assistance is that given on the basis of need alone and makes no distinction as to race, creed, nationality, sex, age, physical or mental disability.

Indicator

'Signals' that show whether a standard has been attained. They provide a way of measuring and communicating both the impact, or result, of programmes as well as the process, or methods, used. The indicators may be qualitative or quantitative.

Local authorities

Government or leaders recognised to be in control in the country or region in which the disaster-affected population is located.

Minimum standard

The minimum level (of service) to be attained in humanitarian assistance.

Sexual violence

All forms of sexual threat, assault, domestic violence, interference and exploitation including involuntary prostitution, statutory rape and molestation without physical harm or penetration.

Staff

Employees of humanitarian agencies.

Stakeholder

Anybody affected by, or who can affect, humanitarian assistance.

The humanitarian principle

Prevention and alleviation of suffering, protection of life and health and respect for human dignity.

Transparency

Openness and accessibility of humanitarian agencies, their systems and information.

2 Acronyms

ACC/SCN:

United Nations Administrative Committee on Coordination/Subcommittee on Nutrition

ACT:

Action by Churches Together

ALNAP:

Active Learning Network for Accountability in Practice

CDC:

Centers for Disease Control and Prevention

DAC:

Development Assistance Committee (OECD)

FAO:

Food and Agriculture Organization

IAPSO:

Inter-Agency Procurement Services Office (UNDP)

ICRC:

International Committee of the Red Cross

INFCD:

International Nutrition Foundation for Developing Countries

LWF:

The Lutheran World Federation

MISP:

Minimum Initial Service Package

MSF:

Médecins Sans Frontières

NCHS:

National Centre for Health Statistics

NGO:

Non-governmental organisation

OCHA:
UN Office for Coordination of Humanitarian Affairs

OECD:
Organization for Economic Cooperation and Development

OFDA:
Office of Foreign Disaster Assistance (USAID)

PTSS:
Programme and Technical Support Section (UNHCR)

SCHR:
Steering Committee for Humanitarian Response

UNDP:
United Nations Development Programme

UNDRO:
United Nations Disaster Relief Organization

UNEP:
United Nations Environment Programme

UNHCR:
United Nations High Commissioner for Refugees

UNICEF:
United Nations Children's Fund

USAID:
United States Agency for International Development

WCRWC:
Women's Commission for Refugee Women and Children

WFP:
World Food Programme

WHO:
World Health Organization

WMO:
World Meteorological Organization

3 Acknowledgements

Sphere Project

Staff team

Chair, Project Management Committee - Nicholas Stockton, Oxfam, UK

Project Coordinator - Peter Walker, IFRC, Switzerland

Project Manager, Phase I - Susan Purdin, Switzerland

Project Manager, Phase II - Nan Buzard, Switzerland

Project Assistant, Phase II - Catherine Blum, Switzerland

Training Manager, Phase II - Sean Lowrie, UK

Project Management Committee

James K Bishop, InterAction, USA ◊ Peter Hawkins, Save the Children Alliance, UK ◊ Graham Miller, CARE International, Switzerland ◊ Jean-Marie Kindermans, MSF International, Belgium ◊ Rebecca Larson, The Lutheran World Federation (ACT), Switzerland ◊ Gianni Ruffini, VOICE, Belgium ◊ Nancy Lindborg, Mercy Corps International, USA ◊ Miriam Lutz, Action by Churches Together (ACT), Switzerland ◊ Gerald Martone, International Rescue Committee, USA ◊ Joel McClellan, SCHR, Switzerland ◊ Pierre Perrin, ICRC, Switzerland ◊ Ed Shenkenberg, ICVA, Switzerland ◊ Karel Zelenka, Caritas Internationalis, Vatican City

Donors

In addition to contributions by the member organisations of SCHR and by InterAction through a grant provided by the Ford Foundation, funding for the Sphere Project has been provided by:

The Australian Agency for International Development (AusAID) ◊ The Belgian Ministry of Development ◊ The Canadian International Development Agency (CIDA) ◊ Danish International Development Assistance (DANIDA) ◊ The United Kingdom Department for International Development (DFID) ◊ The European Community

Humanitarian Office (ECHO) ◊ The Netherlands Ministry of Foreign Affairs Humanitarian Aid Division ◊ The New Zealand Ministry of Foreign Affairs and Trade ◊ The Swedish International Development Cooperation Agency (Sida) ◊ The Swiss Agency for Development and Cooperation (SDC) ◊ The United States Department of State Bureau of Population, Refugees and Migration (US-BPRM) ◊ The United States Agency for International Development Office of Foreign Disaster Assistance (US-OFDA)

Chapter 1: Water Supply and Sanitation

Sector Manager: John Adams, Oxfam GB

John Adams and the Sphere Project would like to thank the peer review group for their contributions to this chapter:

Riccardo Conti, International Committee of the Red Cross, Switzerland ◊ Eric Drouart, Action Contre La Faim, France ◊ Jeff Eames, CARE International UK, UK ◊ Denis Heidebroek, MSF Holland, The Netherlands ◊ Uli Jaspers, International Federation of Red Cross and Red Crescent Societies, Switzerland ◊ Richard Luff, Oxfam GB, UK ◊ Daniel Mora-Castro, UNHCR, Switzerland ◊ Claude Rakotomalala, UNHCR, Switzerland ◊ Paul Sherlock, Oxfam GB, UK

Other contributors:

Astier Almedom, London School of Hygiene and Tropical Medicine, UK ◊ Andy Bastable, Oxfam, UK ◊ Eveline Bolt, IRC International Water and Sanitation Centre, Holland ◊ Paul Borsboom, SAWA, Agro Business, Holland ◊ Bernard Broughton, Relief Development Services Pty, Australia ◊ Sandy Cairncross, London School of Hygiene and Tropical Medicine, UK ◊ Art Carlson, International Rescue Committee, Rwanda ◊ M T Chanyowedza, Christian CARE (ACT), Zimbabwe ◊ Desmond Chavasse, London School of Hygiene and Tropical Medicine, UK ◊ Sara Davidson, People in Aid, UK ◊ Tom de Veer, Independent Consultant, Holland ◊ Florence Descacq, ACF - Côte d'Ivoire, France ◊ Ben Fawcett, Institute of Irrigation Studies, University of Southampton, UK ◊ Suzanne Ferron, Independent Consultant, UK ◊ Tim Foster, RedR International, Switzerland ◊ Pierre

Part 3

Fourcassier, ACF - Côte d'Ivoire, France ◊ Banteyehun Haile, American Refugee Committee, Rwanda ◊ Alden Hendersen, Health Studies Branch, CDC, National Center for Environmental Health, USA ◊ Robert Hodgson, Exeter University, UK ◊ Mark Hogan, Concern Worldwide, Ireland ◊ Sarah House, Water and Engineering Development Group, Loughborough University of Technology, UK ◊ Modhakkiru Katakweba, Oxfam, Tanzania ◊ Vincent Koch, Oxfam UK and Ireland, Angola ◊ Bobby Lambert, RedR, UK ◊ Sue Lim, DRA, Holland ◊ Peter Lochery, CARE, USA ◊ Woldu Mahary, Oxfam, UK ◊ Duncan Mara, Department of Civil Engineering, University of Leeds, UK ◊ Laura Marks, International Rescue Committee, USA ◊ Tom McAloon, International Rescue Committee, USA ◊ Bob Reed, Water and Engineering Development Group, Loughborough University of Technology, UK ◊ Philippe Rey, ICRC, Switzerland ◊ Les Roberts, Independent Consultant, USA ◊ David Saunders, IRC International Water and Sanitation Centre, Holland ◊ Stefan Spang, ICRC, Switzerland ◊ Madeleine Thomson, MALSAT Research Group, Liverpool School of Tropical Medicine, UK ◊ Roger Yates, Oxfam, Tanzania ◊ MSF Belgium

Chapter 2: Nutrition

Sector Manager: Lola Gostelow, SCF UK

Sector Researcher: Anna Taylor, SCF UK

Lola Gostelow and the Sphere Project would like to thank the following people for their substantial contributions to this chapter:

Ken Bailey, World Health Organisation, Switzerland ◊ Rita Bhatia, UNHCR, Switzerland ◊ Annalies Borrel, Concern Worldwide, Ireland ◊ Anne Callanan, World Food Programme, Italy ◊ Pieter Djikhuizen, World Food Programme, Italy ◊ Michael Golden, University of Aberdeen, UK ◊ Yvonne Grellety, Action Contre La Faim, France ◊ Susanne Jaspars, independent consultant, UK ◊ Marion Kelly, UK Department for International Development, UK ◊ Clare Schofield, London School of Hygiene and Tropical Medicine, UK ◊ John Seaman, Save the Children Fund UK, UK ◊ Jeremy Shoham, independent consultant, UK ◊ Arnold Timmer, UNHCR, Switzerland ◊ Saskia van der Kam, MSF Holland, Holland ◊ Zita Weise-Prinzo, World Health Organisation, Switzerland ◊ Helen Young, Oxfam GB, UK

Other contributors:

Carla Abou-Zahr, WHO, Switzerland ◊ Lesley Adams, Oxfam GB ◊ Tahmid Ahmed, ICDDR, Bangladesh ◊ David Alnwick, UNICEF ◊ A M M Anisul Anwal, Ministry of Health and Family Welfare, Bangladesh ◊ Iqbal Anwar, Radd MCH FP Centre Bangladesh ◊ Judith Appleton, Independent Consultant, UK ◊ Selena Bajraktarevic, UNICEF, Bosnia ◊ Theresa Banda, Ministry of Health, Malawi ◊ Hilary Baroi, Church of Bangladesh Social Development Programme, Bangladesh ◊ George Beaton, independent consultant, Canada ◊ Nathan Belete, World Vision ◊ Chris Besse, Merlin, UK ◊ Aminul Haque Bhuyan, University of Dhaka, Bangladesh ◊ John Borton, Overseas Development Institute, UK ◊ Dominique Bounie, Lille Institute of Food and Agriculture, France ◊ Francesco Branca, Istituto Nazionale della Nutrizione, Italy ◊ Andre Briend, INSERM, France ◊ Vincent Brown, Epicentre, France ◊ Kate Bruck, Dr Cynthia's Clinic, Thailand ◊ Judy Bryson, Africare, USA ◊ Ann Burgess, independent consultant, UK ◊ Brent Burkholder, CDC, USA ◊ Christine Cambrezy, WFP, Somalia ◊ Kathy Carter, Institute of Child Health, UK ◊ Jenny Cervinskas, Micronutrients Initiative, Canada ◊ Gene Charoonruk and Uraiporn Chittchang, Mahidol University, Thailand ◊ Françoise Chome, Sustain, USA ◊ Ian Christopholos, SIDA, Sweden ◊ Ed Clay, Overseas Development Institute, UK ◊ William Clay, FAO, Italy ◊ Graeme Clugston, WHO, Switzerland ◊ Karen Codling, UNICEF, Thailand ◊ Bruce Cogill, IMPACT ◊ Marc Cohen, Bread for the World Institute ◊ Steve Collins, Independent Consultant, UK ◊ Suzanne Cotter, WHO, Bosnia ◊ Joanne Csete, UNICEF, USA ◊ Ariane Curdy, ICRC, Switzerland ◊ Helena Dalton, International Rescue Committee, Thailand ◊ Frances Davidson, USAID Nutrition Section, USA ◊ Austin Davis, LSE/MSF, UK ◊ Danielle Deboutte, WHO/EHA, Switzerland ◊ Vicki Denman, CRS, USA ◊ Pat Disket, Cranfield University, UK ◊ Rhoda Eliasi, National Economic Council, Malawi ◊ Mendez England, FFP, USA ◊ Linda Ethangatta, UNICEF OLS, Kenya ◊ Margie Ferris-Morris, formerly USAID, USA Anna Ferro-Luzzi, National Institute of

Nutrition, Italy ◊ Lourdes Fidalgo, Ministry of Health, Mozambique ◊ Aida Filipovic, Institute of Public Health, Sarajevo ◊ Wilma Freire, PAHO, USA ◊ David Garms, FFP/USAID, USA ◊ Veronique Genaille, UNHCR, Kenya ◊ Laura Guimond, Mercy Corps International Child Survival Program, USA ◊ Alistair Hallam, Overseas Development Institute, UK ◊ John Hammock, Tufts University, USA ◊ Steven Hansch, Refugee Policy Group, USA ◊ Pirko Heinonen, UNICEF, Somalia ◊ Jeya Henry, Oxford Brookes University, UK ◊ Hege Hetzberg, NORAD, Norway ◊ Moazzem Hossain, Save the Children UK, Bangladesh ◊ Janet-Marie Huddle, World Vision, Canada ◊ Zahidul Islam, Grameen Health Programme, Bangladesh ◊ Safia Jama, UNICEF, Somalia ◊ Omanic Jasna, Public Health Institute, Bosnia ◊ Linley Karlton, Uppsala University, Sweden ◊ Lawson Kasamale, Red Cross, Malawi ◊ Judit Katona-Apte, WFP, Italy ◊ Kathy Krasovec, USAID ◊ Fred Kuhila, Programme Against Malnutrition, Zambia ◊ Natehalai (Kitty) Lanmg, ARC TRAT, Thailand ◊ Bruce Laurence, Merlin, UK ◊ Bernt Lindtjorn, University of Bergen, Norway ◊ Dr Luecha, Department of Health, Thailand ◊ Mary Lung'aho, CRS, USA ◊ Jane Macaskill, Nairobi/Somalia ◊ Sharon MacDonall, CDC Nutrition Division, USA ◊ Kandarasee Malanong, Ministry of Public Health, Thailand ◊ Gabrielle Maritim, University of Nairobi, Kenya ◊ David Marsh, Save the Children US, USA ◊ Rabia Mathai, IFRC, Bangladesh ◊ Fedai Mawlar, Voluntary Health Services Society, Bangladesh ◊ Jenny McMahon, ICRC, Kenya ◊ Judiann McNulty, CARE ◊ Cathy Mears, independent consultant, UK ◊ David Meek, World Vision, USA ◊ Andrea Menefee, International Rescue Committee, Thailand ◊ Zahra Mirghani, UNHCR, Tanzania ◊ Sheikh Mohiuddin, Ad-din Hospital, Bangladesh ◊ Alain Moren, RNSP, Belgium ◊ Saul Morris, IFPRI ◊ Yasmine Motarjemi, WHO, Switzerland ◊ Ellen Muehlhoff, FAO, Italy ◊ Chizuru Nishida, WHO, Switzerland ◊ Eric Noji, WHO, Switzerland ◊ Ted Okada, Food for the Hungry International, USA ◊ Ben Okech, Ministry of Health, Kenya ◊ Omawale Omawale, UNICEF, DPRK ◊ OMNI, USAID Project ◊ Fiona O'Reilly, Emergency Nutrition Network, Ireland ◊ Christophe Paquet, Epicentre, France ◊ Abe Parvanta, CDC, USA ◊ Chris and Monika Pearson, Uppsala University, Sweden ◊ Nina Pillai, Overseas Development Institute, UK ◊ Rachel Pinniger, Tribhuvan University,

Nepal ◊ Claudine Prudhon, ACF, France ◊ Randy Purviance, ADRA, USA ◊ Sonya Rabenack, ACC/SCN, Switzerland ◊ Shah Mahfuzur Rahman, Institute of Public Health, Bangladesh ◊ Anne Ralte, IMPACT, USA ◊ Emma Roberts, TEAR Fund, UK ◊ Anna de Roos, ECHO, Bangladesh ◊ Aileen Robertson, WHO Regional Office Europe, Denmark ◊ S K Roy, ICDDR, Bangladesh ◊ Terrence T J Ryan, Food Aid Management, USA ◊ Serge Rwamasirabo, USAID Rwanda ◊ Abdus Sabur, Save the Children UK, Bangaldesh ◊ Erminio Sacco, WFP, Somalia ◊ Helen Samatebele, Programme Against Malnutrition, Zambia ◊ Andy Seal, Institute of Child Health, UK ◊ Mary Serdula, CDC, USA ◊ Louise Serunjogi, Makere University, Uganda ◊ Dr Shazahan, Helen Keller Institute, Bangladesh ◊ S Shao, Tanzania Food and Nutrition Centre, Tanzania ◊ Catherine Siandwazi, Commonwealth Regional Health Secretariat, Tanzania ◊ Sangsom Sinawat, Ministry of Public Health, Thailand ◊ Jose Solis, PAHO, USA ◊ Bernhard Staub, Tanganyika Christian Refugee Service, Tanzania ◊ Anne Swindale, IMPACT, USA ◊ Kerry Sylvester, independent consultant, Mozambique ◊ Judith Tagwira, Ministry of Health, Zimbabwe ◊ M Q K Talukder, Institute of Mother and Child, Bangladesh ◊ Haile Selassi Tekie, Relief Society of Tigray, Ethiopia ◊ Andy Tembon, SCF UK, Rwanda ◊ Aster Tesfaye, Jesuit Refugee Service, Ethiopia ◊ Andrew Tomkins, Institute of Child Health, UK ◊ Michael Toole, MacFarlane Burnet Centre for Medical Research, Australia ◊ Benjamin Torun, INCAP, Guatemala ◊ Stuart Turner, World Vision, UK ◊ Daniel Valle, Red Cross, USA ◊ Albertine van der Veen, Independent Consultant, Holland ◊ Michel van Herp, MSF International, Belgium ◊ Fabienne Vautier, MSF Belgium ◊ Anna Verster, WHO/EMRO, Egypt ◊ M A Wahed, ICDDR, Bangladesh ◊ Jane Wallace, ACC/SCN, Switzerland ◊ Boonyuen Warasai, Ministry of Public Health, Thailand ◊ Fiona Watson, Institute of Child Health, UK ◊ Katy Watt, Nutrition Consultant, UK ◊ Elizabeth Westaway, Cardiff University, UK ◊ Carole Williams, Nutrition Consultant, UK ◊ Rukia Abdillahi Yacoub, UNICEF, Sudan ◊ Oliver Yambi, UNICEF, Kenya ◊ Tayech Yimer, Save the Children UK, Ethiopia

Part 3

Chapter 3: Food Aid

Sector Manager: Harlan Hale, CARE USA

Harlan Hale and the Sphere Project would like to thank the following people for their substantial contributions to this chapter:

Rita Bhatia, UNHCR, Switzerland ◊ Delphine Borione, World Food Programme, Italy ◊ Analies Borrel, Concern Worldwide, Ireland ◊ Rick Brennan, Centre of Excellence in Disaster Management ◊ Lola Gostelow, Save the Children Fund, UK ◊ Charles Kelly, independent consultant ◊ Isabelle Le Normand, Action Contre La Faim, France ◊ Thomas J Ryan, Food Aid Management, USA ◊ Anne Ralte, consultant to USAID, USA ◊ Anna Taylor, Save the Children Fund, UK

Other contributors:

Ibrahim (Abe) Parvanta, CDC, USA ◊ Lesley Adams, Independent Consultant ◊ Rennata Becker, German Agro-Action ◊ François Belanger, Epicentre, France ◊ Bob Bell, CARE ◊ Mark Bowden, Save the Children, UK ◊ Ann Callanan, WFP, Italy ◊ Thoric Cederstrom, Save the Children, USA ◊ Jendra Cekan, CRS ◊ Willian Clay, FAO-Nutrition ◊ Bruce Cogill, Impact Project USAID ◊ Jim Cornelius, CFGB ◊ Annegre de Roos, Independent Consultant ◊ Serge Depotter, MSF International, Belgium ◊ Agnes Dhur, ICRC, Switzerland ◊ Tim Frankenberger, CARE, USA ◊ Georg Frerks, Agricultural University, Wageningen, Holland ◊ Michael Golden , University of Aberdeen, UK ◊ Jennifer Graef, FAM, USA ◊ Yvonne Grellety, ACF, France ◊ Dave Hagen, USAID/FFP-ER ◊ Steve Hansch, Independent Consultant ◊ David J. Garms, USAID, USA ◊ Susan Jaspars, Independent Consultant, UK ◊ Al Kehler, CFGB ◊ Marion Kelly, DFID, UK ◊ Anders Ladekarl, Danish Refugee Council, Denmark ◊ Lauren Landis, SCF, USA ◊ Francoise Ledru, VOICE, Belgium ◊ Sean Lowrie, CARE, Canada ◊ Mary Lung'aho, Catholic Relief Services, USA ◊ Frances Mason, ACF, France ◊ Paul Maurie Boulanger, AEDES ◊ Catherine Mears, independent consultant, UK ◊ Walter Middleton, World Vision ◊ Chizuru Nishida, WHO ◊ Mario Ochoa, ADRA ◊ Stefan Peterson, MSF/Upsala University, Sweden ◊ Veronique Priem, MSF, France ◊ Bill Ralston, CIDA ◊ Jeremy Shoham, ENN/RNIS/LSHTM, UK ◊ Piet

Spaarman, Caritas, Holland ◊ Stein Stoa, Norwegian Refugee Council, Norway ◊ Jo Thomas, Concern Worldwide, Ireland ◊ Marge Tsitouris, CARE ◊ Bernd V Dreesmann, EuronAid, Holland ◊ Albertien van der Veen, Independent Consultant, Holland ◊ Michel van Herp, MSF International, Belgium ◊ Saskia van der Kam, MSF Holland ◊ Rudy von Bernuth, Save the Children, USA ◊ Jane Wallace, ACC/SCN ◊ Shaun Walsh, FHI ◊ Jackie Wood, CARE, Canada ◊ Helen Young, Oxfam, UK ◊ Dutch Interchurch Aid (ACT) ◊ Global Network on Food Security

Chapter 4: Shelter and Site Planning

Sector Manager: Philip Wijmans, The Lutheran World Federation (ACT), Cambodia

Sector Researcher: Tom Corsellis, University of Cambridge, UK

Philip Wijmans and the Sphere Project would like to thank the following people for their substantial contributions to this chapter:

Ad Hordijk, Matrix Consultants for Development, The Netherlands ◊ Gatachew Jembere, The Lutheran World Federation (ACT), Zambia ◊ Barend Leeuwenberg, MSF Holland, The Netherlands ◊ John Nduna, The Lutheran World Federation (ACT), Tanzania ◊ Brian Neldner, The Lutheran World Federation (ACT), Australia ◊ Wolfgang Neumann, UNHCR, Switzerland ◊ Todd Stowell, The Lutheran World Federation (ACT), Nepal ◊ Elizabeth Umlas, UNHCR, Switzerland ◊ Gerro Vonk, MSF Holland, The Netherlands

Other contributors:

Krister Åkesson, Church of Sweden Aid (ACT), Sweden ◊ Jaap Aantjes, LWF (ACT), Rwanda ◊ Richard Agullas, ELCSA-LWF, South Africa ◊ Allen Armstrong, LWF (ACT), Nepal ◊ Inu Arya, LWF (ACT), Cambodia ◊ Dirk Bakker (ZA), ICCO (ACT), Holland ◊ Henk Bakker, ICCO (ACT), Holland ◊ John Barrett, AIT, Thailand ◊ Krishan Batra, UNDP/IAPSO, Denmark ◊ Andrew Chalinder, UNICEF, Botswana ◊ Arno Coerver, LWF (ACT), Mauritania ◊ John Cosgrave, InterWorks Europe, Ireland ◊ Howard Dalzell, Concern Worldwide, Ireland ◊ John

Part 3

Damerell, LWF (ACT), Angola ◊ Rudelmar de Faria, LWF (ACT), El Salvador ◊ Martin Dillon, LWF (ACT), Uganda ◊ Paevo Faerm, LWF (ACT), Ethiopia ◊ Tim Foster, RedR International, Switzerland ◊ Dennis Frado, Lutheran Office for World Community, USA ◊ Laura Gibbons, ODI, UK ◊ Hannelore Hensle, Bread for the World Projects (ACT), Germany ◊ Mark Hogan, Concern Worldwide, Ireland ◊ Hossein Kalali, University of Geneva/ Swiss Cooperation for Development, Switzerland ◊ Kroslak, LWF, Russia ◊ Sean Lowrie, CARE Emergency Unit, Canada ◊ Ingela Lundborg, Church of Sweden Aid (ACT), Sweden ◊ Meena-Mbvumbe, LWF (ACT), Malawi ◊ Jim Mason, LWF (ACT), Kenya ◊ Cyrus Mechkat, University of Geneva/ Swiss Cooperation for Development, Switzerland ◊ Pamela Meggitt, Lutheran Development Service, Swaziland ◊ Enos Moyo, ELCSA-LWF (ACT), South Africa ◊ Babar Mumtaz, Development Planning Unit, University College London, UK ◊ Gail Neudorf, CARE, Kenya ◊ Hermine Nikolaison, LWF (ACT), Croatia ◊ Stichting Oecomenische Hulp, Dutch Interchurch Aid (ACT), Holland ◊ Patrick Oger, MSF ◊ Lars Olsson, WHO, Switzerland ◊ Duane Poppe, LWF (ACT), Tanzania ◊ William Power, Concern Worldwide, Ireland ◊ Eric Ram, World Vision International, Switzerland ◊ Joe Riverson, World Vision International, Liberia ◊ Craig Sanders, UNHCR, Switzerland ◊ Tapio Saraneva, Finnchurchaid (ACT), Finland ◊ Don Schramm, Disaster Management Center of the University of Wisconsin-Madison, USA ◊ Sarah Scott, ODI, UK ◊ David Shearer, Institute of Strategic Studies, UK ◊ Paul Sitnam, LWF (ACT), Angola ◊ Rudi Slooff, WHO, Switzerland ◊ Atle Sommerfeldt, Norwegian Church Aid (ACT), Norway ◊ Bernard Staub, LWF (ACT), Bosnia ◊ Mamane Sukati, Lutheran World Development Service, Swaziland ◊ John Svendsen, UNDP-IAPSO, Denmark ◊ Jens Tang, Meteorologist, Denmark ◊ Gerrit ten Velde, LWF (ACT), Mozambique ◊ Reinier Thiadens, UNHCR, Switzerland ◊ Paul Thomson, Disaster Management Center of the University of Wisconsin-Madison, USA ◊ Jan v Bentum, ICCO, Holland ◊ Koenraad Van Brabant, ODI, UK ◊ John Watt, IFRC, Switzerland ◊ Jacques Willemse, Dutch Interchurch Aid (ACT), Holland ◊ Henk Zomer, Dutch Interchurch Aid (ACT), Holland ◊ MSF Holland ◊ Canadian Lutheran World Relief (ACT), Canada ◊ DanChurchAid (ACT), Denmark ◊ Christian Aid (ACT) ◊ Evangelical Lutheran Church in America (ACT),

USA ◊ Evangelische Zentralstelle für Entwicklungshilfe (Protestant Association for Cooperation in Development), Germany ◊ LWF (ACT), Haiti ◊ LWF(ACT), India ◊ LWF (ACT), Jerusalem ◊ LWR (ACT), Kenya ◊ PLWF/LWF (ACT), Peru ◊ Leo Siliamaa, LWF (ACT), Zimbabwe

Chapter 5: Health Services

Sector Managers: Joachim Kreysler, IFRC, Switzerland and Jean Roy, CDC/IFRC, USA and Switzerland

Joachim Kreysler, Jean Roy and the Sphere Project would like to thank the following people for their substantial contributions to this chapter:

Sue Chowdhury, Oxfam GB, UK ◊ Carole Collins, Oxfam GB, UK ◊ Daniel Deboutte, World Health Organization, Switzerland ◊ Myriam Henkens, MSF Belgium, Belgium ◊ Sandra Krause, American Refugee Committee, USA ◊ Bruce Laurence, Merlin, UK ◊ Jean Long, Concern Worldwide, Ireland ◊ Serge Malé, UNHCR, Switzerland ◊ Eric Noji, World Health Organization, Switzerland ◊ Jean Marc Olivé, World Health Organization, Switzerland ◊ Pierre Perrin, International Committee of the Red Cross, Switzerland ◊ Stefan Seebacher, International Federation of Red Cross and Red Crescent Societies, Malaysia ◊ Harald Siem, Emergency and Humanitarian Action, World Health Organization, Switzerland ◊ Ronald Waldman, Columbia University, USA

Other contributors:

Andrea Ammon, Robert Koch Institute, Germany ◊ Thomas Baker, Red Cross, USA ◊ Rita Bhatia, UNHCR, Switzerland ◊ Vincent Brown, Epicentre, France ◊ Brent Burkholder, CDC, USA ◊ Gilbert Burnham, Johns Hopkins University School of Hygiene and Public Health, USA ◊ Kate Burns, UNHCR, Switzerland ◊ Manuel Carballo, ICMHC, Switzerland ◊ Christine Chevalier, MSF Switzerland ◊ Maire Connolly, WHO/ICA, Switzerland ◊ Alphonse daSilva, AMP, France ◊ Claude de Ville de Goyet, PAHO/WHO, USA ◊ Flavio del Ponti, Swiss Disaster Policy, Switzerland ◊ Pat Disket, Cranfield University, UK ◊ Kolude Doherty, UNHCR, Switzerland ◊ Mohamed Dualeh, UNHCR,

Part 3

Switzerland ◊ Marcel Dubouloz, HDCA, Switzerland ◊ Marcel Furic, Caritas Internationalis, Switzerland ◊ Anne Golaz, CDC, USA ◊ Lola Gostelow, Save the Children, UK ◊ Brian Gushulak, IOM Medical Services, Switzerland ◊ Harlan Hale, CARE, USA ◊ Hilde Haug, UNFPA, Switzerland ◊ Nobuhide Hayashi, AMDA, Kenya ◊ Jean Herve Bradol, MSF, France ◊ Mark Hogan, Concern, Ireland ◊ Kjura Inomzoda, Red Crescent Society, Tajikistan ◊ Hector Jalipa, World Vision - Somalia, Kenya ◊ Nenad Javornik, Croatia ◊ Robert Kesala, IFRC Regional Health Delegate, Zimbabwe ◊ Jean-Marie Kindermans, MSF International, Belgium ◊ Renee Kotz, American Red Cross, USA ◊ Nance Kyloh, USAID, Switzerland ◊ Mary Lange, US BPRM, Switzerland ◊ Rebecca Larson, The Lutheran World Federation (ACT), Switzerland ◊ Jennifer Leaning, Medicine and Global Survival, USA ◊ Philippe Leborgne, ACF, France ◊ Maura Lennon, GOAL, Ireland ◊ Annie Lloyd, Oxfam, UK ◊ Jean-Dominique Lormond, MSF International, Switzerland ◊ William Lyerly, USAID, USA ◊ Alexander Malyavan, UNICEF, Switzerland ◊ Michael Marx, University of Heidelberg, Germany ◊ Jean-Paul Menu, WHO, Switzerland ◊ Eric Mercier, UNICEF, USA ◊ Nancy Mock, Tulane University, USA ◊ Alain Moren, Epicentre, France ◊ Cleopas Msuya, IFRC Regional Health Delegate, Kenya ◊ Jayne Mutonga, AMREF, Kenya ◊ Geir Nergard, IFRC Regional Delegation, Kazakstan ◊ David Newberry, CARE, USA ◊ Ishmael Noko, The Lutheran World Federation (ACT), Switzerland ◊ Michael Pelly, IFRC, Switzerland ◊ Lyle Petersen, Robert Koch-Institut, Germany ◊ Mit Philips (Kinshasa assignee), MSF, Belgium ◊ Daniel Pierotti, UNFPA, Switzerland ◊ Jean Pierre Revel, IFRC, Switzerland ◊ Peter Poore, Save the Children, UK ◊ Eric Ram, World Vision International, Switzerland ◊ Arthur Reingold, University of California at Berkeley, USA ◊ Remi Russbach, Geneva Foundation to Protect Health in War, Switzerland ◊ Hakan Sandbladh, IFRC, Switzerland ◊ Khalid Shibib, WHO, Switzerland ◊ Ola Skuken, IFRC, Somalia Delegation, Kenya ◊ Barbara Smith, International Rescue Committee, USA ◊ Paul Spiegel, Johns Hopkins University, USA ◊ Robert Steinglass, BASICS, USA ◊ Philippe Stoeckel, Association pour l'Aide à la Médecine Préventive, France ◊ Peter Strebel, Centers for Disease Control and Prevention, USA ◊ Michael Toole, Macfarlane Burnet Centre for Medical Research, Australia ◊ Maarten Van Cleeff,

Royal Tropical Institute, Netherlands ◊ Laetitia Van Haren, Refugee Policy Group, Switzerland ◊ Carlos Wandscheer, Médecins du Monde, France ◊ Ralph Watts, ADRA, USA ◊ Christopher Wood, AMREF, Kenya ◊ Brad Woodruff, Centers for Disease Control and Prevention, USA ◊ Takako Yasukawa, WHO Emergency and Humanitarian Action, Switzerland

Other Contributors

Mike Aaronson, Save the Children Fund, UK ◊ Imadulddin Abdulrahim, Islamic African Relief Agency, Ethiopia ◊ Susanta Adhikari, Christian Commission for Development (ACT), Bangladesh ◊ Gilberto Aguirre, Council of Evangelical Churches (ACT), Nicaragua ◊ Juana Albornoz G .Confraternidad Cristiana de Iglesia de Chile (ACT), Chile ◊ Kate Alley, UNICEF, Switzerland ◊ Mary Anderson, Local Capacities for Peace Project, USA ◊ Tim Andrews, World Vision, Guinea ◊ Oldrich Andrysek, IFRC ◊ Jennifer Ashton, UNHCR, Switzerland ◊ Marie-Pierre Auger, ECHO, Guinea ◊ Helen Awan, Overseas Development Institute, UK ◊ Tom Baker, American Red Cross ◊ Rebecca Bardach, America Refugee Committee, Sarajevo ◊ Mikael Barfod, ECHO, Belgium ◊ David Bassiouni, UNOCHA, USA ◊ Luntan Bayarmaa, IFRC ◊ Dana Beegun, InterAction, USA ◊ Claude Belleau, UNV, Switzerland ◊ Judy Benjamin, Women's Commission for Refugee Women and Children, USA ◊ Jon Bennet, Norwegian Refugee Council ◊ Choloka Beyani, Oxfam, UK ◊ Helen Bishop, Concern Universal, Guinea ◊ Dounia Bitar, UNHCR, Switzerland ◊ Richard Blewitt, British Red Cross, UK ◊ Lucie Blok, MSF, Switzerland ◊ Myra Blyth, World Council of Churches (ACT), Switzerland ◊ Ian Bray, Oxfam, UK ◊ Marie Breton-Ivy, The Lutheran World Federation (ACT), Switzerland ◊ Rachel Brett, Quaker UN Office, Switzerland ◊ Lucy Brown, American Red Cross ◊ William Brownfield, US Bureau for Population, Refugees and Migration, Switzerland ◊ David Bryer, Oxfam, UK ◊ Margie Buchanan-Smith, ActionAid, UK ◊ Skip Burkle, University of Hawaii Center for Excellence, USA ◊ Polly Byers, USAID, USA ◊ Edmund Cain, UNDP, USA ◊ Sara Canna, IFRC, Switzerland ◊ David Cardan, UNOCHA, Guinea ◊ Kevin Carew, American Refugee Committee, Sarajevo ◊ Andrew Carl, Conciliation Resources, UK ◊

Part 3

Chris Carr, IFRC, Switzerland ◊ Rob Carr, UNICEF, USA ◊ Nils Cartensen, ACT, Switzerland ◊ Matthew Carter, CAFOD, UK ◊ Louisa Chan, WHO, Switzerland ◊ David Church, VOICE, Belgium ◊ Roger Clark, Department for International Development, UK ◊ Maureen Connelly, UNHCR, Switzerland ◊ Peggy Creese, UNICEF, Switzerland ◊ Diane Crocombe, Oxfam, UK ◊ Chris Cushing, UN Staff College, Italy ◊ Marc D'Silva, Catholic Relief Services, Guinea ◊ Gary Dahl, America Refugee Committee, Thailand ◊ James Darcy, Oxfam, UK ◊ Steve Davey, IFRC ◊ Sara Davidson, People In Aid, UK ◊ Will Day, CARE, UK ◊ Gloria De Sagarra, UNHCR, Switzerland ◊ Sean Deely, IFRC, Switzerland ◊ Sarah Degnan Kambou, Ethiopia ◊ Flavio Del Ponte, Swiss Disaster Relief, Switzerland ◊ Penny Panayiota Deligiannis, Diaconia Agapes (ACT), Albania ◊ Kerry Demuz, Oxfam, Sri Lanka ◊ Gregorie De Sachy, Solodarites, Sarajevo ◊ Mary Diaz, Women's Commission for Refugee Women and Children, USA ◊ Deborah Doane, British Red Cross, UK ◊ Karen Donovan, Independent Consultant, UK ◊ Bernard Doyle, UNHCR, Switzerland ◊ Joelle Dubois, Oxfam, Belgium ◊ Jon Ebersole, CETI, Switzerland ◊ Jan Eijkenaar, ECHO, Belgium ◊ Hussein El Obeid, Humanitarian Aid Commission, Sudan ◊ Judy El-Bushra, Acord, UK ◊ Cirre Emblen, American Red Cross ◊ Paul Emes, IFRC, Switzerland ◊ Liz Eyster, UNHCR, Switzerland ◊ Christine Forgière, Rights and Humanity, UK ◊ Salamo Fulivai, YWCA, Fiji ◊ Sarah Galietsky, Overseas Development Institute, UK ◊ Michael Golden, University of Aberdeen, UK ◊ Elena Gonzalez-Romero, ECHO, Belgium ◊ Lorelei Goodyear, International Rescue Committee, USA ◊ Brewster Grace, Quaker UN Office, Switzerland ◊ Sean Greenaway, ECHO, Belgium ◊ Andres Griekspoor, MSF, Switzerland ◊ Martin Griffiths, UNOCHA, USA ◊ Birte Hald, Danchurchaid/Folkekirkens Nodhjaelp (ACT), Denmark ◊ Teresa Hanley, British Red Cross, UK ◊ Caroline Harford, Red Cross/Red Crescent Country Delegation, Russia ◊ Julia Hausermann, Rights and Humanity, UK ◊ Robert Hayward, Christian Aid (ACT), UK ◊ Ralph Hazleton, CARE International, Switzerland ◊ Pirkko Heinonen, UNICEF, East Africa ◊ Daniel Helle, ICRC ◊ Peter Henderson, USAID, USA ◊ Peter Herby, ICRC ◊ Maurice Herson, Oxfam, UK ◊ Rudolph Hinz, The Lutheran World Federation (ACT), Switzerland ◊ Michael Hoffman, American Red Cross, USA ◊ Mary

Hope Schwoebel, InterAction, USA ◊ Nap Hosang, University of California at Berkeley, USA ◊ Shamsul Huda, Association of Development Agencies in Bangladesh, Bangladesh ◊ Janet Hunt, ACFOA, Australia ◊ Salvatore Ippolito, UNHCR, Switzerland ◊ Bernard J Vrban, Red Cross/Red Crescent Country Delegation, Sarajevo ◊ Safia Jama, UNICEF, East Africa ◊ Riad Jarjour, Middle East Council of Churches (ACT), Cyprus ◊ Samardic Jasna, Red Cross/Red Crescent Country Delegation, Sarajevo ◊ Rome Johan Ketlers, Caritas International ◊ Sally Johnson, Oxfam, UK ◊ Gerry Jones, American Red Cross, USA ◊ Ivan Joseph, Caritas, India ◊ Kristin Kalla, Independent Consultant, USA ◊ Mukesh Kapila, Department for International Development, UK ◊ Geshe Karrenbrock, UNHCR, Switzerland ◊ Innocent Kaseke, Christian Care (ACT), Zimbabwe ◊ Lex Kassenberg, CARE International, Belgium ◊ Chris Kaye, UNOCHA, Switzerland ◊ Jim Kelly, Catholic Relief Services, Sarajevo ◊ Randolph Kent, Independent Consultant, USA ◊ Michael Kiernan, InterAction, USA ◊ Suzanne Kindervatter, InterAction, USA ◊ Andrew Kishindo, AACC (ACT), Kenya ◊ Alimamy Koroma, Council of Churches (ACT), Sierra Leone ◊ Michele Kuhn, ICRC ◊ Sasi Kumar, Oxfam, Sudan ◊ Peter R Kunze, ADRA, Switzerland ◊ Jane Kusin, Royal Tropical Institute, Holland ◊ Sarah Lachat, IFRC ◊ Philip Lam, Hong Kong Christian Council (ACT), China ◊ Warren Lancaster, British Red Cross, UK ◊ Natalia Langlais, Department for International Development, UK ◊ Jones Laviwa, Churches Action in Relief and Development (ACT), Malawi ◊ Nick Leader, Overseas Development Institute, UK ◊ Françoise Ledru, VOICE, Belgium ◊ Gail Lerner, World Council of Churches, USA ◊ Iain Levine, Amnesty International United Nations Office, USA ◊ Reynold Levy, International Rescue Committee, USA ◊ Tan Li Ying, Amity Foundation, China ◊ Claire Light, Oxfam, UK ◊ Santhe Loizos, InterAction, USA ◊ Jean Long, Trinity College, Ireland ◊ Barbara Luckhurst, RedR International, UK ◊ Paula Lynch, US Bureau for Population, Refugees and Migration, USA ◊ Joanna Macrae, Overseas Development Institute, UK ◊ Kirsi Madi, UNICEF, Switzerland ◊ Jok Madut Jok, University of California at Los Angeles, USA ◊ Gianni Magazzeni, UNCHR, Switzerland ◊ John Magrath, Oxfam GB ◊ Kaanaeli Makundi, The Lutheran World Federation (ACT),

Part 3

Switzerland ◊ Juan Manuel Acena, Movimiento Por La Paz El Desarme Y La Libertad, Spain ◊ Gabrielle Martim, University of Nairobi, Kenya ◊ Simon Maxwell, Overseas Development Institute, UK ◊ Monique McClellan, Independent Consultant, Switzerland ◊ Peter McDermott, UNICEF, Switzerland ◊ Therese McGinn, Columbia University, USA ◊ John McGrath, Oxfam, UK ◊ Jennie Meadows, Save the Children Fund, UK ◊ Bob Medrala, CCSDPT, Thailand ◊ Anita Menghetti, USAID, USA ◊ J K Michael, Church's Auxiliary for Social Action (ACT), India ◊ Larry Minear, Brown University, USA ◊ Dahawi, Ministry of Social Planning, Sudan ◊ John Mitchell, British Red Cross, UK ◊ Barbara Monahan, CARE, USA ◊ Moises Moraga, Accion Medica Cristiana (ACT), Nicaragua ◊ Nicholas Morris, UNHCR, Switzerland ◊ Pat Morris, InterAction, USA ◊ Jeremy Mortimer, IFRC, Switzerland ◊ Mutawa Musyimi, National Council of Churches (ACT), Kenya ◊ Doris Mwangi, Equipe d'Urgence de la Biodiversité ◊ Andrew Natsios, World Vision Relief and Development, USA ◊ Gawher Nayeem Wahra, Oxfam, Bangladesh ◊ Paula Nersesian, BASICS, USA ◊ Wolfgang Neumann, UNHCR, Switzerland ◊ Kathleen Newland, Carnegie Endowment for International Peace, USA ◊ Ackbar Noor, ICVA , Sarajevo ◊ Emmanuel Nsabimana, Council of Churches (ACT), Rwanda ◊ Mary O'Reilly, America Refugee Committee, Uganda ◊ Ron Ockwell, Independent Consultant, France ◊ Xavier Ortegat, VOICE, Belgium ◊ Karen Otsea, IPAS, USA ◊ Robert Painter, UNOCHA, Guinea ◊ Dragana Pandurevi, Red Barnet, Sarajevo ◊ David Pardoe, Canadian Red Cross ◊ Jeffrey Pereira, Caritas, Bangladesh ◊ Katherine Perkins, US Bureau for Population, Refugees and Migration, USA ◊ Karen Perrin, Handicap International, Sarajevo ◊ Sue Pfiffner, IFRC ◊ Ian Piper, IFRC ◊ William Power, Concern, Ireland ◊ Marion Pratt, USAID, USA ◊ Zoran Radic, International Rescue Committee, Sarajevo ◊ K Rajaratnam, United Evangelical Lutheran Churches (ACT), India ◊ White Rakuba, Council of Churches (ACT), South Africa ◊ Angela Raven-Roberts, UNICEF, USA ◊ Stephen Richards, International Rescue Committee, USA ◊ Marie-Jeanne Richiardione, IFRC, Switzerland ◊ Cyril Ritchie, InterAid International, Switzerland ◊ Peterson, Robert Koch Institute, Germany ◊ Lloyd Rollins, UMCOR (ACT), USA ◊ Berta Romero, InterAction, USA ◊ Giovanni Rufini, VOICE, Belgium ◊ Sharon Rusu, UNHCR,

Switzerland ◊ Frank Rwakabwohe, Church of Uganda, Uganda ◊ Serge Rwamashirabo, USAID, Rwanda ◊ Salomon S Sanny, Association Beninoise de Lutte Contre La Faim et La Misère du Peuple, Republic du Benin ◊ Muhodzic Sanela, WFP, Sarajevo ◊ Baldo Santo Lucherini, Caritas, Chile ◊ David Shearer, Institute for Strategic Studies, Switzerland ◊ Ed Shenkenberg, ICVA, Switzerland ◊ Shoko Shimozawa, UNHCR, Switzerland ◊ Christine Simon, EU/CE Regional Food Security, Ivory Coast ◊ Hugo Slim, Oxford Brookes University, UK ◊ Gavic Smilijka, Centre for Torture Victims, Sarajevo ◊ Thomas Soderman, Sweden Red Cross ◊ Holly Solberg, CARE, USA ◊ Jacques Stroun, ICRC ◊ Meinrad Studer, ICRC ◊ Jane Swan, InterAction, USA ◊ Brita Sydhoff, Norwegian Refugee Council, Switzerland ◊ Julia Taft, US Bureau for Population, Refugees and Migration, USA ◊ Nermina Tankovic, Sphere Project Intern, Bosnia/UK ◊ Yousef Tariq, Irish Refugee Council ◊ John Telford, Independent Consultant, Ireland ◊ Niall Tobis, Trocaire, Ireland ◊ Susan Toole, Women's Commission for Refugee Women and Children, USA ◊ Luc Trouillard, Caritas International ◊ Herman Van Aken, Dutch Interchurch Aid/Stichting Oecumenische Hulp (ACT), Holland ◊ Sergio Veirra de Mello, UNOCHA, USA ◊ Rudy Von Bernuth, Save the Children Fund, USA ◊ Carlo Von Flue, ICRC ◊ Margareta Wahlstrom, IFRC, Switzerland ◊ Bill Warnock, World Vision, Sarajevo ◊ John Watt, IFRC, Switzerland ◊ Peter Webber, CARE, Guinea ◊ George Weber, IFRC, Switzerland ◊ Merri Weinger, WHO, Switzerland ◊ Hannah Weiss, Sphere Project Intern, USA/Switzerland ◊ Thomas Weiss, Brown University, USA ◊ Monica Wernette, UNAIDS, Switzerland ◊ Joe William, Caritas, Sri Lanka ◊ Chandran Williams, YGRO Ltd., Sri Lanka ◊ Roy Williams, USAID, USA ◊ June Wyer, World Council of Churches (ACT), UK ◊ Robert Yallop, CARE, Australia ◊ Jennifer Yumie Song, Sphere Project Intern, USA/Korea ◊ Anthony Zwi, London School of Hygiene and Tropical Medicine, UK ◊ Médecins du Monde, France, Ivory Coast, Spain, USA ◊ AMREF, Kenya, USA ◊ Canadian Food Grains Bank, Canada ◊ Church World Service (ACT), USA ◊ DROP, India ◊ ENDA-Tiers Monde, Senegal ◊ Hungarian InterChurch Aid (ACT), Hungary ◊ KWAHO, Kenya ◊ London School of Economics ◊ Ministry of Health, Benin ◊ Ministry of Health, Tanzania ◊ Ministry of Water, Zambia ◊ National Centre for Disaster Management, India ◊ National

Part 3

Economic Council, Malawi ◊ Non-governmental Organizing
Committee (NGOCC), Zambia ◊ Norwegian Church Aid (ACT),
Norway ◊ SMSF, Zaire ◊ Water and Sewage Corporation, Ghana

Sphere Participating Agencies

Steering Committee for Humanitarian Response

CARE International (CARE Australia, CARE Austria, CARE Canada,
CARE Denmark, CARE France, CARE Germany, CARE Italy, CARE
Japan, CARE Norway, CARE UK, CARE USA) ◊ Caritas
Internationalis ◊ International Federation of Red Cross and Red
Crescent Societies ◊ International Save the Children Alliance ◊
Médecins Sans Frontières International (MSF Belgium, MSF France,
MSF Holland, MSF Spain, MSF UK, MSF USA) ◊ Oxfam ◊ The
Lutheran World Federation (ACT) ◊ Save the Children Alliance ◊
World Council of Churches (ACT)

InterAction members

Action Against Hunger ◊ Adventist Development and Relief Agency
International ◊ African Medical and Research Foundation ◊ Africare ◊
Aga Khan Foundation USA ◊ American Friends Service Committee ◊
American Jewish Joint Distribution Committee, Inc ◊ American Jewish
World Service ◊ American Near East Refugee Aid ◊ American Red Cross,
International Services Department ◊ American Refugee Committee ◊
Ananda Marga Universal Relief Team ◊ Baptist World Alliance (ACT) ◊
CARE ◊ Catholic Medical Mission Board, Inc ◊ Catholic Relief Services
- USCC ◊ Child Health Foundation ◊ Children's Survival Fund, Inc ◊
Christian Children's Fund ◊ Christian Reformed World Relief
Committee ◊ Church World Service, Inc (ACT) ◊ Council of Jewish
Federations ◊ Counterpart International, Inc ◊ Direct Relief International
◊ Doctors of the World ◊ Doctors Without Borders USA / MSF-USA ◊
Episcopal Church of the USA (ACT) ◊ Presiding Bishop's Fund for
World Relief (ACT) ◊ Food for the Hungry International ◊ Friends of
Liberia ◊ Grassroots International ◊ Interchurch Medical Assistance, Inc
◊ International Aid, Inc ◊ International Executive Service Corps ◊
International Medical Corps ◊ International Orthodox Christian

Charities (ACT) ◊ International Rescue Committee ◊ Islamic African Relief Agency USA ◊ Latter-day Saint Charities ◊ Lutheran World Relief (ACT) ◊ MAP International ◊ Mercy Corps International ◊ National Peace Corps Association ◊ OIC International ◊ Operation USA ◊ Oxfam America ◊ Planning Assistance ◊ Points of Light Foundation ◊ Refugees International ◊ Relief International ◊ Salvation Army World Service Office ◊ Save the Children ◊ Service and Development Agency, Inc ◊ SHARE Foundation: Building a New El Salvador Today ◊ Solar Cookers International ◊ Unitarian Universalist Service Committee ◊ United Israel Appeal ◊ United Methodist Committee on Relief (ACT) ◊ US Committee for Refugees ◊ US Committee for UNICEF ◊ Volunteers in Technical Assistance ◊ World Relief Corporation ◊ World Vision Relief and Development

International Committee of the Red Cross

VOICE members

Osterreichisches Hilfswerk International ◊ SOS Kinderdorf International ◊ World Vision-GEV ◊ Caritas Secours International ◊ Handicap International Bureau De Liaison ◊ Oxfam Solidarité en Belgique ◊ ASF Dansk Folkehjælp ◊ Danchurchaid (ACT) ◊ Danish Refugee Council ◊ Suemen World Vision ◊ Action Contre La Faim ◊ Aide Medicale Internationale ◊ ATLAS ◊ France Libertés ◊ Medécins du Monde International ◊ Pharmaciens Sans Frontières ◊ Secours Catholique/Caritas France ◊ Secours Populaire Français ◊ Triangle "Generation Humanitaire" ◊ Adventist Development and Relief Agency ◊ Arbeiter-Samartiter-Bund Deutschland E V ◊ Caritas Deutsche ◊ Deutsche Welthungerhilfe E V ◊ Diakonie Emergency Aid (ACT) ◊ Johanniter-Unfall-Hilfe E V ◊ Malteser Hilfsdienst E V ◊ Medico International E V ◊ World Vision Deutschland E V ◊ Concern Worldwide ◊ GOAL ◊ Trocaire ◊ World Vision Ireland ◊ Associazione Amici dei Bambini ◊ Associazione Volontari per il Servizio Internazionale-Milano ◊ Centro Regionale d'Intervento per la Cooperazione-CRIC ◊ Cesvi-Cooperazione e Sviluppo ◊ Comitato Collaborazione Medica ◊ Coordinamento delle Organizzazioni Non Governative per la Cooperazione Inernazionale allo Sviluppo ◊ Comitato di Cordinamento delle Organizzazioni per il Servizio Volontario ◊ Comitato Internazionale per lo Sviluppo dei Popoli ◊ Comitato Italiano Permanente Emergenze Oltremare ◊ Cooperazione Internazionale ◊ Intersos ◊ Movimento Laici Americo Latina ◊ Movimondo ◊ Volontari Nel Mondo-FOCSIV ◊ Caritas-NL ◊ Dutch Relief and Rehabilitation Agency ◊ Dutch Interchurch Aid (ACT) ◊ Memisa Medicus Mundi ◊ World Vision Nederland ◊ ZOA Refugee Care ◊ Norwegian People's Aid ◊ Assistencia Medica Internacional ◊ Caritas ◊ Medicus Mundi Navarra ◊ Movimiento por la Paz el Desarme y la Libertad ◊ Paz y Tercer Mundo ◊ Caritas-Sverige ◊ Lutherhjalpen Church Of Sweden Aid (ACT) ◊ PMU Interlife ◊ Star of Hope International ◊ Action by Churches Together (ACT) ◊ The Lutheran World Federation (ACT) ◊ ActionAid ◊ CAFOD ◊ Christian Aid UK (ACT) ◊ Concern Universal ◊ Health Unlimited ◊ Helpage International UK ◊ Mercy Corps International/Scottish European Aid ◊ Oxfam GB ◊ Save the Children Fund UK ◊ Tear Fund UK ◊ World Vision UK ◊ International Rescue Committee

ICVA members

ActionAid ◊ Adventist Development and Relief Agency, International ◊ Afghan NGOs Coordination Bureau ◊ Africa Humanitarian Action ◊ African Association for Literacy and Adult Education ◊ All Africa Conference of Churches (ACT) ◊ Amel Association ◊ American Joint Distribution Committee ◊ Anatolian Development Foundation ◊ Asian Institute for Rural Development ◊ Asian NGO Coalition for Agrarian Reform and Rural Development ◊ Asociacion Latinoamericana de Organizaciones de Promcion ◊ Asociacion Latinoamericana para los Derechos Humanos ◊ Asociacion Nacional de Centros de Investigacion, Promocion Social y Desarrrollo ◊ Asociacion Regional para las Migraciones Forzadas ◊ Associacion Beninoise de Lutte Contre La Faim et La Misere du Peuple ◊ Association of Development Agencies in Bangladesh ◊ Association for Sarva Seva Farms ◊ Association for Social Advancement ◊ Association of Voluntary Agencies for Rural Development ◊ Australian Council for Overseas Aid ◊ British Refugee Council ◊ Canadian Council for International Cooperation ◊ Canadian Council for Refugees ◊ CARE International ◊ CARE USA ◊ Chinese Refugees' Relief Association ◊ Christian Children's Fund, Inc. ◊ Christian Relief and Development Association (ACT) ◊ Church World Service (ACT) ◊ Confederation of Environmental and Development

NGOs of Central Africa ◊ Conseil des Organisations Non Gouvernementales d'Appui au Developpement ◊ Consejo de Educacion de Adultos de America Latina ◊ Consejo de Instituciones de Desarrollo ◊ Convergencia de Organismos Civiles por la Democracia ◊ Coordinacion de ONG y Cooperativas para el Acompanamiento de la Poblacion Damnificada por el Conflicto Armado Interno ◊ Danish Refugee Council ◊ Diakonia (ACT) ◊ EMO-BARAKA, Union Pour la Promotion du Paysan ◊ Encuentro de Entidades no Gubernamentales para el Desarrollo ◊ Episcopal Church Center of the USA (ACT) ◊ Equilibre Suisse ◊ European Association of Non Governmental Organisations for Food Aid and Emergency Aid ◊ Federacion de Organismos no Gubernamentales de Nicaragua ◊ Feed the Children International ◊ Forum of African Voluntary Development Organizations ◊ Fundacion Augusto Cesar Sandino ◊ General Union of Voluntary Societies ◊ Gonoshahajjo Sangstha ◊ Handicap International ◊ Human Appeal International ◊ Indian Institute of Youth and Development ◊ Individuell Manniskohjalp ◊ InterAction ◊ Inter-Africa Group ◊ InterAid International ◊ International Catholic Migration Commission ◊ International Islamic Relief Organisation ◊ International Rescue Committee ◊ International Social Service ◊ Islamic Relief Agency ◊ Jesuit Refugee Service ◊ Lebanese NGO Forum ◊ LINK-NGO Forum ◊ Lutheran Immigration and Refugee Service ◊ The Lutheran World Federation (ACT) ◊ Mauritius Council of Social Service ◊ National NGO Council of Sri Lanka ◊ Netherlands Organisation for International Development Cooperation ◊ Non-Governmental Organisation Coordinating Committee ◊ Norwegian Refugee Council ◊ Organisation for Industrial Spiritual and Cultural Advancement-International ◊ PACS/PRIES/Instituto Politicas Alternativas para o Cone Sul ◊ Philippine Development NGOs for International Concerns ◊ Queen Alia Fund for Social Development ◊ Réseau Africain Pour le Developpement Intègre ◊ Rural Development Foundation of Pakistan ◊ Lanka Jathika Sarvodaya Shramadana Sangamaya Inc ◊ Secours Populaire Français ◊ Sudanese Women General Union ◊ Voluntary Health Association of India ◊ World Council of Churches (ACT) ◊ World University Service/Servicio Universitario Mundial ◊ World Vision International ◊ Yayasan Indonesia Sejahtera

Part 3

ICVA Associate Members

Refugee Studies Programme, Oxford University ◊ Caritas Internationalis ◊ International Committee of the Red Cross ◊ International Federation of Red Cross and Red Crescent Societies ◊ Médecins du Monde ◊ Médecins Sans Frontières International

4 Summary of the Minimum Standards

This section provides an overview of the minimum standards for each of the five sectors described in chapters 1 – 5: water supply and sanitation, nutrition, food aid, shelter and site planning, and health services. Each chapter provides indicators, guidance notes and contextual information, all of which are essential to the interpretation and application of the standards.

Minimum Standards in Water Supply and Sanitation

1 Analysis

Analysis standard 1: initial assessment

Programme decisions are based on a demonstrated understanding of the emergency situation and on a clear analysis of the health risks and needs relating to water supply and sanitation.

Analysis standard 2: monitoring and evaluation

The performance of the water supply and sanitation programme, its effectiveness in responding to health problems related to water and sanitation, and changes in the context are monitored and evaluated.

Analysis standard 3: participation

The disaster-affected population has the opportunity to participate in the design and implementation of the assistance programme.

2 Water Supply

Water supply standard 1: access and water quantity

All people have safe access to a sufficient quantity of water for drinking, cooking and personal and domestic hygiene. Public water points are sufficiently close to shelters to allow use of the minimum water requirement.

Water supply standard 2: water quality

Water at the point of collection is palatable, and of sufficient quality to be drunk and used for personal and domestic hygiene without causing significant risk to health due to water-borne diseases, or to chemical or radiological contamination from short term use.

Water supply standard 3: water use facilities and goods

People have adequate facilities and supplies to collect, store and use sufficient quantities of water for drinking, cooking and personal hygiene, and to ensure that drinking water remains sufficiently safe until it is consumed.

3 Excreta Disposal

Excreta disposal standard 1: access to, and numbers of toilets

People have sufficient numbers of toilets, sufficiently close to their dwellings to allow them rapid, safe and acceptable access at all times of the day and night.

Excreta disposal standard 2: design and construction

People have access to toilets which are designed, constructed and maintained in such a way as to be comfortable, hygienic and safe to use.

4 Vector Control

Vector control standard 1: individual and family protection

People have the means to protect themselves from disease vectors and nuisance pests when they are estimated to be a significant risk to health or well-being.

Vector control standard 2: physical, environmental and chemical protection measures

The number of disease-bearing vectors and nuisance animals that pose a risk to people's health and well-being are kept to an acceptable level.

Vector control standard 3: good practice in the use of chemical vector control methods

Vector control measures that make use of pesticides are carried out in accordance with agreed international norms to ensure that staff, the people affected by the disaster and the local environment are adequately protected, and to avoid creating resistance to pesticides.

5 Solid Waste Management

Solid waste management standard 1: solid waste collection and disposal

People have an environment that is acceptably free of solid waste contamination, including medical wastes.

Solid waste management standard 2: solid waste containers/ pits

People have the means to dispose of their domestic waste conveniently and effectively.

6 Drainage

Drainage standard 1: drainage works

People have an environment that is acceptably free from risk of water erosion and from standing water, including storm water, flood water, domestic wastewater and wastewater from medical facilities.

Drainage standard 2: installations and tools

People have the means (installations, tools etc) to dispose of domestic wastewater and water point wastewater conveniently and effectively, and to protect their shelters and other family or communal facilities from flooding and erosion.

7 Hygiene Promotion

Hygiene promotion standard 1: hygiene behaviour and use of facilities

All sections of the affected population are aware of priority hygiene practices that create the greatest risk to health and are able to change them. They have adequate information and resources for the use of water and sanitation facilities to protect their health and dignity.

Hygiene promotion standard 2: programme implementation

All facilities and resources provided reflect the vulnerabilities, needs and preferences of all sections of the affected population. Users are involved in the management and maintenance of hygiene facilities where appropriate.

8 Human Resource Capacity and Training

Capacity standard 1: competence

Water supply and sanitation programmes are implemented by staff who have appropriate qualifications and experience for the duties involved, and who are adequately managed and supported.

Minimum Standards in Nutrition

1 Analysis

Analysis standard 1: initial assessment

Before any programme decisions are made, there is a demonstrated understanding of the basic nutritional situation and conditions which may create risk of malnutrition.

Analysis standard 2: response

If a nutrition intervention is required, there is a clear description of the problem(s) and a documented strategy for the response.

Analysis standard 3: monitoring and evaluation

The performance and effectiveness of the nutrition programme and changes in the context are monitored and evaluated.

Analysis standard 4: participation

The disaster-affected population has the opportunity to participate in the design and implementation of the assistance programme.

2 General Nutritional Support to the Population

General nutritional support standard 1: nutrient supply

The nutritional needs of the population are met.

General nutritional support standard 2: food quality and safety

Food that is distributed is of sufficient quality and is safely handled so as to be fit for human consumption.

General nutritional support standard 3: food acceptability

Foods that are provided are appropriate and acceptable to the entire population.

General nutritional support standard 4: food handling and safety

Food is stored, prepared and consumed in a safe and appropriate manner, both at household and community level.

3 Nutritional Support to Those Suffering From Malnutrition

Targeted nutritional support standard 1: moderate malnutrition

The public health risks associated with moderate malnutrition are reduced.

Targeted nutritional support standard 2: severe malnutrition

Mortality, morbidity and suffering associated with severe malnutrition are reduced.

Targeted nutritional support standard 3: micronutrient deficiencies

Micronutrient deficiencies are corrected.

4 Human Resource Capacity and Training

Capacity standard 1: competence

Nutrition interventions are implemented by staff who have appropriate qualifications and experience for the duties involved, and who are adequately managed and supported.

Capacity standard 2: support

Members of the disaster-affected population receive support to enable them to adjust to their new environment and to make optimal use of the assistance provided to them.

Capacity standard 3: local capacity

Local capacity and skills are used and enhanced by emergency nutrition programmes.

Minimum Standards in Food Aid

1 Analysis

Analysis standard 1: initial assessment

Before any programme decisions are made, there is a demonstrated understanding of the basic conditions that create risk of food insecurity and the need for food aid.

Analysis standard 2: monitoring and evaluation

The performance and effectiveness of the food aid programme and changes in the context are monitored and evaluated.

Analysis standard 3: participation

The disaster-affected population has the opportunity to participate in the design and implementation of the assistance programme.

2 Requirements

Requirements standard

The food basket and rations are designed to bridge the gap between the affected population's requirements and their own food sources.

3 Targeting

Targeting standard

Recipients of food aid are selected on the basis of food need and/or vulnerability to food insecurity.

4 Resource Management

Resource management standard

Food aid commodities and programme funds are managed, tracked, and accounted for using a transparent and auditable system.

5 Logistics

Logistics standard

Agencies have the necessary organisational and technical capacity to manage the procurement, receipt, transport, storage and distribution of food commodities safely, efficiently and effectively.

6 Distribution

Distribution standard

The method of food distribution is equitable, and appropriate to local conditions. Recipients are informed of their ration entitlement and its rationale.

7 Human Resource Capacity and Training

Capacity standard 1: competence

Food aid programmes are implemented by staff who have appropriate qualifications and experience for the duties involved, and who are adequately managed and supported.

Capacity standard 2: local capacity

Local capacity and skills are used and enhanced by food aid programmes.

Minimum Standards in Shelter and Site Planning

1 Analysis

Analysis standard 1: initial assessment

Programme decisions are based on a demonstrated understanding of the emergency situation and on a clear analysis of people's needs for shelter, clothing and household items.

Analysis standard 2: monitoring and evaluation

The performance and effectiveness of the shelter and site programme and changes in the context are monitored and evaluated.

Analysis standard 3: participation

The disaster-affected population has the opportunity to participate in the design and implementation of the assistance programme.

2 Housing (shelter)

Housing standard 1: living quarters

People have sufficient covered space to provide protection from adverse effects of the climate. They have sufficient warmth, fresh air, security and privacy to ensure their dignity, health and well-being.

3 Clothing

Clothing standard

The people affected by the disaster have sufficient blankets and clothing to provide protection from the climate and to ensure their dignity, safety and well-being.

4 Household Items

Household items standard 1: items for households and livelihood support

Families have access to household utensils, soap for personal hygiene and tools for their dignity and well-being.

Household items standard 2: environmental concerns

Fuel-economic cooking implements and stoves are made available, and their use is promoted.

5 Site Selection

Site standard 1: site selection

The site is suitable to host the number of people involved.

Site standard 2: site planning

Site planning ensures sufficient space for household areas and supports people's security and well-being. It provides for effective and efficient provision of services and internal access.

Site standard 3: security

Site selection and planning ensures sufficient personal liberty and security for the entire affected population.

Site standard 4: environmental concerns

The site is planned and managed in such a way as to minimise damage to the environment.

6 Human Resource Capacity and Training

Capacity standard 1: competence

Shelter and site interventions are implemented by staff who have appropriate qualifications and experience for the duties involved, and who are adequately managed and supported.

Capacity standard 2: local capacity

Local skills and capacity are used and enhanced by shelter and site programmes.

Minimum Standards in Health Services

1 Analysis

Analysis standard 1: initial assessment

The initial assessment determines as accurately as possible the health effects of a disaster, identifies the health needs and establishes priorities for health programming.

Analysis standard 2: health information system - data collection

The health information system regularly collects relevant data on population, diseases, injuries, environmental conditions and health services in a standardised format data in order to detect major health problems.

Analysis standard 3: health information system - data review

Health information system data and changes in the disaster-affected population are regularly reviewed and analysed for decision-making and appropriate response.

Analysis standard 4: health information system - monitoring and evaluation

Data collected is used to evaluate the effectiveness of interventions in controlling disease and in preserving health.

Analysis standard 5: participation

The disaster-affected population has the opportunity to participate in the design and implementation of the assistance programme.

2 Measles Control

Measles control standard 1: vaccination

In disaster-affected populations, all children 6 months to 12 years old receive a dose of measles vaccine and an appropriate dose of vitamin A as soon as possible.

Measles control standard 2: vaccination of newcomers

Newcomers to displaced settlements are vaccinated systematically. All children 6 months to 12 years old receive a dose of measles vaccine and an appropriate dose of vitamin A.

Measles control standard 3: outbreak control

A systematic response is mounted for each outbreak of measles within the disaster-affected population and the host community population.

Measles control standard 4: case management

All children who contract measles receive adequate care in order to avoid serious sequellae or death.

3 Control of Communicable Diseases

Control of communicable diseases standard 1: monitoring

The occurrence of communicable diseases is monitored.

Control of communicable diseases standard 2: investigation and control

Diseases of epidemic potential are investigated and controlled according to internationally accepted norms and standards.

4 Health Care Services

Health care services standard 1: appropriate medical care

Emergency health care for disaster-affected populations is based on an initial assessment and data from an ongoing health information system, and serves to reduce excess mortality and morbidity through appropriate medical care.

Health care services standard 2: reduction of morbidity and mortality

Health care in emergencies follows primary health care (PHC) principles and targets health problems that cause excess morbidity and mortality.

5 Human Resource Capacity and Training

Capacity standard 1: competence

Health interventions are implemented by staff who have appropriate qualifications and experience for the duties involved, and who are adequately managed and supported.

Capacity standard 2: support

Members of the disaster-affected population receive support to enable them to adjust to their new environment and to make optimal use of the assistance provided to them.

Capacity standard 3: local capacity

Local capacity and skills are used and enhanced by emergency health interventions.

Part 3

5 The Code of Conduct for the International Red Cross and Red Crescent Movement and NGOs in Disaster Relief

Prepared jointly by the International Federation of Red Cross and Red Crescent Societies and the ICRC[1]

Purpose

This Code of Conduct seeks to guard our standards of behaviour. It is not about operational details, such as how one should calculate food rations or set up a refugee camp. Rather, it seeks to maintain the high standards of independence, effectiveness and impact to which disaster response NGOs and the International Red Cross and Red Crescent Movement aspires. It is a voluntary code, enforced by the will of the organisation accepting it to maintain the standards laid down in the Code.

In the event of armed conflict, the present Code of Conduct will be interpreted and applied in conformity with international humanitarian law.

Note

1. Sponsored by: Caritas Internationalis*, Catholic Relief Services*, The International Federation of Red Cross and Red Crescent Societies*, International Save the Children Alliance*, Lutheran World Federation*, Oxfam*, The World Council of Churches*, The International Committee of the Red Cross (* members of the Steering Committee for Humanitarian Response).

The Code of Conduct is presented first. Attached to it are three annexes, describing the working environment that we would like to see created by Host Governments, Donor Governments and Inter-governmental Organisations in order to facilitate the effective delivery of humanitarian assistance.

Definitions

NGOs: NGOs (Non-Governmental Organisations) refers here to organisations, both national and international, which are constituted separately from the government of the country in which they are founded.

NGHAs: For the purposes of this text, the term Non-Governmental Humanitarian Agencies (NGHAs) has been coined to encompass the components of the International Red Cross and Red Crescent Movement – The International Committee of the Red Cross, The International Federation of Red Cross and Red Crescent Societies and its member National Societies – and the NGOs as defined above. This code refers specifically to those NGHAs who are involved in disaster response.

IGOs: IGOs (Inter-Governmental Organisations) refers to organisations constituted by two or more governments. It thus includes all United Nations Agencies and regional organisations.

Disasters: A disaster is a calamitous event resulting in loss of life, great human suffering and distress, and large scale material damage.

The Code of Conduct

Principles of Conduct for The International Red Cross and Red Crescent Movement and NGOs in Disaster Response Programmes

1 The Humanitarian imperative comes first

The right to receive humanitarian assistance, and to offer it, is a fundamental humanitarian principle which should be enjoyed by all citizens of all countries. As members of the international community, we recognise our obligation to provide humanitarian assistance wherever it is needed. Hence the need for unimpeded access to affected populations is of fundamental importance in exercising that responsibility. The prime motivation of our response to disaster is to alleviate human suffering amongst those least able to withstand the stress caused by disaster. When we give humanitarian aid it is not a partisan or political act and should not be viewed as such.

2 Aid is given regardless of the race, creed or nationality of the recipients and without adverse distinction of any kind. Aid priorities are calculated on the basis of need alone

Wherever possible, we will base the provision of relief aid upon a thorough assessment of the needs of the disaster victims and the local capacities already in place to meet those needs.

Within the entirety of our programmes, we will reflect considerations of proportionality. Human suffering must be alleviated whenever it is found; life is as precious in one part of a country as another. Thus, our provision of aid will reflect the degree of suffering it seeks to alleviate.

In implementing this approach, we recognise the crucial role played by women in disaster-prone communities and will ensure that this role is supported, not diminished, by our aid programmes.

The implementation of such a universal, impartial and independent policy, can only be effective if we and our partners have access to the necessary resources to provide for such equitable relief, and have equal access to all disaster victims.

3 Aid will not be used to further a particular political or religious standpoint

Humanitarian aid will be given according to the need of individuals, families and communities. Not withstanding the right of NGHAs to espouse particular political or religious opinions, we affirm that assistance will not be dependent on the adherence of the recipients to those opinions.

We will not tie the promise, delivery or distribution of assistance to the embracing or acceptance of a particular political or religious creed.

4 We shall endeavour not to act as instruments of government foreign policy

NGHAs are agencies which act independently from governments. We therefore formulate our own policies and implementation strategies and do not seek to implement the policy of any government, except in so far as it coincides with our own independent policy.

We will never knowingly – or through negligence – allow ourselves, or our employees, to be used to gather information of a political, military or economically sensitive nature for governments or other bodies that may serve purposes other than those which are strictly humanitarian, nor will we act as instruments of foreign policy of donor governments.

We will use the assistance we receive to respond to needs and this assistance should not be driven by the need to dispose of donor commodity surpluses, nor by the political interest of any particular donor.

We value and promote the voluntary giving of labour and finances by concerned individuals to support our work and recognise the independence of action promoted by such voluntary motivation. In order to protect our independence we will seek to avoid dependence upon a single funding source.

5 We shall respect culture and custom

We will endeavour to respect the culture, structures and customs of the communities and countries we are working in.

6 We shall attempt to build disaster response on local capacities

All people and communities – even in disaster – possess capacities as well as vulnerabilities. Where possible, we will strengthen these capacities by employing local staff, purchasing local materials and trading with local companies. Where possible, we will work through local NGHAs as partners in planning and implementation, and co-operate with local government structures where appropriate.

We will place a high priority on the proper coordination of our emergency responses. This is best done within the countries concerned by those most directly involved in the relief operations, and should include representatives of the relevant UN bodies.

7 Ways shall be found to involve programme beneficiaries in the management of relief aid

Disaster response assistance should never be imposed upon the beneficiaries. Effective relief and lasting rehabilitation can best be achieved where the intended beneficiaries are involved in the design, management and implementation of the assistance programme. We will strive to achieve full community participation in our relief and rehabilitation programmes.

8 Relief aid must strive to reduce future vulnerabilities to disaster as well as meeting basic needs

All relief actions affect the prospects for long-term development, either in a positive or a negative fashion. Recognising this, we will strive to implement relief programmes which actively reduce the beneficiaries' vulnerability to future disasters and help create sustainable lifestyles. We will pay particular attention to environmental concerns in the design and management of relief programmes. We will also endeavour to minimise the negative impact of humanitarian assistance, seeking to avoid long-term beneficiary dependence upon external aid.

9 We hold ourselves accountable to both those we seek to assist and those from whom we accept resources

We often act as an institutional link in the partnership between those who wish to assist and those who need assistance during disasters. We therefore hold ourselves accountable to both constituencies.

All our dealings with donors and beneficiaries shall reflect an attitude of openness and transparency.

We recognise the need to report on our activities, both from a financial perspective and the perspective of effectiveness.

We recognise the obligation to ensure appropriate monitoring of aid distributions and to carry out regular assessments of the impact of disaster assistance.

We will also seek to report, in an open fashion, upon the impact of our work, and the factors limiting or enhancing that impact.

Our programmes will be based upon high standards of professionalism and expertise in order to minimise the wasting of valuable resources.

10 In our information, publicity and advertising activities, we shall recognize disaster victims as dignified humans, not hopeless objects

Respect for the disaster victim as an equal partner in action should never be lost. In our public information we shall portray an objective image of the disaster situation where the capacities and aspirations of disaster victims are highlighted, and not just their vulnerabilities and fears.

While we will cooperate with the media in order to enhance public response, we will not allow external or internal demands for publicity to take precedence over the principle of maximising overall relief assistance.

Part 3

We will avoid competing with other disaster response agencies for media coverage in situations where such coverage may be to the detriment of the service provided to the beneficiaries or to the security of our staff or the beneficiaries.

The Working Environment

Having agreed unilaterally to strive to abide by the Code laid out above, we present below some indicative guidelines which describe the working environment we would like to see created by donor governments, host governments and the inter-governmental organisations – principally the agencies of the United Nations – in order to facilitate the effective participation of NGHAs in disaster response.

These guidelines are presented for guidance. They are not legally binding, nor do we expect governments and IGOs to indicate their acceptance of the guidelines through the signature of any document, although this may be a goal to work to in the future. They are presented in a spirit of openness and cooperation so that our partners will become aware of the ideal relationship we would seek with them.

Annex I: Recommendations to the governments of disaster-affected countries

1 Governments should recognise and respect the independent, humanitarian and impartial actions of NGHAs

NGHAs are independent bodies. This independence and impartiality should be respected by host governments.

2 Host governments should facilitate rapid access to disaster victims for NGHAs

If NGHAs are to act in full compliance with their humanitarian principles, they should be granted rapid and impartial access to disaster victims, for the purpose of delivering humanitarian assistance.

It is the duty of the host government, as part of the exercising of sovereign responsibility, not to block such assistance, and to accept the impartial and apolitical action of NGHAs.

Host governments should facilitate the rapid entry of relief staff, particularly by waiving requirements for transit, entry and exit visas, or arranging that these are rapidly granted.

Governments should grant over-flight permission and landing rights for aircraft transporting international relief supplies and personnel, for the duration of the emergency relief phase.

3 Governments should facilitate the timely flow of relief goods and information during disasters

Relief supplies and equipment are brought into a country solely for the purpose of alleviating human suffering, not for commercial benefit or gain. Such supplies should normally be allowed free and unrestricted passage and should not be subject to requirements for consular certificates of origin or invoices, import and/or export licences or other restrictions, or to importation taxation, landing fees or port charges.

The temporary importation of necessary relief equipment, including vehicles, light aircraft and telecommunications equipment, should be facilitated by the receiving host government through the temporary waving of licence or registration restrictions. Equally, governments should not restrict the re-exportation of relief equipment at the end of a relief operation.

To facilitate disaster communications, host governments are encouraged to designate certain radio frequencies, which relief organisations may use in-country and for international communications for the purpose of disaster communications, and to make such frequencies known to the disaster response community prior to the disaster. They should authorise relief personnel to utilise all means of communication required for their relief operations.

Part 3

4 Governments should seek to provide a coordinated disaster information and planning service

The overall planning and coordination of relief efforts is ultimately the responsibility of the host government. Planning and coordination can be greatly enhanced if NGHAs are provided with information on relief needs and government systems for planning and implementing relief efforts as well as information on potential security risks they may encounter. Governments are urged to provide such information to NGHAs.

To facilitate effective coordination and the efficient utilisation of relief efforts, host governments are urged to designate, prior to disaster, a single point-of-contact for incoming NGHAs to liaise with the national authorities.

5 Disaster relief in the event of armed conflict

In the event of armed conflict, relief actions are governed by the relevant provisions of international humanitarian law.

Annex II: Recommendations to donor governments

1 Donor governments should recognise and respect the independent, humanitarian and impartial actions of NGHAs

NGHAs are independent bodies whose independence and impartiality should be respected by donor governments. Donor governments should not use NGHAs to further any political or ideological aim.

2 Donor governments should provide funding with a guarantee of operational independence

NGHAs accept funding and material assistance from donor governments in the same spirit as they render it to disaster victims; one of humanity and independence of action. The implementation of relief actions is ultimately the responsibility of the NGHA and will be carried out according to the policies of that NGHA.

3 Donor governments should use their good offices to assist NGHAs in obtaining access to disaster victims

Donor governments should recognise the importance of accepting a level of responsibility for the security and freedom of access of NGHA staff to disaster sites. They should be prepared to exercise diplomacy with host governments on such issues if necessary.

Annex III: Recommendations to inter-governmental organisations

1 IGOs should recognise NGHAs, local and foreign, as valuable partners

NGHAs are willing to work with UN and other inter-governmental agencies to effect better disaster response. They do so in a spirit of partnership which respects the integrity and independence of all partners. Inter-governmental agencies must respect the independence and impartiality of the NGHAs. NGHAs should be consulted by UN agencies in the preparation of relief plans.

2 IGOs should assist host governments in providing an overall coordinating framework for international and local disaster relief

NGHAs do not usually have the mandate to provide the overall coordinating framework for disasters which require an international response. This responsibility falls to the host government and the relevant United Nations authorities. They are urged to provide this service in a timely and effective manner to serve the affected state and the national and international disaster response community. In any case, NGHAs should make all efforts to ensure the effective co-ordination of their own services.

In the event of armed conflict, relief actions are governed by the relevant provisions of international humanitarian law.

Part 3

3 IGOs should extend security protection provided for UN organisations, to NGHAs

Where security services are provided for inter-governmental organisations, this service should be extended to their operational NGHA partners where it is so requested.

4 IGOs should provide NGHAs with the same access to relevant information as is granted to UN organisations

IGOs are urged to share all information, pertinent to the implementation of effective disaster response, with their operational NGHA partners.

Índex